IN TUNE
WITH
HEAVEN

THE REPORT
OF
THE ARCHBISHOPS' COMMISSION ON
CHURCH MUSIC

D0896709

IN TUNE
WITH
HEAVEN

THE REPORT
OF
THE ARCHBISHOPS' COMMISSION ON
CHURCH MUSIC

Published jointly by

CHURCH HOUSE PUBLISHING
LONDON

Hodder & Stoughton
LONDON SYDNEY AUCKLAND

Scripture quotations in this work are taken from the Revised Standard Version ©
Division of Christian Education of the National Council of the Churches of Christ in
the United States of America.

Cover extract from C. H. H. Parry's *Blest Pair of Sirens* (SATB version edited by
C. S. Lang) reproduced by permission of the copyright owners, Novello and Co. Ltd.

British Library Cataloguing in Publication Data is available for this title.

  ISBN 0-340-57046-6 (Hodder & Stoughton)
      0-7151-3744-1 (Church House Publishing)

Copyright © The Central Board of Finance of the Church of England 1992

First published in Great Britain 1992

Published jointly by:

Church House Publishing, Church House, Great Smith Street, London SW1P 3NZ

Hodder and Stoughton, a division of Hodder and Stoughton Ltd, Mill Road,
Dunton Green, Sevenoaks, Kent TN13 2YA. Editorial Office: 47 Bedford Square,
London WC1B 3DP.

Photoset by Rowland Phototypesetting Ltd, Bury St. Edmunds, Suffolk.

Printed in Great Britain by St. Edmundsbury Press Ltd, Bury St. Edmunds, Suffolk.

O may we soon again renew that Song,

And keep in tune with Heaven, till God ere long

To his celestial consort us unite,

To live with him, and sing in endless morn of light.

John Milton
'At a Solemn Music'

Contents

Foreword

The original suggestion for an Archbishops' Commission on Church Music came from Dr. Lionel Dakers whose tireless work when he was Director of the Royal School of Church Music has put the whole Church in his debt. The opportunity to follow up the suggestion was provided through the generosity of the Proprietors of *Hymns Ancient and Modern*. Our first task, therefore, must be to thank those who persuaded the two Archbishops that the time for a new and comprehensive report on church music had arrived.

In Tune with Heaven shows how right they were. The forty years since the publication of the last report have witnessed a social, liturgical and musical revolution. It has become imperative to take stock of where we are, and the Commission is to be congratulated on its wise and sensitive handling of an impressively broad agenda.

The needs are great. Music has a high profile in today's society. Good quality performances are easily available to almost everybody. Music is as important in worship as it has always been, perhaps more so. Yet the resources of the Church for producing music are under pressure, and there is evidence in some circles that standards are falling and interest diminishing. Our hope is, therefore, that this timely report will be read, not only by those involved directly in the musical life of the Church, but by all who share in the ordering of worship and the education of clergy and laity.

Our greatest contribution to the Commission's work was to invite the Bishop of Portsmouth to be its Chairman. He has by all accounts been exemplary in his leadership, in his commitment to the task, which has included doing much of the drafting, and in his ability to make it enjoyable.

We accept the Report with much gratitude to him, to the members of the Commission, and to all those who have assisted them in their work.

✠ GEORGE CANTUAR   ✠ JOHN EBOR

Preface

To be given a commission by the Archbishops of Canterbury and York to review the present state of church music, to offer reflections and to make recommendations is a daunting task. Not only is the brief a far-reaching one and the subject diffuse, but there is widespread and well-informed interest on the part of most of those who will read this Report. Moreover, people hold strong views about the music which is used in worship, as is shown by the many letters the Commission has received.

We are enormously grateful to all our correspondents, as we are to the various organisations and associations who have made submissions to us. We have also been greatly helped by those who have shared both time and expertise in coming to talk with us at our meetings. These people are named in Appendices 2.2–2.4.

Much of the evidence came to us in response to a general invitation issued by the Chairman by means of letters to a number of journals and periodicals (see Appendix 2.1). More specific letters were written to various individuals and organisations listed in Appendices 2.6–2.11.

One of the Commission's major sources of information was a parish survey undertaken by means of a questionnaire, in the completion and interpretation of which we were greatly assisted by the Statistics and Computer Department of the Central Board of Finance of the Church of England. A balanced sample, as employed by them, was used and the results are given both in Chapter 9 and in Appendix 2.5. We express our thanks to the staff of the department and to Ms. Jacqui Cooper in particular, and to Mr. Nicholas Wills who generously provided a grant to pay the costs of the survey. We are most grateful, too, to all those who completed yet another questionnaire which landed on their desk.

In addition to the information received by the Commission, members undertook visits to churches and congregations, in order to experience for themselves their worship and to observe the place and use of music within it.

The Commission also drew upon the varied expertise and experience of its own members, and we were particularly glad to have two people appointed by the Free Churches and by the Roman Catholic Church respectively. Although the membership was not fully representative of every constituency of those concerned with the

Church's worship and music (and a number of letters to the Commission made this point forcibly, with suggestions of others who might be asked to serve), the Commission hopes that it has not overlooked or misunderstood any significant group within the worshipping community of the Church of England. It would not have been sensible to increase a membership already fifteen strong.

The funding of the Commission's work was mainly through the generosity of the Proprietors of *Hymns Ancient and Modern*. We express our sincere thanks to them and hope that, on reading this Report, they will consider their money to have been well spent. We also thank others who have made contributions and grants and whose names are recorded in Appendix 1.4.

The Commission met fourteen times between July 1988 and October 1991. Of these six were meetings for the inside of a day and eight were in residence overnight. We are grateful for the hospitality received from the Sisters at St. Columba's, Woking, the Church Commissioners, the Dean and Chapter of Westminster, the Director and his staff at Addington Palace, the Dean and Chapter of York, the Headmaster of the Minster School at York, Messrs. Lee, Bolton and Lee in London, the Dean and Chapter of Liverpool and a number of private hosts in York and Liverpool.

The Chairman's thanks go to the members of the Commission who, in addition to all the other responsibilities in their busy lives, have given so generously of their time and expertise to the work and meetings of the Commission. Particular appreciation is recorded for Mr. Patrick Salisbury, the Secretary of the Commission. His has been the hard work of arranging and recording the work of the meetings, of seeing to its finance and conducting its correspondence. We could not have managed without him. Nor could we have managed without the secretarial help given by Miss Virginia Vincent of Sutton Courtenay and Miss Jennifer Robinson of Fareham, who has typed all the drafts of the Report, together with Mrs. Jean Maslin. To these as well go our sincere thanks.

So, with much gratitude (not least for the privilege and enjoyment which have been ours), and with a proper sense of humility, we offer this Report to the Archbishops. We hope that it may be of some help to the Church in leading people to experience a little more of God's glory, through the use of music in worship.

✝ TIMOTHY PORTSMOUTH
8th November 1991

The Plan of the Report

This Report is in six parts. In Part 1 an introductory chapter describes the two previous church music reports and suggests why a third is necessary. That is followed by a summary of the history of church music from its beginning to the present day in this country. This provides, for those who require it, the background and context for the Commission's task.

In Part 2 (Chapters 3–8) there is some exploration of the theological and theoretical issues relating to music, and consideration is given to its place in the created order as well as to its uses in worship. There is also some discussion of the meaning of worship and the relationship of music to speech, together with a look at the people, buildings, instruments and other components which are associated with it. Something is said, too, on the difficult question of making judgments between 'good', appropriate music and that which is 'bad' and unsuitable.

Part 3 (Chapters 9–17) is the most factual section of the Report, in which the findings of the Commission as to the present state of church music are summarised under various headings. These findings are the result of correspondence, submissions, presentations and conversations, visits and questionnaires, as well as the personal experience and observations of members of the Commission. Chapters are devoted to music in parish churches, cathedrals, other churches and congregations, the church overseas, and Anglican religious communities. Attention is also given to the musical training offered in schools, and to church musicians and ordinands.

Part 4 (Chapters 18–20) describes some of the musical instruments and other equipment appropriate for use in church and examines the role of the electronic media. Issues relating to the composition, publication and copyright of music, and insurance are also included in this section.

Part 5 (Chapters 21–28) contains the heart of the Commission's work, consisting of its comments and reflections as it seeks to relate the contents of Part 2 with the realities portrayed in Parts 3 and 4. These lead into a summary of recommendations which are contained, with a conclusion, in Part 6. Much detailed information is given in the Appendices which follow.

The Commission is only too well aware of its limitations and it anticipates two criticisms in particular. Some will regard much of what it says, particularly in Part 2, as obvious and therefore unnecessary in a report of this kind. Both for its own work, however, and for others who read the Commission's conclusions, it was necessary to establish certain agreed criteria relating to worship and music, as the basis for what was to follow. Without them, members of the Commission could have found themselves speaking at cross-purposes, and some people reading this report might have been left wondering why its comments and recommendations have come out as they have.

Because each chapter of the Report is based on one or more working papers written by members of the Commission (see Appendix 1.5), and sometimes re-worked several times, the reader may notice some differences in style and content, levels of writing, attitudes and assumptions in parts of the Report. There are also some instances of overlapping and repetitiveness, although the Commission hopes that there are no inconsistencies or contradictions. However, if the Report is used as a resource book, rather than as something to be read through in one sitting, the repetitions should not prove too obtrusive.

A last point is that in making its suggestions and recommendations, the Commission has primarily addressed the needs it perceives in the parishes of this country. For it is in them that the strength of the Church of England lies and its future depends upon the quality of their worship.

PART 1

INTRODUCTION
The Background to the Report

1

Another Report

1.   Future historians of the Church of England will surely note that this century has been marked, more than any other, by the appointment of commissions on any number of topics and the publication of their reports. They may further remark that these have greatly increased since the inauguration of synodical government in 1970, and that an ever-increasing proportion of the Church's time, energy and resources is taken up with considering them.

2.   Some explanation, therefore, is required for the setting up of what is the third Commission on Church Music this century and for the appearance of yet another report. This is especially so when some would question the need to discuss a subject about which, for them, there is nothing new to be said. They know what they expect and like in church and it is simply, as they see it, a matter of maintaining (or improving) standards. Others may regard a Church Music Commission as at best irrelevant and at worst wasteful: the Church has so many more pressing questions than that of music in church, and precious resources should be devoted to improving her efforts in the fields of mission and evangelism.

3.   This Report will show, however, that in view of the many other changes that have taken place, to reject the possibility of changes in the use of music in today's services is neither realistic nor desirable. Moreover, the worship of the Church is the foundation for her work and witness in the world, and music can be a powerful means not only for the inspiration of worshippers but also for reaching out into society. In any case, the clergy, musicians and others who are responsible for the services of the Church know at first hand the increasing difficulties of providing music appropriately and effectively in worship. They are looking for help and encouragement with an urgency which was absent when the two previous Reports were written.

MUSIC IN WORSHIP 1922

4.   The first Report was that of a Committee appointed by the Archbishops of Canterbury and York in 1922, which consisted of nineteen people. Its chairman was Earl Beauchamp and, in addition to eight well-known church musicians, there were two bishops, an archdeacon, three other clergy and four laity. Its terms of reference were:

> To consider and report upon the place of Music in the Worship of the Church, and in particular the Training of Church Musicians, and the Education of the Clergy in the Knowledge of Music as a branch of Liturgical Study.

5.   The Committee held nine full meetings and worked in sub-committees, relying upon 'a good deal of correspondence' for evidence. Within a year it produced a Report of fifty-five pages, containing twelve chapters, which was reprinted with minor revisions in 1932, 1938 and 1947.

6.   After considering the place of music in the Church's worship and seeking to define the difference between what is 'fitting' and what is 'unsuitable' church music, the committee reports on the music of small town, village and larger town churches, and of cathedral and collegiate churches. Hymn-singing receives detailed attention, as does the 'use and abuse' of the organ. In addition to looking at the need for the training of both church musicians and the clergy, there is a discussion of the relationships between them.

7.   It is an impressive document and the situation, as well as many of the problems which it describes, has a familiar ring about it seventy years later. Words such as 'dignity', 'beauty', 'taste', 'simplicity', and 'restraint' are found throughout and the Committee deprecates music which is 'trivial', 'tawdry', 'superficial', 'inherently poor', 'small-minded' and 'cheaply sentimental'. Serious warnings are uttered against the use of music's unrivalled power to enervate and manipulate human emotions and to attract hearers rather than to be a vehicle of devotion; this accords ill with the 'improvement' in public taste, and the 'idioms of the opera and the concert room' are unacceptable. The public utterances of the Church, together with 'good' sermons, demand 'good' music.

8.   Amongst its practical recommendations is a strong emphasis on the priority of the words and the value of unison music, together with plenty of congregational singing. In order to help with the careful choice of music and its best possible performance, there are suggestions for the establishment of choral societies, hymn festivals and music competitions at a local level and, for the diocese, the arrangement of summer schools or one-day conferences. It is also proposed that each diocese should have an Inspector of Choirs and a diocesan music committee, in addition to a 'Central Council on Church Music'. This would exist for the offering of advice and opinions, the settling of difficulties in relationships and the arrangement of 'proper instruction of ordinands in the essentials of liturgical chant'.

9.   Few of the specific recommendations of the Report were implemented, but its influence was obviously widespread. Possibly the most significant result was in preparing the ground for the foundation by Sydney Nicholson (a member of the Committee) of the School of English Church Music, later the Royal School of Church Music.

MUSIC IN CHURCH 1948

10.   When the Archbishops set up a new Committee in 1948, it consisted of three eminent organists (one of whom was the Director of the Royal School of Church Music), an archdeacon, a parish priest and one layman, who was the Chief Commissioner of the RSCM. Its Chairman was Provost Noël Hopkins of Wakefield and its task was to amend and alter the 1922 Report. In the event it produced 'something akin to a new report'. After nineteen whole-day meetings and two 'extended sessions', it published a document in 1951. This was revised and expanded in 1957 and republished with minor amendments in 1961. Other than a round-the-world tour by the Director of the RSCM, no mention is made of the sources of its evidence.

11.   In response to the 'listlessness' that prevails in parish worship, there is a very strong emphasis on the priority of the words and the 'noble language' of the Book of Common Prayer. Music is complementary to it and should be expressive of strong faith and assurance, even of awe, with 'qualities of nobility and restraint', free from 'sensationalism or mawkishness, and from all suggestions of secularity.' So it is 'unwise' to offer to young people that which is too intimate, personal and emotional, and what is required is music which gives a 'sincere and noble impression', rather than that which is weak and

complacent. To be worthy of its intention, music should be 'offered with sincerity, selected with wise appreciation of its true purpose, and given the best possible interpretation'.

12.   The Report notes a significant advance in the standards of secular music since 1922 and an improvement in taste and performance, so that church musicians rightly reject the 'unreal and conventional' and exercise a growing discrimination in the choice and use of both words and music. It attributes these to the influence of the earlier Report and notes with approval that after the upheavals of two World Wars, the clergy have never given 'so much consideration to the conduct of public worship, or made greater efforts at linking the prayer and praises of their people with the needs of a troubled and bewildered age'. The contribution towards this of both the Church Music Society and the RSCM is acknowledged. Yet there remain the problems of declining attendance at public worship, the difficulties of recruitment to choirs, and the shortage and inadequacy of the training of church musicians.

13.   The Report includes a number of chapters giving detailed advice on the conduct of Morning and Evening Prayer and the choral celebration of Holy Communion, with brief considerations of broadcast and televised services and the use of processions. Psalms and hymns receive similar careful treatment. So does the use of the organ, for which the appropriate substitute may be a piano, rather than a harmonium or American organ with its 'depressing and tiresome' tone. Qualified approval is given to the use of both electronic instruments and the gramophone.

14.   In considering cathedrals, the Committee adds its voice to the pleas of many (including Archbishop Cosmo Lang) for the retention of cathedral choirs and services in the face of a move between the Wars to cut out what was regarded by some as 'a wasteful expense and an esoteric luxury'. It notes that cathedral organists since 1922 had generally become 'men of wide general culture', often with a university degree, and that they ought to be paid a salary equivalent to that of a canon residentiary. In keeping with its strong emphasis on the traditional repertoire, the Report's random list of cathedral composers ends with Charles Wood.

15.   Whilst cathedral organists would be trained in much the same way as before, there were some new resources for the serious parish

musician. The RSCM and the College of St. Nicolas are mentioned, together with the Royal College of Organists, the Church Music Society and the Gregorian Association. The more skilled might obtain the Archbishop of Canterbury's Diploma in Church Music, whilst for the 'amateur' there was little other than what might be available locally.

16.   When discussing the training of ordination candidates, as strong an emphasis is placed upon the ability to read as upon that of singing. Little is said about the clergy's part in the choice of music, which seems generally to belong to the organist or choirmaster. Whilst acknowledgment is made of the 'happy partnership of clergy, organists and choirs . . . in the past', the Report notes continuing problems of pay and conditions of service. Consequently, qualified musicians were increasingly taking appointments outside the Church and a growing shortage of organists was the result.

17.   A shortage is also noted in respect of members of parish choirs, together with the reasons for this. However, on no account should a professional quartet be considered for a parish church and every possible effort should be made to maintain a voluntary choir, with a majority of boys' rather than women's voices. The hope is therefore expressed, in a chapter on music for the young in church and school, that the children might learn music which breeds in them a 'liking for' the Church's worship. As well as hymns, they should be taught canticles, psalms, responses and amens, and the BBC's 'Religious Service for Schools' is offered as an example of good practice.

18.   Overseas, the churches faced many of the same problems as in England, particularly where (as usually) their services and music followed the Church of England pattern. Whilst noting that there were some 'deeply interesting and commendable experiments' in the use of traditional Asiatic and African music, the Report suggests the need for 'a very considerable effort' so that the difficulties in many parts of the Anglican Communion might be overcome.

19.   The Report concludes by saying:

The Committee would, therefore, plead that all the people of the Church should have the opportunity of hearing about the steps which may be taken to raise the standard of its music, to perform it with skill and sincerity, and to make it worthy of its holy purpose.

THE SITUATION TODAY

20.   The Reports of both these Committees reflect in different ways a more settled situation than that which obtains today. Then, there was general acceptance of a more or less common style and repertoire of music for church services. Forty years on, there have been changes of the most radical kind which have affected every part of the Church's life and worship, including its music, together with a marked reduction in its membership, ministry and resources.

21.   Despite this persisting trend, music in church in some respects continues to flourish. Certainly these are different and difficult days for what we might call traditional church music. But there has been in recent years an unprecedented burgeoning of new musical expression for use in worship and a wide range of musical styles has gained acceptance. Moreover, religious music of all kinds has an appeal far beyond the membership of the Church.

22.   It is this very burgeoning which creates the need for a commission. Whereas formerly there was little departure from what was familiar and traditional in the music for worship, there is now the possibility of many different varieties of music. Musical instruments of all kinds are vying with the organ in many places. New hymns are coming off the press and the photocopier as never before, and music, no longer the preserve of the 'qualified', is being composed by people from all walks of life.

23.   Such an increase in musical activity and interest is partly to be explained by an education system which has produced a much more literate musical public, as well as many more instrumentalists, and by radio and recordings. It is also a result of the easy availability at modest cost of electronic and other musical instruments. Many more homes today probably have a 'keyboard' than have a piano.

24.   But the overwhelming consideration is the very great liturgical changes over the past forty years, which have resulted in new forms of service throughout Christendom. These demand much greater vocal participation by congregations and less place for soloists, whether in song or speech. Together with this is the growth in lay leadership and a greater emphasis upon shared responsibility between clergy and laity for the leading of worship. The new services offer more spontaneity and freedom than those of the Book of Common Prayer, and their

language adds to the sense of flexibility, bringing both opportunities and problems for musicians.

25. The churches where most of the new musical developments are taking place are those where most advantage is taken of the new flexibility, and this is particularly true of those which have experienced charismatic renewal. However, many musicians, clergy and people are confused and uncertain over what music is right for their congregation. Pressures are brought to bear by those who want changes, resistance comes from those who do not, and the Church's life and mission are weakened by the resulting polarisation.

26. In whatever way the question is resolved, it is clear that the maintenance of a traditional choir with a repertoire of traditional church music is becoming harder by the year. Even cathedrals report fewer boys attending their voice trials. Whilst cathedral music is possibly more popular than it has ever been, thanks to radio, television and the recording industry, the growing pressures on the education of children and the greatly increased costs of maintaining a choir do not allow us to be too complacent about the future.

27. In addition, it is extremely difficult for many parish churches to recruit and keep a competent organist willing to play throughout the year for a nominal salary. Sociological changes, pressures of work and finance, longer weekends and a greatly increased range of leisure activities make it increasingly hard to persuade people to undertake a regular weekly commitment. Consequently the music may depend either upon a rota of 'occasional' organists or upon the willingness of a pianist to come to the rescue.

28. The improved conditions for security of tenure, provided by General Synod legislation in 1987, may help the situation. Even so, there are still plenty of sad stories of poor, or broken, clergy and organist relationships. This seems to be a problem as perennial as the low salary paid to most church musicians.

29. Because of the difficulty in recruiting competent musicians for the Church's worship there is a temptation to reduce standards and to go for the lowest common denominator in choice and performance, on the principle that what is lacking in excellence, or even adequacy, will be compensated for by sincerity. In such circumstances the absence

altogether of music is sometimes thought to be preferable, and the experience of doing without it can actually liberate the liturgy.

30.   The appeal to sincerity is sometimes used to resist the professional approach of those organisations which exist to help church musicians in the improvement of standards. In spite of this, there is evidence of the effectiveness of such organisations in very many congregations. This is one of the signs of hope, notwithstanding the suspicion in some quarters of what is described as élitism and a consequent sense of guilt in those who insist on high standards.

31.   A last, though not least important, reason for needing to review the present state of church music is the dramatic change in the ecumenical scene since the 1951 Report. Then each Church could and did behave as if the other Churches did not exist. Now there is neither the desire nor the possibility of ignoring each other, and music with its common language can be a powerful encouragement to growth in unity among Christians still divided by theology and tradition. It is our hope that this Report may contribute to the process of ecumenism, and that much of what it contains will be helpful also to musicians, clergy and congregations beyond the Church of England.

2

A Millennium of Church Music
in England

32.   For the first thousand years of the Church's life the music used in worship was the unaccompanied melody of plainsong, or Gregorian chant. Embellishment began when singers found parts of even the simplest tunes to be out of their range and instead sang notes either lower or higher than the melody. The new musical style which resulted was called *organum* and although it was originally confined to the doubling of a melody at the fourth or fifth, it soon became the singing of a counter-melody.

The Middle Ages and the Renaissance

33.   The development of *organum* led to the invention of wholly different counter-melodies, or *faburden*, and so to the rise of polyphony. This soon grew in complexity and, as a result, music became an increasingly powerful ingredient and assumed a new importance within worship. The fears of church authorities were aroused, and Pope John XXII, for example, tried to put a limit to the ingenuity of composers, although he was largely unsuccessful.

34.   England's composers succeeded in defying papal edicts, perhaps because of their distance from Rome. Consequently between 1400 and 1600 English church music was the most lively and colourful in the Western Church. Not only was it very different from secular music, but it was also ahead of it in its technical complexity and emotional content. In the Peasants' Revolt and in John Wycliffe's translation of the Bible there were hints of the forthcoming Reformation, but the singularity of English style is evident in the music of the whole period. There was no diminution in the quality of inspiration from Dunstable to Orlando Gibbons.

35.   By the end of the fourteenth century, composers began to be identified by name. Many of them, like Cornyshe, Fayrfax and

Taverner, were associated with the Chapel Royal. This is the oldest church music foundation in Britain (dating from at least 1135) and is the name of a body of singers, rather than of a building. The singers were under royal patronage, which gave them crucial support at times when it was most needed.

36.   The climax of excellence in pre-Reformation music is to be found in the works of Taverner, notably in his *Western Wynde Mass*, which makes use of a secular song and which contributed to the widespread acceptance of polyphony. This in turn led to the interaction between the secular and sacred, although the melodies of plainsong had always been adapted to the rhythms of the dance. Now, as music became more complex, secular tunes were incorporated in the music for the Mass.

37.   By the end of the Middle Ages the desire to write music without words had become commonplace. Since the only instrument then permitted in churches was the organ, vocal music in the fifteenth century began to employ other embellishments which set a single syllable to many notes. The same device was adopted in later times when Protestant sensitivities, with their special reverence for the Word of God, succeeded in keeping instrumental music out of the services.

Congregational Music and the Reformation

38.   Until the Reformation the performance of music in church was in the hands of the 'professionals', for congregations had little to do in worship except to listen and look, and to pray. Nor had they any part even in hymns, although outside the church they had the carol or sacred song which was usually performed with dancing.

39.   When congregational music was eventually introduced, as one of the fruits of the Reformation, it was in the form of metrical psalms and passages of Scripture which could be construed as songs. Typical of these is the *Genevan Psalter* of 1551, a fundamental source book of good verse set to good, solid tunes; its lasting influence on English hymnody was profound. By contrast, the attempts in England and Scotland to force words from the Bible into the metre of a popular ballad were often unsatisfactory.

40.   If the medieval view of worship had something about it of the theatre, the reformers' priority speaks more of a lecture hall and the need for the human mind to have constant instruction and correction. Not surprisingly, therefore, the use of music in church was severely

restricted and the result was that one dictatorship replaced another. Moreover, the insistence on psalmody alone was as 'Catholic' as the medieval clerics who had used only the Psalms in the Mass.

41. Apart from an interval during the Commonwealth, the Chapel Royal continued to function and ensured continuity, even though its composers conformed to the requirement that music in worship should have the qualities of restraint and distinctiveness. The emphasis of the Reformers on the importance of communication gives the writing of the great Tudor composers its peculiarly English quality, while the unhappy philistinism in the society of their day gave them a kind of freedom. Almost nothing was written for congregations, however, apart from metrical psalms. Even in John Merbecke's settings for Morning and Evening Prayer and for the Holy Communion, much was written for the Clerks.

The Restoration

42. With the coming of Charles II there was a relatively swift transformation. The restoration of the monarchy heralded the arrival in church music of rhetoric in which the solo voice was given the same prominence that it had already achieved in the theatre abroad. Whilst Henry Purcell and the Chapel Royal set a high standard, the freedom to write such dramatic music attracted some composers whose lack of restraint produced some unhappy results.

43. During this period there was a new flowering of music for choirs. An innovation in their repertoire was the Anglican chant, which has come to be seen as perhaps the Church of England's most characteristic musical form. It was derived from the effect upon Gregorian plainsong of metrical and harmonised music. Gregorian chant had been much affected by polyphony, with the introduction of *faburden*, but it was only after 1700 that Anglican chant appeared, using a very short tune with a reciting note to accommodate the varying lengths of verses in the Prayer Book Psalter. It is essentially choral music and in its earliest days it produced nothing for the ordinary worshippers to sing. The metrical psalms remained the only congregational part in services which were often formal, drab and carelessly conducted.

The Evangelical Revival

44. The eighteenth century was the great age of English hymn writing, in which earlier experiments to add to the traditional metrical psalms were succeeded by the work of Isaac Watts and his followers.

27

Watts 'christianised' the psalms, but also versified the individual faith of the Christian. His work was an inspiration to John and Charles Wesley, among others. John Wesley was also influenced by the hymn-singing Moravians whom he met on a voyage to Georgia in 1735. Charles celebrated his own 'conversion' with a hymn, and continued to write magnificently for more than thirty years, expressing evangelical concerns, sacramental beliefs, and the personal experience of the believer. The richness and strength of this eighteenth-century work is without parallel in post-Reformation hymnody, and many of the greatest English hymns date from this period.

45.   Not all the music for these new hymns were of high quality. Moreover, because they were learnt by rote, the original rather restrained flourishes in the tunes easily grew out of proportion and their aesthetic quality diminished as what had originally been choir music became the property of all. At first they were used more like anthems. The various Hospitals (the Foundling, the Magdalen and the Lock) had their own books of hymns, containing a mixture of some very good and some fairly low-grade music.

46.   As often is the case with successful movements, the Evangelical Revival attracted many composers with minimal talent. Many of the Hospital composers had little concern for the purity of their texts and the influence of Handel proved to be not a little harmful. Composers of genius do not always provide the best examples. Handel could make a short text go a long way (as in the 'Amen Chorus' in *Messiah*), but lesser composers tried to do the same with very tedious results.

The Tractarians

47.   With the passage of time, the services of the Established Church once again sank into mediocrity, although Nonconformists maintained some vitality in worship. But the energy of the Oxford Movement came to the rescue and by 1860 its members were beginning to lead the way liturgically. Finding its inspiration in a romanticised return to medieval liturgies, and anxious to invigorate a church in decline, the Movement led the search for high standards in worship. Holy Communion was often given prominence above Morning and Evening Prayer, and whilst the latter offices are not easily overweighted by elaborate music, the eucharistic drama can easily be distorted by it. Far from being a cause for musical impoverishment, however, the excellence in liturgy which was promoted by the Oxford Movement had a beneficial effect on the music of the Church as well.

48.   Other forces were also at work in dispelling the apathy which had settled over the Church and they were led, both musically and practically, by a nephew of Charles Wesley. Samuel Sebastian Wesley was responsible, through his writing, his exhortations and his example, for a considerable raising of standards. Not only in the cathedrals, but also in the parish churches, robed choirs began to appear in chancels and much of their repertoire was derived from cathedral music lists.

49.   Although the last part of the century saw a great flowering of new composers, there were few who could work at the same level as Wesley for cathedrals. He was almost alone in his day in having the ability to write new music of quality, although worthy successors included Stanford, Parry, Charles Wood and Walford Davies.

Hymns and Plainsong

50.   In hymnody, however, there was no dearth of talent and many a Victorian composer knew how to write a good tune. The publication of *Hymns Ancient and Modern* in 1861 was an important event. Indeed, so popular was it (as Erik Routley recounts) that when a new edition came out in 1904, in which 'Abide with me' was no longer 27 but 23, many complained that it was sure to fail; the country, they implied, would not stand for it. In the event, that edition was never popular.

51.   The same period was also a time of much persistent and profound scholarship, especially in Germany, and church musicians in England were not unaffected by it. Revised plainsong texts prepared at Mechlin and Solesmes attracted great interest. Thomas Helmore and Thomas Walmisley were amongst those who brought about the return of plainsong, however bowdlerised, to the Church in England. There was also a revival of the carol through men such as J. M. Neale, H. R. Bramley and John Stainer.

The Twentieth Century

52.   By the end of the nineteenth century, changes were in the air. Composers who were not all orthodox believers began to replace the Church's own musical employees. A surge of scholarly research revealed new treasures and challenged many of the assumptions of previous generations. Nevertheless, elaborate music flourished until the beginning of World War II, and musical attainment in church, school and cathedral was probably at a higher level than it had ever been.

53.   In composition Vaughan Williams, Gustav Holst and Edmund Rubbra had followed the leading Victorians and Edwardians and they in turn were succeeded by Howells and Britten, amongst others. In scholarship the way was led by Woodward, Bridges, Dearmer, Nicholson and Martin and Geoffrey Shaw. Vaughan Williams' memorable words 'good taste is a moral concern' provided the basis of their work. In the non-Anglican churches there was much the same picture of life and growth, and musical ecumenism had begun.

54.   Although attempts were made to continue or re-create after World War II what had been established in the first half of the century, the mood of the 1960s created dissatisfaction in the Church with what was evidently old and tired. A new feeling emerged as to what was suitable for use as music in worship, and cathedrals and those churches with competent choirs began to explore a more modern world. The output of new writing was small but the quality of, for instance, Tippett's *Magnificat and Nunc Dimittis* shows the revolution in thinking.

55.   At the same time, much of the division between sacred and secular had disappeared, with results as disparate as Britten's *Missa Brevis* and Sydney Carter's 'Lord of the Dance'. The re-introduction of instruments other than the organ has brought new opportunities into the worship of the Church. Today the simple effectiveness of the Taizé chant, which makes it instantly popular, and the effects of charismatic renewal have introduced to our services a new style and repertoire of music. Whilst parishes and the churches of other denominations strive to find an answer to the criticism that much of their music is either trivial or complicated, the mainstream of cathedral music continues.

PART 2

WORSHIP AND MUSIC
Some Theological and Theoretical Background to the Report

3

God, Music and Creation

56. Most people would be hard pressed to produce a satisfying definition of music, yet they know instinctively what is meant by the word. In spite of differences in our ability to recognise, appreciate and make it, there is music of some kind within every one of us. It is an experience common to all people and all nations. It is identified variously in the rhythms and tunes of human invention, the songs of birds, the sounds of waters and winds, or even the supposed harmonies of the spheres in space. Religious belief is not necessary to accept that music is part of the natural order. It is something that is there, to be enjoyed or not, as we wish, in the same way as the scent of flowers, the colours of the rocks, the taste of honey or the warmth of the sun.

Creation and Communication

57. For those who believe in a divine Creator, however, the natural order has its origins in God and is no mere chance happening. The beginning of Scripture depicts its being carefully planned and describes everything as being 'very good' (Genesis 1:31), from the division of light and darkness to the creation of the human race. No less than the earth and its resources, music is an integral part of God's great act of creation. Like all manifestations of truth, beauty, goodness and love in their many forms, it has its origin in God. With its place in his design, it has a purpose.

58. At the simplest level that purpose may be described as communication. In this music is not alone. Writing, painting and sculpture also communicate, as do speech, gesture and other means of expression which depend upon neither sound nor sight. Each has its place and each its distinctive way of conveying thoughts, ideas and emotions. But music, which is our concern here, is one of the most accessible and universal languages, being less limited than speech by social, intellectual, national or religious boundaries. It expresses, often more effectively than words, our feelings and aspirations. It is therefore

widely employed in religious rituals, not only to address God but also to express his reality for the worshippers.

A Revelation of God

59. That which is made reveals something about its maker, as a book its writer or a home its occupants. Music may be seen, therefore, as telling us something not only about its composer and performers but also about the God who has given it. In common with other creative gifts, it expresses something of the mystery, the order and the glory of creation and its Creator. Music partakes of the goodness of the Creation and reflects varying aspects of the divine nature. It is thus used by God, both within and outside worship, to speak to us of himself. By means of it we may glimpse his majesty and his simplicity, his righteousness and his mercy, his power and his gentleness, his mystery and his love. One might even suggest that the revelation of God as Trinity is reflected in different kinds of music. So for some the triumphant last movement of a Beethoven symphony conveys the power and transcendence of God the Father; the gentle plaintiveness of an Irish folk song may speak of the humanity and solidarity in suffering of the incarnate Son; and the cheerful appeal of a Strauss waltz might reflect for some people the warmth and encouragement of the indwelling Holy Spirit.

Uses and Abuses of Music

60. In addition to speaking to us of God, music has other uses, including that of simple enjoyment. Indeed, it is not improper to suggest that God may have given it to us largely for that purpose. The fact that most people respond positively to music indicates that it is among those things of this world which are provided for our pleasure. Not surprisingly, therefore, it is widely employed to help people, and even animals, to relax. It can also be of great assistance in the process of healing; David was employed to play in order to soothe the demented Saul (1 Samuel 16:23). It can challenge, too. Thus, Elisha summoned a minstrel to enable him to prophesy (2 Kings 3:15). Shakespeare describes it as 'the food of love' (*Twelfth Night*, I. i) and it is without doubt a potent means of stirring emotions at their deepest level. By music people are easily moved, inspired and uplifted.

61. Like all of God's good gifts, music can be trivialised, as it is so often when it is employed as background noise for gatherings of people. More serious is its actual abuse. For, as a 'language', it is quite

capable of being used to express that which is evil, as well as that which is good. The views and state of mind of those who compose and perform it will influence its content and its effect. Association of ideas is a strong element in musical language; if the ethos of some music is too much associated with a way of life in conflict with the Gospel, its use could even have harmful results. This might be true not only of the more extreme forms of 'pop' music, but also of the very secular and pagan ideas found in some of the music of Wagner, for example. The close connection between some kinds of music and the drug culture may not be coincidental. The use of music as a kind of anaesthetic is well known, even in religious gatherings.

62.   The manipulation of feelings through music is not new, and because of this many of the Church Fathers regarded music as part of our lower nature. St. John Chrysostom, for example, believed it to be sensual and pagan, obstructing our progress towards the 'real world' of the Spirit. There was a concern that people might be moved more by the music than by the Reality for whose worship it is used. Such concern was not without foundation, and Erasmus in the sixteenth century anticipated the view of the Protestant Reformers when he complained that the English were obsessed with the performance of fine music in church. Calvin allowed only 'utility' music in the Genevan Psalm tunes. Lutheranism generally encouraged much fuller artistic expression and created a climate in which great music could flourish. There were nevertheless those who objected to the liturgical pieces of composers such as Bach and Buxtehude, because of their being too 'elaborate'.

63.   Certainly it was, and is, possible for people to be drawn more to the means than to the End. But even St. Augustine, who worried a good deal about the worldly nature of music, had to admit to a profound experience as a result of it:

> How I wept to hear your hymns and songs, deeply moved by the voices of your sweet singing in church. Their voices penetrated my ears, and with them truth found its way into my heart; my frozen feeling for God began to thaw, tears flowed and I experienced joy and relief. (*Confessions* IX.6.14)

64.   Nevertheless, it has to be recognised that music, and our use of it, is not perfect. It is part of a universe which waits with 'eager longing' for redemption, in which all humans and their gifts are to find their

fulfilment in Christ, together with their physical environment (Romans 8:18–23). Until that time, we recognise the imperfections of a 'fallen' creation. Whilst acknowledging the dangers of allowing his many gifts to interrupt the direct relationship between God and his children, we use those gifts as responsibly as we may. To do otherwise would be to reject without gratitude what God has provided for us.

The Necessity of Music

65.   As gifts of God, therefore, music and the other arts should not be seen as luxuries or optional extras, to be indulged only when all the other needs of daily living have been met. Even in times of hardship, danger or oppression, people paint the walls of caves, whittle pieces of wood, make up prison poems, tell and act stories, create simple musical instruments or sing songs of freedom. We need, as those made in the likeness of God (Genesis 1:27), an outlet for that creative instinct which all of us share with our Creator. To regard music as an unnecessary indulgence not only denigrates one of God's gifts, but also suppresses human creativity.

66.   Since the Church has a concern for the redemption of the whole human person, physical, spiritual, intellectual, emotional and aesthetic, it has the responsibility to encourage to the full the cultivation of musical and other artistic gifts. Indeed, our western culture is the result of such encouragement in the past. But there needs to be the recognition that different people have different gifts and that musical tastes vary widely. As Jesus asserts, each person has individuality and unique worth within the vast complexity of the universe (Luke 12:6–7).

Music and Worship

67.   A further reason why the Church has a responsibility for encouraging the arts arises from our understanding of worship. In that activity everyone offers to God a personality whose gifts are artistic and creative as well as spiritual. The offering of music as one of these gifts rests upon a firm biblical foundation. The Christian Church has been singing since the time of Jesus and the Apostles (Mark 14:26). They in turn were within a long Jewish musical tradition in which the Song of Moses (Exodus 15:1–18) and the Song of Deborah (Judges 5) are among the oldest parts of Scripture. Hymns of praise are found within the Psalter too, but that also contains outpourings of sorrow, complaint and anger. Indeed, the whole gamut of human emotion had its poetic and

musical expression in the worship of the Jewish people. However, references to music in Scripture and quotations from early Christian hymns in the New Testament Epistles, as well as the songs of the redeemed in Revelation, show music mostly as a means of giving glory to God. It communicates the thanksgiving and joy of the created to their Creator.

Sacred and Secular

68.   The Fathers believed that in order to be acceptable in worship music had to be 'purified' and 'seized' by the life-giving power of the Spirit. This belief is not widely held today, any more than the view that music is irretrievably tainted as part of fallen creation. But there is considerable debate, and much prejudice, as to what music is suitable for use in church. For example, there is common disagreement between those who believe that the only appropriate music is that which is instantly communicable to all the faithful, and others who hold that an insistence on vocal participation by everybody underrates the use, demanded by much music of the European classical tradition, of the mind and senses.

69.   For many of the latter the music preferred by proponents of 'full participation' is not properly 'religious' in its feel. It has too much of the world about it. But that is true also of much of the more traditional repertoire, even if it does not reach the proportions of Gounod's somewhat operatic *Messe Solennelle*. If a secular musical idiom is compatible with a Christian view of life, there seems no reason why it should not be used and consecrated in worship as part of a whole human offering. Given the belief that music itself is part of a fundamentally good creation, and not merely a means of understanding it, and given that it is capable of enhancing rather than detracting from the bond between God and his people, it is difficult to draw a line between what is sacred and what is secular. It is dangerous to make too clear-cut a separation of life inside and outside a church building. Too great a concern to have only 'religious' music in church may limit the worshipper's response to God's goodness in creation. It is understandable that people whose life and work is largely 'secular' should wish to use the world's idioms at least occasionally in their worship. What is an acceptable secular activity for the Christian surely becomes sacred through its conscious offering to God.

70.   The ability to discern is listed as one of the gifts of the Holy Spirit (1 Corinthians 12:10). It is as necessary for church musicians as for

anyone else to seek that gift, in their choice of music. Moreover, God's Spirit is mentioned in Scripture as having a part both in the Creation, and in the bestowal of artistic talents on human beings (Genesis 1:2; Exodus 35:30–35). From him we derive our many and varied abilities, including the gift of music which is commonly regarded as being amongst the highest manifestations of human creativity. Whether or not music is used in the context of worship, it remains a gift of God to the world. Its pervasiveness in every human society is indicative of its importance.

4

Worship, Prayer and the
Liturgy of the Church

71. We have referred to worship several times in the preceding pages, but there is more to be said. Worship provides the context for the music which is the concern of this Report. It is an activity which expresses an attitude fundamental to human life. Many people experience, deep within themselves, the need to give glory to God and an urge to have communion with him. St. Augustine identifies the reason for this in his oft-quoted words: 'Thou hast made us for thyself, and the heart of man is restless until it finds its rest in thee' (*Confessions* I.i). It is not, however, only a matter of instinct. We worship God because we know him to be worthy of worship, and because he both desires and enables us to offer it. This is a truth which all Christians believe, even though their responses to it vary according to differing traditions.

72. The most common form of response is to praise God and to thank him because of the salvation which he offers us in Jesus Christ. Thanksgiving is indeed the characteristic form of corporate worship, both in the Eucharist and on other occasions. So the Ephesians were enjoined to be 'filled with the Spirit . . . always and for everything giving thanks in the name of our Lord Jesus Christ to God the Father' (Ephesians 5:18–20). Whilst other forms of devotion may be helpful in taking us deeper into the mystery of prayer, thanksgiving marks Christian liturgical worship at its best. In it we give glory to God in response to his mighty acts. The act of thanksgiving reminds us that even in worship the initiative lies not with us but with God.

THE PURPOSE OF WORSHIP

73. In its proper sense worship is not confined to an activity in church, or to when one seeks to be consciously 'religious'. Genuine faith expresses itself in the worship of one's whole life, as is suggested by St. Paul when he writes, 'I appeal to you . . . by the mercies of God,

to present your bodies as a living sacrifice, holy and acceptable to God, which is your spiritual worship' (Romans 12:1). Nevertheless, the worship of daily life is expressed and focused in the liturgical worship of the Church. That worship not only reflects the worship of everyday living but also helps to form it. For this reason it is vital that the Church's services be services of *worship* before they be anything else.

Teaching, Fellowship and Evangelism

74.   Often, however, there would seem to be other priorities in the minds of those responsible for the worship in our churches. Three are common. The first is when a service is used for 'teaching', so that the Sunday liturgy is principally a time to communicate the Faith. Thematic lectionaries, and hymn lists to complement them, encourage such thinking, and the structure of the traditional Morning and Evening Prayer of Anglicanism seems to lead towards a climax of the expounding of the Word. For some people it is the preaching which determines their attendance at a particular church. Yet the public reading and exposition of the Scriptures, which themselves give glory to God, are as much directed towards him in worship as towards the people for their edification. There are other occasions and contexts for the latter.

75.   Another, and increasingly popular, view is that of worship as a means of promoting fellowship within the Christian community. Appropriate hymns and songs bind the people together in solidarity and love, which may be further expressed and fostered by movement and ritual. The whole atmosphere speaks of welcome, of belonging and friendship. There is no denying the enormous gain that has been brought by the rediscovery of church services as the normative context for Christian fellowship, but that is not the primary purpose of worship.

76.   Nor is its purpose chiefly one of evangelism, even if a service and its music have the undeniable power to convert or inspire. For whilst it is perfectly proper to expect people to be drawn by worship into a first experience of the living God, or to be reconverted in that context, the overriding purpose of worship is not one of mission.

Thanksgiving

77.   There is no doubt that worship does instruct, promote fellowship and present the Gospel to those who have not before been touched by

it and to those whose faith has weakened. It does all these and does them well. But that is because God chooses or allows it for one or more of these purposes. It is his prerogative and activity, not ours. Our responsibility is first and foremost to offer to him 'ourselves, our souls and bodies' in thanksgiving. Nothing matters for us except to give glory and to seek communion with him. The *raison d'être* of the whole enterprise is that worship is for God. In it we consciously stretch up towards heaven, seeking to get in tune with the angels and archangels. We strive to latch on to that worship of the whole company of the redeemed which is depicted in Revelation as being unceasing. For this reason the central part of authentic worship is the offering of thanksgiving, adoration and praise. By this means, above all others, we help people to catch a glimpse of God's glory.

PUBLIC WORSHIP AND PERSONAL PRAYER

78.   Part of the difficulty in achieving this purpose arises from a widely held belief that we have lost a sense of the numinous. It is sometimes suggested that this is a result of 'abandoning' the Book of Common Prayer, or of the fact that the celebrant no longer has his back to the people at a distant East end. But whatever the effects of particular liturgical texts or of architectural and choreographic arrangements, the difficulty in capturing a glimpse of heaven has much to do with the spiritual condition of those who worship.

79.   The quality of the devotional life of the faithful is important, not least because many people see little connection between private prayer and public worship. This is true of some who practise both, but is even more true of the large number of people who either go to church or say their prayers, but do not do both. Yet the liturgy is seriously weakened by such disconnection, since it needs above all to be prayed. Below the level of hymns, psalms, readings and prayers there needs to be an undercurrent or reservoir of prayerfulness. This is not the kind of praying which is turned on by 'Let us pray', and off again by the saying of the Grace. It is a deep spirit of longing for God. It is also rather different from the once popular custom of offering one's own personal prayers, often from a little holy book, at certain points during the liturgy. A private supplement to public worship, or an alternative approach to God in parallel, is not helpful. What is required is a prayerfulness in all who are present, which is wholly integrated with the action of the liturgy and which deepens it at every point.

Music and Silence

80.　Music is one aid to recovering this undercurrent of prayerfulness. An opportunity is provided, for example, by the singing of an anthem during the liturgy. It may well be used by God as a 'word' for people, as they sit quietly and let the music wash over them. Many of those who go to Evensong in a cathedral have learned to use the singing of the choir in just this way. There is no justification for a piece of music's intrusion into the flow of the service, however, unless worshippers are drawn into a deeper sense of God and a closer communion with him. It is not uncommon to find the singing of an anthem which rings more of 'performance' than prayerfulness, as the people sit back after the 'act' has been announced to enjoy (or endure) the result. Anthems should bring us to our knees, but it is not always so. The provision of a text can help people to unite themselves fully with what the choir is doing.

81.　More telling as an aid to prayerfulness, however, is silence. For prayer in worship is not what the minister does, or even what the people do when they join in the set-piece texts. It is what continues when the speaking or the singing stops, and the silence starts. The loss of this sense is illustrated in the way in which the Collect of the day is commonly used. In the classic start to the liturgy, after the president's greeting, the words 'Let us pray' introduced a lengthy silence before the praying of the Collect. However, 'Let us pray' has come to be understood as an instruction about posture, instead of expressing an attitude of mind and heart. No longer does it allow silent prayer by the people to take place during a substantial pause. The Collect, no longer a collective summing up of all the individual praying, is left on its own, to 'collect' something which has not happened. All that remains of the people's praying is the 'amen' at the end of it.

82.　The loss of silence has been a serious impoverishment of the liturgy for a thousand years and we need to recover its use, together with music, as a means of deepening the prayerfulness of worshippers. For participation in worship does not consist in being singled out to do something apart, or even in joining vocally in as much of the service as possible, whether singing or saying. Our profoundest offering is often to be silent and still. In such apparent passivity, we may contribute that undercurrent of prayer which is absolutely crucial and which gives worship its authenticity. This is as true of public liturgy as it is of private devotion. The recovery of this truth will help significantly in regaining a sense of the numinous.

Transcendence and Immanence

83.   In speaking of the numinous (and some would prefer to speak of catching a glimpse of heaven as being more concrete and biblical), it needs to be remembered that in the Incarnation we have an expression of the numinous in human form. Unlike those who belong to non-incarnational religions, Christians believe that in Jesus Christ the transcendent has been embodied and that we have received a full revelation of the God who has made heaven on earth. For this reason there is danger in drawing too sharp a distinction between the vertical and the horizontal in our faith and worship. In Jesus they have come together. A blessing used at Christmas expresses it: 'Christ . . . by his incarnation gathered into one things earthly and heavenly . . .'. In trying to catch a glimpse of heaven, we do so as those who have in a sense received it and are surrounded by it. In reaching up to God in our worship we respond to the one who has reached, and continues to reach, down to us.

God's Use of our Worship

84.   In our worship God often takes what we are trying to give him, no matter how inadequately, transforms it and makes of it a gift to us. We think we are doing one thing, only to find that God has turned the tables on us and given us much more than we have been able to give to him. This is his nature and character. So worship is after all a means of teaching. The whole experience, including the readings and preaching, teaches us of God, not because of our plans but because God chooses to accept what we offer and to use it in this way. Similarly, we do not set out to use worship as a means of fostering fellowship. But it develops into that, and at a level as deep as the reality and quality of the worship which is being offered. In the same way, we seek to worship rather than intend to evangelise at a Sunday Eucharist. But we often find that God so fills the assembly with grace that people can discover him, either for the first time or more deeply than before.

Giving Glory to God

85.   In the end, therefore, worship *is* a means of teaching, fellowship, mission and much else besides (for example, encouragement, Hebrews 10:25), but the *reason* for our worship nevertheless matters. Giving glory to God is not just one, or even the first, of a long string of reasons. It is the fundamental, deepest and truest reason, all-sufficient in itself. All the other reasons that are given for worship are to be seen,

43

not as products of our own contriving, but as the gifts of God in return for our response of giving him the glory.

86.   This means that in the preparation for the Sunday liturgy there needs to be (especially on the part of those who lead it) a desire above all to worship God. They will long to experience a glimpse of heaven and to have communion at a level that is only in part about bread and wine. In response to such yearning of the soul, God is able to work the miracle which makes it possible to speak of worship in terms of teaching, fellowship and mission.

87.   The primacy of praise and adoration remains, however, and is well expressed in Bishop Thomas Ken's familiar doxology:

> Praise God, from whom all blessings flow,
> Praise him, all creatures here below,
> Praise him above, ye heavenly host,
> Praise Father, Son, and Holy Ghost.

5

Music and Worship

88.   Almost all Christian traditions include the use of music in their worship. Worship can happen without it, but the recognition that music is one of God's gifts which we have to offer in worship has ensured its place in the services of the Church from biblical times onwards. There are many examples and exhortations in Scripture, and those who employ music in worship belong to the mainstream of Christianity, both East and West. We are able to draw on a rich tradition.

89.   If the fundamental purpose of worship is to give glory to God, this must be the overriding reason for the use of music within that context. However, as has been noted, what begins as our offering to God often becomes his giving to us. Thus he accepts the offering of our hymns, songs, anthems and settings and returns it to us transformed and enriched for our benefit. This may be so as to reveal something of himself, and in order that we may have a glimpse of heaven. It may also be for blessings of other kinds. Two in particular, unity and evangelism, were mentioned in the previous chapter, and are dealt with more fully here.

Unity

90.   Music, as has been said, may be a means of creating, fostering and deepening the fellowship of the congregation. Those who have experienced the singing of a crowd at the Cup Final, or of the audience at the Last Night of the Proms, know that music binds people together more deeply than almost anything else. It is, perhaps, part of St. Paul's concern for unity amongst his readers that leads him to urge them, whilst singing in their hearts to the Lord, to use 'psalms and hymns and spiritual songs' to address one another, and even to teach and admonish (Ephesians 5:19; Colossians 3:16). Whilst some may find it a strange notion, it may not be inappropriate for those singing in church to look one another in the eye, and even to smile as they do so. By such

means God not only enlarges our awareness of his Word and deepens our confidence in the Faith; he also blends widely differing people together in mutual joy, encouragement and acceptance.

91.   In some traditions this is the more real when the exchange of the Peace in the Eucharist is accompanied by singing, and sometimes dancing as well. The corporate encouragement that may be derived from music sends the worshipper out with a deeper sense of security and a renewed hope. There is something to 'take away' for the facing of the demands of daily life. It is thus valuable in encouraging people in the many areas of mission and Christian caring in society, as well as having important implications for ecumenism.

Evangelism

92.   No less significant is God's use of worship and music to confront those present with the Gospel, with all its promises and demands. For some, his way into their hearts is through music and they are brought to faith, or have their commitment renewed or deepened, because of what they hear or sing.

93.   This is not always an instant process and it may be spread over a long period of time. There are very many people, for instance, who have been brought to Christ, and sometimes to ordained ministry as well, as a result of many years' membership of a choir. Equally, people who attend services because they enjoy the music can one day find that they are there for more than that. God has used it to draw from them their love and obedience to himself. A consequence of such 'conversion' is that a person who has been blessed in this way may be enthused to share a new-found faith with others. Music has considerable potential for evangelism both in itself and through its devotees.

Our Responsibility

94.   Precisely how or when, or even if, the use of music will move worshippers is something that cannot be foreseen, planned or guaranteed. It remains part of the mystery of God's gift. We may neither anticipate nor dictate the ways and occasions on which he will use it. The important and well-planned service does not always 'take off', no matter how great the care that has been lavished upon its preparation. A 'routine' service, on the other hand, sometimes quite unexpectedly catches fire, and people experience something of the numinous. Like

the wind, the Spirit blows where he wills (John 3:8), whatever the results we hope for from our planning.

95.   We are not, however, absolved from the work of planning. Our receptiveness to the 'miracle' to be performed by God is perhaps in direct proportion to the quality of the material we offer him through careful preparation. This makes considerable demands on those who are responsible for the choice and performance of music. Perhaps their chief concern should be to create the right mood, both for the service as a whole and for its constituent parts.

Music and Mood

96.   Film-makers and broadcasters know well the unsurpassable power of music to set a mood, and church musicians may learn much from them. What happens before a service, for example, is important, whether it be silence or the use of worship songs or the playing of an instrumental voluntary. Erik Routley once said that the organ music before a service does for Anglicans what the smoke of incense does (or used to do) for Catholics: 'It lifts you over the threshold and into worship'. Thereafter the average congregation responds well to a well-known and lively piece in which all can join together. This generally gets the service off to a better start than when most of those present are silent, either because they do not know the music or because it is for the choir alone.

97.   At other points in the worship the mood will be different. Something quiet and gentle is called for during those parts of the service which are reflective; or strong, affirmative music for a confession of faith and commitment; or merry and boisterous pieces where the mood is one of celebration and praise. The final piece or the final voluntary is important, too, in influencing the morale of worshippers as they leave the service.

98.   A valuable defence against monotony, prejudice and personal idiosyncrasies is in the themes for the day or season provided by the liturgical year. Even so, one of the Commission's members heard of a church which on Easter Day 1990 had one Easter hymn, two for Passiontide and one for Ascension Day.

99.   The importance of music for setting the appropriate mood, both for and within an act of worship, cannot be over-emphasised. Those who are responsible for its choice and performance wield an influence

which is awesome indeed. They are perhaps helped by the fact that most of the music which is used is written for the enrichment of words. These provide a more concrete vehicle for the expression of human emotion, and most people use words as the primary means of expressing their feelings for God. Music is for the enhancement of their offering.

Singing in Tongues

100.   Something of the same might be said about the phenomenon known as singing in tongues. Particularly used by the Pentecostal churches, this is one of the marks of the charismatic movement which has emerged in some churches within the main-line denominations during the past few decades. It has its theological roots in the New Testament, where it is commonly associated with praising God and is a spontaneous improvisation in a 'language' not previously known by the worshipper. It conveys a depth of worship literally beyond description.

101.   Because of its unfamiliarity, the sound of singing in tongues at first strikes some people as eerie; however, it is not long before most appreciate its beauty and its simplicity. Often it begins by one person singing a melody, either quietly during a silence or at the height of praise which follows joyful hymns and songs. Other people begin to join in, each in an individual given 'language', and they contribute to variations on a common chord with the occasional passing note, or to harmony and counterpoint which may rise and fall in different parts of the church. If there are instruments, they may add their individual melodies, weaving in and out in improvisation.

102.   After a continuous time of worship through music someone may sing in a tongue, either a song of praise to God or a prophecy. In this case, since the solo involves only one voice, the leader is likely to pray for an interpretation to be given. This may be received either by the original singer or by some other person, and is usually a paraphrase rather than a literal translation of the original tongue. It may be spoken or sung. When it is sung it is often an exact repeat of the original melody, in spite of its usually being too long or complicated to be memorised on one hearing even by a trained musician. Or the interpretation is given in music which decorates, answers or complements the original.

103.   Neither the leader of the worship nor the director of music plans, initiates or terminates the period of 'worshipping in the Spirit'.

Nor is there any question of the congregation being out of control, since each individual can start or stop at will. Not all people have the ability or wish to sing in tongues, although many of those who desire this particular gift of the Spirit may well receive it at some time in their lives.

104.   The musician observing this phenomenon might well expect chaos to be the result of such spontaneity by those who are not particularly musical. They seem to be largely unaware of key, rhythm, accuracy of notes and pitch and other 'technical' considerations. Yet many people who cannot normally sing in tune do so perfectly when singing in tongues and produce a pleasing vocal sound. Moreover, the melodies which are sung are normally well-constructed and interesting. Far from there being discords and cacophony, there is such harmonious blending and unity that some would see it as an anticipation of the worship of heaven.

105.   The practice of singing in tongues need not divide a congregation. A sensitive leader will invite all to join together in singing, if not in tongues then in familiar words and phrases such as 'Alleluia', 'Hosanna' or 'We praise you, O God'. What matters is not so much the language used as that a whole congregation offer their spontaneous and heartfelt worship to God.

Liturgical Dance

106.   Words are not the only form of expression for which music provides an accompaniment, for with the introduction of many new songs since the charismatic renewal of the 1970s, there has been an increasing use in church of liturgical dance. It was to be expected that 'folk' music should find additional expression through movement, and its ethos is more one of corporate participation than of 'performance'. Those who present dance in worship are usually amateur enthusiasts rather than highly trained 'balletic' professionals.

107.   Liturgical dance has been described as a 'descant in movement' and that indicates both its subordination to, and its embellishment of, a theme. Frequently it accompanies the spoken word, such as a reading from Scripture. It can also take the form of a silent mime. Most commonly, however, it is accompanied by music. This may be pre-recorded or live, instrumental or vocal.

108.   The appropriate context for liturgical dance is an atmosphere of

worship, sharing and prayer, and the ideas and vision for its use arise naturally from the regular meetings of a committed membership. The underlying principle is that it should fit comfortably into the service. With or without words, it is as much an interpretation or expression of worship as the music which accompanies it.

Performance and Participation

109.   In common with dancers, musicians are commonly described as giving a performance. When this is applied to those who sing in church it can give rise to misunderstanding. For whether or not all those who are present *perform* the music which is employed in worship, it is for the *use* of everyone. When an anthem is sung, that music is offered for use by those who are listening silently to it, quite as much as by its performers. The announcement that 'the choir will sing an anthem' is an invitation to worshippers, not to sit back and relax but to do some 'praying with their ears', as Cardinal Basil Hume has suggested.

110.   Today there is an increasing emphasis on active musical 'participation' by the whole congregation. It should not be forgotten, however, that performance by a smaller number of people is a valid means of participation, which brings its own advantages. It encourages the employment of special musical skills, whilst allowing those who cannot or do not wish to sing to enjoy and meditate upon what is being done by others. Both are part of the worshipping congregation. The word 'performance' is not necessarily a pejorative one. Full participation does not, properly understood, demand speaking or singing by everybody all the time.

Musicians without Faith

111.   Those who accuse choirs of giving 'performances' in church sometimes find justification in the seeming attitude of those whom they criticise. But it is dangerous to make assumptions concerning the quality of their Christian commitment. God alone is the judge of the human heart, and some reticence is required before judging the motives or spiritual qualifications of players and singers.

112.   Nevertheless, not all church musicians are believing Christians and a good musical tradition often attracts those whose interest is more in the music than in the worship. Some argue that only believers should be involved (and perhaps quote John 4:24), whilst others see God as accepting and using a musical contribution for the benefit of the

whole community, whether it is offered by a believer or not. There are many architects, painters, sculptors and embroiderers, as well as musicians, who are not believers but who want to make a contribution to the Church's worship. Dare we say that God does not wish to make his gifts available to us through them?

113.   Music as a means or vehicle for worship is not the sole preserve of those who gather in Church. Its use in a service clearly makes it an offering to God by those who are there on that occasion. But it may also be an expression of worship by those not present who are responsible for its composition and even perhaps its publication. God gives music as much to those who write and propagate it as to those who perform and listen to it in church. There are composers for whom the writing of a piece of music is an act of response to God; there are secular musicians who regard their performances in terms of glorifying God. People can encounter God within a concert hall as well as in a church building. There is always a danger when we restrict God and his power to our own preconceptions.

Conclusion

114.   The attempt to describe the role of music in worship can be neither tidy nor precise. It is impossible to define the point at which our offering of music to God becomes his offering to us, since both usually happen at the same time. *We* use it to create an atmosphere helpful to worshippers and as a vehicle to express our feelings for God, with or without words or dance. *He* uses it simultaneously to reveal something of his nature to us, or in some other way to 'speak' to his people, or to draw people to himself, or to bring the congregation together. What is important is that we hold to our belief that music is a gift from God. As we offer the other gifts of creation to him in worship, so we offer and use this one. It is a gift which communicates chiefly in the area of human emotion, as well as being immensely satisfying to the intellect. There is nothing wrong with that. As Spurgeon, the great Baptist preacher, said in reply to a question about what kind of music should be used in church, 'Why, music which gives the *heart* the most play'.

6

Words and Music

115.   In almost all Christian traditions speech predominates in church services. Consequently, music in worship is nearly always used in conjunction with words and is commonly seen as subordinate to the words to which it is set. There is no doubt that an appropriate musical setting can greatly enhance the power of speech. As has been said, 'he who sings prays twice'.

Language and Expression

116.   The emphasis on verbal communication is understandable in a society as dependent as ours upon speech. Words are plentiful and are employed cheaply. They are necessary for philosophical thought, for the exchange of ideas and for the formulation and definition of anything beyond the vaguest feeling.

117.   Words are also used both for the creation of beauty and to allow the feelings of awe and wonder, joy and laughter, to be discovered and refined. The practice of poetry is the discovery of human ability to give language to what was hitherto inexpressible, and T. S. Eliot describes it as 'a raid on the inarticulate' (*Four Quartets*).

118.   So, although music has perhaps a greater capacity for expressing the subtleties of human emotions, we need words on most occasions in order to express what we hope or feel. Used in worship, they can exalt and proclaim, excite and delight. They allow our souls to express themselves 'Till we cast our crowns before thee, Lost in wonder, love and praise'.

119.   But speech can also oversimplify issues, and ill-chosen words can debase them by their coarseness, their lack of finer feelings, their insensitivity, their use of cliché or their sheer quantity. When the mind and spirit flag because of words ill-used in worship, music, as well as silence, provides blessed relief. It may also heighten the value and significance of the surrounding speech.

Variety and Flexibility

120.   Many of the traditional patterns of worship (associated for Anglicans with Matins, Evensong and the 1662 service of Holy Communion) have disappeared, taking with them much of the fine language of former days, and have made way for styles which give greater emphasis to spontaneity, variety and freedom of choice. Congregations differ in their styles of worship and 'churchmanship' and in their composition, according to age, ethnic make-up or social situation. Consequently, the same language is made to sound different in different contexts, by pronunciation and rhythm. The English of Radio 1 or 2 sounds different from that broadcast on Radio 3 or 4, and the kind of music used with that language differs as well.

121.   Those who adopt the idiom of Radio 1 or 2 and of the tabloid newspapers do so because these are the media with which their congregations are familiar. However, there is danger in any approach which aims for what is most widely acceptable. To hold to the level of the popular press and radio is liable in the long run to lead to the debasing of worship. But the cultural and intellectual approach of the other radio stations and 'quality' newspapers clearly has its dangers as well. For many, the language of the Book of Common Prayer is unsurpassed in its beauty, but for others it is antiquated and out of touch with contemporary needs. For that reason there is widespread support for those who, like the Jubilate Group, set out to provide 'modern words for modern people'.

122.   As with music, so language has to meet the varied demands of different styles of worship. There are registers and styles for prayer and reflection, for celebration and adoration. There are languages for sermons and for hymns. There are biblical languages of many kinds, prophetic, poetic, narrative, philosophical and mystical. The words used in church, therefore, have to satisfy a number of needs. They have to be clear, literal and down to earth in order to express the doctrines and grounds of belief; to be metaphorical and beautiful in order to express mystery and holiness; to be familiar in order to provide a right kind of security; to be fresh in order to offer a challenge; to be gentle for prayer and joyful for praise.

123.   All this underlines the need to be flexible in the use of language in worship and to take account of every occasion and every mood. It is no longer assumed that worship can or should be the same for all cultures and communities, or for all time, in a society which is multi-

cultural and multi-racial and in which words and their meanings are continually changing. For this reason words, as well as music, have to be more adaptable today than in the past. Modern and experimental language in worship has to exist side by side with that which is traditional.

Sexism in Language

124.   One of the most significant agreements among those writing texts today is the recognition that exclusively masculine language is no longer satisfactory. To the widespread recognition of the equality of the sexes has been added an awareness that attitudes to women continue to be influenced by the traditional language of a patriarchal society. Religious and official documents seem to imply that women are less important than men. Inclusive language is a necessary corrective. Sometimes the traditional language also has militaristic overtones (an example is 'Soldiers of Christ, arise', based on Ephesians 6:10–17) which compound the offence.

125.   Awareness of this poses little problem for present-day writers, but some people find difficulty using hymns which refer in masculine terms to the human race. There are those who find it offensive to refer even to the Persons of the Holy Trinity as male. Whilst it is possible to make simple amendments to some texts, collects and hymns without doing violence to the language or musical setting, there are many which cannot be altered appropriately. In such cases it is preferable to recognise the language as being normal to the age in which they were written. It would be a pity if our sensitivities caused them to fall into disuse.

The Psalms

126.   The oldest form of hymnody is the Psalter. This is one of the greatest treasures of Christian worship inherited from Judaism, in which human yearning and a full range of emotions are powerfully expressed in noble words. The Reformers valued the Psalms because, 'whereas al other scriptures do teach us what God saith unto us, these praiers . . . do teach us what we shall saie unto God'. Calvin described them as 'the anatomy of all parts of the soul'.

127.   Use of the Psalms in church is common to all traditions. Although the quality of their poetry and the range and depth of their feeling ensure their effectiveness when spoken, they are commonly

used with music. This usage varies in difficulty and appropriateness, ranging from plainsong, metrical and Anglican chants to Gelineau, Taizé, responsorial and polyphonic settings, and modern song. Of these, Anglican chant is one of the harder forms to master and, unless it is sung fluently, the music may be a hindrance rather than a help to devotion.

Hymnody

128.   Of all the new writing of texts for the Church today, that of hymns and worship songs is the most common and important. It is an art form which seems more readily accessible to both writer and singer than any other. So recent years have seen what is commonly called a hymn explosion, with a boom in the publishing of new books which shows no sign of abating.

129.   Hymns have been part of Christian worship since the earliest times. They feature at the Last Supper, in St. Paul's writings (for example, Ephesians 5:14, Philippians 2:5–11), and are mentioned by Pliny the Younger (early second century). The *Didache*, of the first or second century, includes some prayers written in rhythmical prose. In the Western Church, the *Te Deum* (traditionally ascribed to St. Ambrose) was one of the earliest Latin hymns. Almost every part of the Christian world had its hymns, written by poets and monks such as Venantius Fortunatus and Rabanus Maurus (who probably wrote *Veni Creator Spiritus*), by Prudentius in Spain, and by St. Patrick and St. Columba among the Celts. St. Augustine says:

> If you praise God, and do not sing, you utter no hymn. If you sing, and praise no god, you utter no hymn. If you praise anything which does not pertain to the praise of God, though in singing you praise, you utter no hymn.

130.   To this day, through the Reformation and with high periods during the eighteenth and nineteenth centuries, hymns have retained their popularity. It is not difficult to see why. They provide opportunities for varieties of self-expression by the worshippers, in verse as against prose, sound as against silence, singing as against saying. They draw upon the Psalms or other passages of Scripture, which they paraphrase, versify and expound. They articulate personal spiritual experience, with its difficulties as well as its joys. They reveal the inner weather of the human heart.

131.   Hymns are used to complement lessons, prayers and sermon. They allow the congregation to be vocally active in standing and expressing their praise, thought and emotion in words and music. They help worshippers to experience a deeper unity through making music together and singing the same words simultaneously. For preachers they can be a valuable resource in supplementing their message, in quotations from their statements of doctrine and ideas about belief.

132.   Dr. Johnson thought hymns to be restricted in their expression. Although they are written within the strict constraints of tempo and metre, they are capable of great variety in the hands of craftsmen such as Watts and Wesley. Congregations have come to accept that their style and their deviations from normal speech are part of a special rhetoric. They sing, without a flicker of hesitation, inversions of normal word order such as 'To his feet thy tribute bring'. Distortions of syntax and unusual juxtapositions were a marked feature of the metrical psalms (especially the 'Old Version' of Sternhold and Hopkins) which had a long dominance in the worship of this country.

133.   Whatever the origin of this trait, the linguistic and stylistic organisation of hymns has worked well for centuries and has become part of the consciousness of ordinary people in worship. Hymns provide a rich resource for personal devotion and can be recited as poetry. However, inasmuch as they are written for corporate singing, many of them feel rather flat when spoken; they need to be sung if they are to come to life. For they are what Roland Barthes would call 'Image-Music-Text', the unique combination of words and music which exists in a hymn book but which only truly exists when it is performed in worship. The hymn is written down, but the writing does not come off the page until the congregation sings it and it enters the body, the lungs and the blood. Through the sound made by the mouth and breath the writing becomes 'speech' again.

Music's Significance

134.   'Church music' means hymns for very many people, not so much because the music enhances the words as because music and words are inseparably linked. Indeed, a hymn tune is sometimes more memorable than its words, since associations are generally more readily evoked by music than by a text. Consequently, some hymns and songs retain their place in collections, in spite of words of doubtful literary or theological merit, because their tunes are popular.

56

135.   This situation is seldom reversed, although one sometimes comes across a hymn in which both text and music are of poor quality but which nevertheless keeps its place in the repertoire, perhaps for 'old times' sake'. In such cases it is often the familiarity of the tune which carries the day. Further evidence of the significance of the music of hymns and songs is that few things upset regular worshippers more than changing the traditional partnership of words and music in a particular piece. This suggests the need for great sensitivity in the increasingly common practice of either 'borrowing' a well-known tune for new words or introducing a new tune to a familiar text.

136.   Music is also of service to hymns because it is an aid to memory. Many a former cathedral chorister knows how a particular Anglican chant brings to mind at least some of the words to which it was set when he was a boy. Opera singers are able to cope with a long and complex libretto because of the wedding of the words to music. So the music used in church on Sunday can provide material for the worshipper during the week. A snatch of a canticle may be hummed and pondered, or a fragment of a chorus, or a phrase from a hymn. Familiar music may well be the major factor in the enormous popularity of television programmes such as 'Songs of Praise'. People take the opportunity to hear their long-loved favourite tunes again and again.

The Independence of Music

137.   Before leaving the question of the words, it should be pointed out that on occasions music in church has a life of its own, and even a significance greater than words. As has been suggested, it is capable of expressing the full variety of human emotions, without verbal under-girding. A piece played by a music group, a voluntary on the organ, or a Mozart symphony may 'speak'. It may express what we want to 'say' to God as much as 'Rejoice, Rejoice, Christ is in you' or Nunc Dimittis or *Messiah*. To stress overmuch the importance of words is to forget that music is an effective form of communication in its own right. It has the power to create an atmosphere for prayer and contemplation, and to set the tone for a celebration.

138.   Nevertheless, words will continue to have priority in our worship. Music will be used primarily for their enhancement. There can be no more powerful partnership than these two forms of expression, but that depends on their being used with imagination and awareness of their creative potential.

139.   Words and music are important as symbols in themselves, but they need to become more than that and to *live*. To cite Coleridge's use of the imagery of Ezekiel, 'The truths and the symbols that represent them move in conjunction and form the living chariot that bears up (for *us*) the throne of the Divine Humanity'. Those concerned with the use of language in worship need to remember that words are capable of bearing such an imaginative charge. For God reveals himself through them, as he does through music.

7

The Worshipping Community
and its Building

140.   Church buildings have a wide and varied significance. For surrounding communities they are both landmarks and the setting for public, local and national religious rites. For preservationists they are objects of beauty and repositories of art and history. For families they are associated with birth, marriage and death. For all manner of folk they are places of memories and dreams. Benefactors use them as an outlet for their generosity. Visitors look for interest within and on their walls. Hungry souls seek stillness and solitude in their space. The people of God meet there for Sunday and daily worship, and it is this last function which concerns us here. Among the many reasons and purposes for our churches, they are first and foremost the meeting-places, consecrated for worship, of the Christian community.

The Church Building

141.   Corporate worship is not confined to churches, but in Europe they provide the usual setting. Although necessity sometimes dictates the use of the town hall or a large classroom, buildings designed and dedicated for worship are much preferred. The building exists to serve the liturgy and its music rather than *vice versa*. This should be a guiding principle both in the adaptation of existing buildings and in the construction of new churches. For flexibility is required, to meet differing liturgical traditions, ever-shifting views, and variations in the content and structure of congregations.

142.   At its most basic the building provides a weatherproof meeting-place for church services, as well as storage for what is used in worship, which in the case of musicians consists chiefly of instruments, music, books and robes. But the significance which a church derives from the wider associations suggested above often makes its local community both possessive and narrowly 'parochial'. It is generally from this local community that the congregation is drawn, but it must never forget

that it belongs also to a worldwide *secular* society. Christians are 'called out' not only for the worship of God, but also for intercession, service, witness and mission towards the world to which they belong. Their purpose is to fulfil God's plan to unite in Christ *all* things in heaven and on earth (Ephesians 1:10). For this they need to have a vision beyond their often limited horizons.

Congregations and the Wider Community

143.   Enlarged awareness is assisted by the local congregation's belonging to the wider Christian community. As part of a denominational body of national or international scale, it inherits liturgical and musical traditions. By these it is sometimes constrained as well as supported, through authoritative instructions, an approved liturgy, a denominational hymn book, or simply the force of tradition. Its membership, with other denominations, of the universal Church on earth creates possibilities for yet wider learning. It is able to draw upon the resources of other traditions, and its musicians participate in choral festivals and courses run by various denominational or interdenominational bodies. Again, the significance of music for fostering ecumenism should not be overlooked. Nor, in a secular context, should one lose sight of its value in bringing together believers and non-believers in a common pursuit.

144.   Most important of all, is that those who worship in their own local church know themselves to be part of the great company of heaven whose worship is depicted in Revelation (especially in chapters 4 and 5). This can offer great reassurance to small congregations. Through the prayers and hymns of worshippers there is a sense of oneness with the communion of saints. Like them, they 'come to the Father through Jesus the Son'. He is the High Priest in heaven and the Minister in the true sanctuary (Hebrews 8:1–2) for all alike. In him all are one, whoever and wherever they are.

Unity and Diversity

145.   Music is not only one of the means of expressing unity both within and beyond the local congregation. It also reflects and fosters the diversity of which the Church consists (1 Corinthians 12:4–6). Most of the music with which we are familiar itself exemplifies the combination of diversity within unity, and the imaginative use of its different styles enriches the worship of a congregation which consists of people of different kinds. The way it is used may also reflect the ecclesiology of

a particular church. Thus denominations which teach strongly the equality in status and function of their members may use music in a similarly undifferentiated way. For example, the Free Church of Scotland has the Psalms sung by all who are present, in unison and unaccompanied. On the other hand, Lutheran churches use the music of Bach, and Roman Catholics the masses of Mozart and Haydn. With their soloists, choir and orchestra, these churches reflect their recognition of a hierarchy of status, functions and skills.

146. The usual reason for a wide range between starkness and complexity, however, is the matter of musical resources available. The music of Church of England services can vary between the simplicity of a small village church and the grandeur of a cathedral. Services differ, too, in their contexts and one cannot properly compare a said weekday service with a royal wedding.

The Congregation

147. The greatest diversity to be found in most churches is amongst those who are known as the congregation. Strictly speaking, all who are gathered for a service form the congregation. Though a distinction is commonly made between the congregation (or the people), and the musicians and others who lead the worship, the leaders nevertheless are part of the congregation and their contribution is intended to be for the benefit of *all* who are present. Notwithstanding their leadership, the tastes and expectations of the congregation are usually the biggest influence upon a Church's liturgical and musical policy. In most cases the people expect to play an 'active' part in the service, and the ordering of the building, together with the placing of leaders, is determined for their benefit.

Sound and Reverberation

148. For worshippers one of the important features of a church is its acoustic, as this determines whether speech and music are audible and intelligible. Music, perhaps more than speech, demands the right amount of reverberation. Too much will confuse, irritate or overwhelm, whilst too little will deaden. The right level will give vitality, in the same way that resonance gives life to an instrument. The provision of a proper acoustic is not a luxury. It improves the performance of expert and non-expert alike, and increases the pleasure of all.

149. The choice of music, the musical resources and the manner of

performance may be influenced by the acoustic. But modern techniques enable acoustics to be changed or, in a new building, designed for a particular result. Electronic amplification has brought a whole range of new possibilities, so that the amount of resonance required for the best musical effect does not make speech impossible. Frequently the acoustic varies from one part of the building to another, and this is an important factor in the siting of musicians. However, the use of sound reinforcement for performers allows considerable flexibility.

Furnishing

150.   A more subtle influence upon the style of a congregation's worship is exercised by the provision and arrangement of furniture and instruments within the building. These have considerable visual effect and power of association even when they are not in use. In a typical nineteenth-century Free Church chapel the organ may be directly behind the pulpit, reflecting the importance of music in its service of the Word in that tradition. Similarly, the array of choir stalls in a traditional Anglican chancel proclaims what was once the prominence in that church's life of Matins and Evensong, and of the robed choir that supported it. Today a raised altar or table at the front of the nave speaks of an emphasis on the Family Communion and the sharing of fellowship.

151.   Because of the difficulties in making changes to fixed seating and other arrangements, and because the furnishings and adornment of a church have their effect upon the psychology of a congregation, strict control is exercised by diocesan chancellors through Faculty Jurisdiction. Problems are usually avoided when parishes use the services of sensitive architects as consultants, as well as qualified advisers on matters affecting the organ.

The Organ and Other Instruments

152.   The position and the bulk of the organ, particularly where it is a nineteenth- or early twentieth-century instrument, offers one of the most intractable problems in re-ordering a church's interior. Tucked away in an alcove or encroaching into the vestry space it may be out of sight but it is not heard to best advantage. Free-standing at the end of an aisle or in a transept, it may sound well but be visually obtrusive. New instruments and new techniques often make it possible to overcome these difficulties, but most churches have to make do with what they have and plan the arrangement of the furniture around the organ.

Where there is an electronic instrument there is considerably more flexibility.

153.   Increasingly, churches are drawing upon the skills of other musicians besides organists. In some respects this is a recovery of the once-common practice, immortalised by Thomas Hardy in *Under the Greenwood Tree*, of having a church band. In addition to providing an accompaniment for hymns and songs, instrumental music encourages the active involvement of a larger number of musicians. It has its own place and value in worship, although traditions vary considerably in their use of it. It also makes for greater flexibility in the siting of those responsible for leading the music.

The Placing of Musicians

154.   The positioning of musicians in church is primarily a musical matter, with the aim of achieving the best musical effect. However, most choirs have more than one role. The same position may not be ideal both for leading the singing of the congregation and for singing on their own. Similarly, many organs are so placed as to make them effective in accompanying either the choir or the congregation, but not both. So the placing of singers and instruments is not always as simple a matter as it appears. Permanent positions make for stability and enable performers to be familiar with the sound they produce. But the space allocated by the constraints of the building is not always the best from a musical point of view.

155.   It is possible to vary the position of singers and instrumentalists during a service, and small organs can be mobile. Some churches are familiar with the choral procession and a Palm Sunday procession often takes the musicians out into the streets, together with the congregation. Occasionally, a whole service, like an Advent Carol Service, is in processional form, where the effect is greatly heightened by musicians moving to different places in the building.

156.   If musical effectiveness is the main consideration in the placing of musicians, there are others as well. For upon their position depends their ability to be associated with the action of the service. A West gallery can painfully distance a choir from the altar at the Eucharist. Singers in seats behind the pulpit are generally ignored by preachers. Similarly, an organist in a remote loft or behind curtains can be detached from almost everything that is going on. In present day re-ordering arrangements some musicians are returning to the gallery,

but it is more common for them to be positioned alongside the congregation (perhaps in a side aisle) or even within it.

157.   Musicians need to be seen as well as heard. Their visibility helps them to give a better musical lead to the congregation, and they can set an important example to the congregation in respect of posture, attitude, attention and general bearing during the service.

Special Dress

158.   Where the musicians are easily visible, what they are wearing becomes a matter of some significance. There are arguments for and against a distinctive dress. At a practical level, fewer children today have 'Sunday best' clothes, and robes can cover wide variations in individual taste in old as well as young. However, in an informal age the robing of musicians is frequently questioned, not least on the grounds of expense. Special dress for a choir certainly indicates its special role, in the minds both of its members and of others. In addition to other considerations, there is the question of how much differentiation between musicians and the rest of the congregation is desirable or appropriate. The decision by any one church will depend upon the answer to that question, as well as upon pastoral and social considerations. Musicians, whilst not being separate, are nevertheless a specialised part of the worshipping community.

159.   The musicians' distinctiveness consists in having musical gifts, to be used corporately and individually as an offering to God, and to assist the worship of all. They may lead and strengthen the congregations' singing, or they may sing or play alone, that others may worship silently. There are variations between these two roles. What they offer may serve both as a revelation from God to all those present and as a message to God from his people, as has already been suggested. The gifts which they place at the disposal of God and the congregation in worship are both those which they have 'naturally' and those which have been developed by hard work. Considerable commitment is required of them, including attendance at practices as well as services. They are rightly regarded as being in one way or another 'experts' in the field.

Other Leaders in Worship

160.   The same may be said of the individuals who lead the worship as readers (with a small or large 'r'), intercessors, officiants or celebrants.

In some traditions musical demands are made upon them in, for example, the Versicles and Collects of the Office or the Gospel and *Sursum Corda* in the Eucharist. The singing of these items by one person was originally in order to make them audible to the worshippers in a large building, before the use of the vernacular and without modern acoustic aids. Today they are sung to enhance the worship and are effective so long as they are adequately performed. Conversely, unsatisfactory singing weakens the liturgy, and where the leaders cannot sing, their parts are commonly delegated to others, where the rubrics permit, or they are said.

161.   Among the most influential people in a service is the one who is in charge of the music. From its selection to its rehearsal and use, the director contributes at least as much as anyone else to the quality of the worship of a church. In many cases directors of music provide the instrumental accompaniment for congregation and choir, or lead a music group. Occasionally they also sing in the choir. Those churches which give a prominent place to their specialist singers generally have their director as a clearly visible conductor. Whatever is the case, the attitude and quality of the director's work profoundly affects all those present in church. That person's influence on the Christian community is also powerfully exercised in everyday working relationships with others.

Professionalism, Payment and Patronage

162.   The expertise of musical directors calls for proper respect. Rarely, however, are they given encouragement, means and opportunities to develop their abilities further. Most receive some kind of payment or honorarium and in some churches others, too, are paid to sing or play. The question of remuneration is not necessarily related directly to the standard of music produced. There are some very gifted amateurs whose skill and dedication result in music of an extremely high quality. Because payment involves terms of employment and contracts and the respect due to a professional, the salaried musician's membership of the worshipping community is a complex one, which may be further complicated by membership of a union. For this reason some churches reject the notion of paying their musicians. They believe that worship, and the offering of music within it, must spring from membership of the Church and personal commitment to the Christian faith. Apart from considerations which have been mentioned earlier, the payment of people to produce music in church has some

benefit for the wider community. It is a relic of that patronage of the arts which has been so essential and so beneficial to society as a whole.

163.　Today the Church's patronage consists not so much in the modest payment of its musicians as in making its buildings available for concerts and musicians of all kinds. The use of churches and cathedrals in this way is worth noting. The demand would seem to be growing for beautiful ecclesiastical venues for music which makes no claim to be religious. Roman Catholic authorities question the appropriateness of the performance of non-religious music in church and lay down firm guidelines for concerts of sacred music. Other churches show less concern about the choice of works to be performed or charging for admission and applause by the audience. The church may become a concert hall. But it is one with a special atmosphere in which God may be glorified and humanity uplifted.

8

Quality, Styles, Standards and Choice

164.   The choice of music in worship is a responsibility greater than is often recognised. It does not always rest alone with those who direct its use or performance in church; in many situations it involves the clergy and musical director in consultation. Increasing use is made of worship sub-committees which include 'ordinary' members of the congregation as well as those with musical or liturgical expertise. Circumstances differ greatly from place to place, but a healthy church should have no difficulty in achieving a proper balance between its specialists and the rest of the worshipping community, where the expertise of the special-ist will be recognised and the wishes of the non-experts will be respected by the specialist. When there is a lack of acceptance on either side, or a failure to recognise the right of all to participate in worship, there will probably be trouble.

Only the Best

165.   Perhaps the least satisfactory discussion in connection with any art form is in reply to the question, 'what is good art . . . painting . . . sculpture . . . poetry . . . music?' Except in a few cases, there is unlikely to be a conclusion with which all will agree, and it has to be recognised that judgment depends primarily on personal taste. We may not expect too definite an answer in reply to 'what is good church music?' There is difficulty even in trying to define exactly what we mean by saying that only the best is good enough for God. Of course it is, but how do we know what is best in his eyes? Who dare presume to describe the aesthetic tastes of the Almighty? Who other than he can finally judge the quality of our offering in worship?

166.   Yet some judgment of quality has to be made by the people responsible for the choice of music. Such discernment is highly subjective. Deciding on pieces of music by merit or quality is often difficult. It is always subject to the danger of arbitrariness based on prejudice or preference. But it is some comfort to recognise that often

that which is really good stands out just as clearly as that which is of poor quality. Moreover, the bad does not on the whole survive. Publishers' catalogues in the last century contained quantities of dross, together with the gems that are still part of the standard repertoire.

167. In the end the choice is best based not on personal preferences but on asking the question, 'Within the style which is suitable, comprehensible and helpful to my congregation, is this piece of the best quality that I can find?' The answer to that question may not always be easy. But there should never be a suspension of sensible critical judgment because the music is for use in church.

Appropriate Styles

168. The question of quality is further complicated because the church musician is faced with an almost bewildering variety of musical styles. The point has already been made that none of these can safely be said to be outside God's inspiration. Potentially, any of them might be appropriate for a particular act of worship. In addition to 'church' music, folk music (real or imitation), classical music, rock, pop and jazz have all been used with varying degrees of success.

169. As well as being an offering to God, the particular musical style adopted in a church is intended to help people in their worship, rather than obtrude or be a source of irritation and dissatisfaction. Consequently most churches have a repertoire which is limited and, some would say, unimaginative. That each church and cathedral should develop its own musical tradition is to be expected. Some will find rock music offensive in church, whilst others are bored or even alienated by the more traditional forms.

The Needs of People

170. Diversity of preferences is explained by the fact that people differ enormously in their temperaments and personalities, and therefore in their responses to different kinds of music. The significance of these differences has long been known to those interested in the relationship of psychology and spirituality. In recent years it has become more widely known through the Jungian Myers-Briggs Type Indicator.

171.   This suggests that there are sixteen basic personality types with many subtle differences within each type. Broadly, each person is somewhere on a continuum between extroverted and introverted, sensing and intuiting, thinking and feeling, judging and perceiving. Consequently, in a congregation some people will not want to change anything in their worship; for others, the more change there is the happier they will be. Some long for more silence and know how to use it creatively; others find silence difficult and need to have their minds and their worship channelled. Some will happily accept what is offered them; others will want answers to innumerable theological and liturgical questions before making up their minds. Some will be drawn to worship through the power and beauty of a performance of Bach's *St. Matthew Passion*; others will be reached through Christian pop music.

172.   People therefore differ in temperament as well as according to any temporary state of happiness, anxiety, grief, anger, depression or exhilaration. They differ, too, in their preferences and needs according to where they are in their spiritual journey. As an individual moves from one stage to the next it is normal to enjoy a different kind of musical expression. Progress in maturity may well be marked by a greater catholicity of taste.

173.   It is not a question of one way being superior to another. Different people have their own preferred ways of worshipping, in which they can feel at ease. Such differences have to be taken seriously, not only by church musicians but by all who plan and lead worship. All of us are created in the image of God. But each is a unique personality, with the need to respond to the worth and love of God as oneself and not as a stereotype. This is obviously more possible in the context of individual devotion than in that of public worship. Knowledge of the many temperamental differences within a congregation, however, explains why a particular musical piece attracts some but repels others. It calls for great sensitivity on the part of those responsible for the music.

174.   We have also to accept that what once appeared to be a common musical language in which all could participate has been curtailed. Thus, familiar hymns and psalms which were part of most church people's upbringing before 1950 are not known by a younger generation. In any case the congregation will probably contain people of significantly differing tastes.

69

175.   In the large town or city, there are enough places for people to find the kind of worship which is most helpful and congenial to them. But in small centres of population and rural communities, where there is only one place of worship, the question of musical styles has to be faced particularly sensitively and imaginatively. There is no reason why all the music in all the services should have the solemnity popularly associated with church music. It should be possible to use varying styles, either on the same occasion or at different services. People may need to learn that their indifference or antipathy to a particular style does not mean that it is unsuitable for others. Preferences will be expressed, but there has also to be tolerance of other tastes. One style of hymn is not necessarily 'better' or 'worse' than another.

Standards of Performance

176.   In the performance of a musical piece, no matter what the quality and style of the writing and whether it be simple or complex, there should always be the aim of achieving the highest possible standard. This is because music in worship is part of the Church's offering to God. It is also because a poor performance can distract the congregation and be destructive of worship. Poorly played hymns, strident singing, insensitive amplification, poor intonation, or insecure part-singing can all intrude and will unsettle the worshipper no less seriously than an unsatisfactory sermon. Moreover, performers are likely to be judged increasingly by the standard of the many recordings of church and other music which are widely available today.

177.   Because perfection is unattainable here on earth, there is bound to be some falling short of the ideal. Worshippers readily forgive minor blemishes, but this should not be made an excuse for shoddy performances. Nor is there any justification for a popular notion that the standard of performance does not matter as long as it is sincere. It is not sincerity before God on the part of musicians if they ignore the right notes or do not attempt to fulfil the intentions of the composer. After all, the skills of performers and composer alike are God-given and it is no glory to him to be musically careless. God may not be glorified by a congregation which has been set on edge by a needlessly low standard of singing or playing.

Making the Choice

178.   Standards are dictated in the first place by the choice that is made of the music to be performed. That choice is determined by a

number of factors, but it is always subject to the overriding consideration that worship is first and foremost an offering to God, whether it be
in the simplicity of a country church with a 'reluctant organist' and no
choir, or in the grandeur of a Perpendicular cathedral with a team
of thirty-six professional musicians. The music is neither community
singing nor is it a concert performance. It is the raising of the hearts and
minds of the congregation, whether they take part silently or with their
voices.

179.   Of the other considerations which guide the choices to be made,
the most important is the necessity of tailoring one's selection to the
resources which are available. Pieces which are beyond the skill of
players or singers or an over-ambitious anthem can seriously detract
from an otherwise admirable service. Although it is often stated, it
remains true that a simple piece well, or even adequately, performed is
much more effective than one which is too difficult for the performers
and leaves performers and listeners alike with a feeling of dissatisfaction.

180.   It is important to take account both of the styles of music which
meet the requirements of that particular congregation, and of the
quality of music within those styles, if there is to be a worthy act of
worship. There is also the need to be sensitive to the moods of the
seasons of the year, of the service as a whole and of the different parts of
the service. Moreover, it is essential to have some understanding of the
effect that music can have upon the human being.

Music's Power

181.   The power of music to heal is familiar to those who use it for
therapy. The wide range of people helped in this way includes those
with mental, physical or emotional handicaps, sufferers from disease
and those with other disadvantages. There is a biblical precedent in the
story of David's playing for Saul when he was under the influence of an
'evil spirit from God' (1 Samuel 16:23). The therapist 'uses music, in a
therapeutic environment, to influence changes in the patient's feelings
and behaviour' (Flashman and Fryear, *The Arts in Therapy*. Chicago:
Nelson Hall, 1981). It is also used for self-enrichment.

182.   Therapists analyse the effects on their clients of the basic components of music, such as pitch, duration, loudness and timbre. Most
people, for example, are most comfortable with the middle range of
pitches. A high range creates tension and a lower one brings relaxation.

Tempi of 70–80 beats per minute echo the average beat of the human heart. An accelerating tempo may speed up the pulse-rate and provide stimulation, but a lower one will relax the listener. Loud music may give the client a sense either of being safe and surrounded or of being excluded or of feeling frightened. Reactions differ widely, too, to timbre and tone colour. The sound of a bagpipe, for example, affects different people in very different ways. Moreover, individual associations, such as the words of a song or the familiarity of a piece, will determine the response of the listener. If music can be used to heal and to help, it can also, therefore, be harmful.

183. The implications of this for church musicians are obvious. Because music is a powerful tool which can affect people deeply, even when that is not perceived or intended, those responsible need to be aware of its influence. It may not be realistic to incorporate instruction on the psychology of music, or the basic principles of music therapy, in the training of musicians and clergy. But it should be possible to observe the reactions of congregations during worship. Also, members of the congregation might be given some opportunity to respond to the choice of music, and even to have some part in it. This is one of the principles of music therapy, and it would provide for greater co-operation and participation in the planning of services, which in turn could bring benefits to the worshipping life of the church.

Censorship

184. From time to time the suggestion is made that 'the Church' should ban certain pieces of music from use in worship. Apart from being practically difficult, such prohibition is highly undesirable. For congregations differ in their ethos and tradition and they need to address God through the music of their choice. Furthermore, if God can reveal something of himself through many styles of music, whether it be Mozart or the Beatles, we might be in danger of limiting both God and church musicians were we to compile an index of forbidden pieces. We could also be in danger of creating a musical élite with the right to bind or loose.

185. But it is important that neither within a congregation nor within the wider Church should there be a single group which assumes that it alone has the right approach. In this area, as in many, no one has the authority finally to judge others. Tolerance of different approaches is essential. We are, unhappily, accustomed to condemning or despising

the forms of worship unfamiliar to us, but it can be deadly to the life of the Church. Whilst preferences are both allowable and necessary, judgmentalism is not.

Conclusion

186. Every effort should be made to educate fully those who are responsible for music in church. It is so important an ingredient of worship that the greatest care needs to be taken over its choice, in order to ensure that the varying temperamental, spiritual and cultural needs of the congregation are respected. Above all, the quality and style of music must assist the community to worship in a way that will lift their hearts and minds as an offering to God.

PART 3

THE PRESENT SITUATION
The Evidence Received by the
Commission

9

Music in Parish Churches

187.   In undertaking its survey of the current state of music in worship, the Commission has attempted to be as comprehensive and as accurate as possible. It has tried to place as much weight on authenticated fact as on hearsay and opinion, and has sought to take a rounded and impartial view of the evidence at its disposal. The means of obtaining such evidence has already been mentioned in the Preface, but among them the Parish Survey is factually the most significant. This, together with other representations, correspondence and observations, forms the basis for an assessment of the music in our parish churches, rural, urban and suburban.

THE OVERALL PICTURE

188.   A questionnaire was compiled and sent to 4% of the parishes in the Church of England (see Appendix 2.5). Although this is statistically small, the scientific choice of the sample has ensured a reasonable representation of the situation as it pertains to our subject. Replies were received from 524 parishes, and of these 63% came from rural parishes, the other 37% being urban (including suburban). Of the total, 23% described themselves as 'evangelical', 36% as 'catholic' and 41% as 'central'.

The Purpose of Music

189.   In reply to a question about the role of music in worship, the most popular reason given is 'to worship and praise God'. Second to that is 'to uplift the soul', and the third, particularly favoured in urban evangelical and central churches, is 'to promote corporate awareness and fellowship'.

Choirs and Music Groups

190.   Nearly two-thirds of the churches have a choir, and 71% of these churches are in urban areas. Most of them wear robes and their average

size is fifteen members, more than half of whom are female. A fifth of the churches also have a 'music group'.

Organists and Clergy

191. In just under half of the parishes, responsibility for the music is shared between the incumbent and the music director. In just over a third of them, the incumbent undertakes this himself. Of the incumbents, 97% consider themselves to enjoy good personal relations with their directors of music. But several correspondents speak of tensions and power struggles. An incumbent suggests that the musician may ignore the feelings and needs of others because he is anxious 'to define his position in a hierarchy'. One organist feels that his integrity is threatened by parish priests who 'run with the tide' in a desperate bid to retain congregations. Another notes that some clergy too readily acquire the belief that standards of performance are not of great importance; 'so what if all the notes are wrong? God won't mind!'

Remuneration

192. Although over half the musical directors mentioned in the Survey have musical qualifications, only 21% of them earn their living wholly as musicians. With a very few exceptions (and those mostly in evangelical churches) none receives from the Church a salary sufficient to live on. Only 5% of parishes pay their directors of music more than £1,000 per annum, 16% offering a sum of between £600 and £1,000. The remaining 79% provide less than £600. Just under one in three urban churches pays more than £600 and 'catholic' churches are more likely to pay at the top end of the scale. Both they and 'evangelical' parishes have a music budget which averages £350 per annum. 'Central' parishes spend a little over one-third of this amount.

193. A few correspondents were opposed to church musicians receiving any remuneration. Many others felt that, as professional directors of music were being increasingly employed as 'ministers of music', their remuneration should be at least on the same basis as that of the clergy. In its evidence to the Commission, the Royal College of Organists speaks of the 'difficulty of choir recruitment and the shortage of organists'. It suggests that there are factors in the Church itself which act as a deterrent, and this 'at a time when our own best young organists are reaching remarkable standards of excellence' and when European liturgical music from the past is more popular than ever before. A larger gap now exists between parish and cathedral music

than hitherto. As the RCO notes, 'the middle [has] dropped out of the market', and in consequence the career structure for professional church musicians has been seriously curtailed.

Handling Change

194.　Many correspondents complain, often with a real sense of hurt, about peremptory change and innovation in parish church music. But the *status quo* has not altered as much as is sometimes claimed. Opportunities for vocal participation by the congregation are certainly on the increase, and most parishes accept the need for healthy evolution. Occasionally it is clear that changes have been made with insufficient consultation and with a lack of diplomacy. Consequently attitudes have hardened and real offence has been taken by those who feel their point of view has been ignored. Fewer than 30% of the parishes have a worship committee.

Repertoire and Standards of Performance

195.　Overall, the Eucharist is the most common service. At least one congregational setting is used by 68% of the churches, while only 18% still use those which are sung exclusively by the choir. Psalms sung to Anglican chant are still to be heard in 74% of the churches. This is particularly favoured by those of the central tradition, but other settings of psalmody are more usually found in evangelical churches. More than half the churches regularly have anthems sung either by the choir or, sometimes, by a less formal singing group. Organ music retains its popularity in 85% of the parishes, with other forms of instrumental music occurring chiefly in the urban areas.

196.　BBC producers of religious programmes have suggested to the Commission that, at a time when the musical standards achieved by cathedral choirs are higher than they were thirty years ago, it is 'increasingly difficult to find good music at parish level'. They claim that too often the repertoire of the indifferent parish church choir is dominated by the cathedral ethos. The aspirations of some choirs are too often 'a triumph of optimism over ability' and they should rather attempt music 'broadly within their competence that can be rendered with integrity'.

197.　One correspondent registers concern that in the future many churches will find themselves increasingly obliged to base their choice of hymns upon the repertoire currently being offered in primary schools. The popularity of the two volumes of the BBC's *Come and Praise*, as used each week by a million children taking part in the 'Together' assembly, sets a limit to their taste for religious songs and hymns. Some have welcomed such material and use it extensively in Sunday School or Junior Church. Others, however, are anxious lest children are being denied the opportunity to encounter at an early age some of the finest examples of hymnody.

Styles of Music

198.   Where there is difficulty, it is clear that much of the debate revolves around deciding what is appropriate in church music. Most people agree that standards need to be maintained, both in the choice of material and in the quality of performance. But they see personal taste as being a large factor in making any judgment. This, as one correspondent put it, is conditioned by one's own particular experience and background; 'what *I* feel good with' is not necessarily right for others.

199.   Many of those who wrote to the Commission made the point that church musicians are the 'transmitters of the vital and rich heritage of liturgical music', and they obviously had a particular style of music in mind. One of them had little time for 'religious observances indistinguishable from . . . forms of commercial entertainment'. Another wondered whether God's glory could adequately be expressed 'by the tawdry words and music of modern pop culture'. One couple in their seventies had abandoned the church where they had worshipped for many years when the 'traditional and reverent approach to worship turned into a jolly social discothèque atmosphere'.

200.   One assistant priest and former church musician suggests that 'music is part of the expression of the relationship between the risen Christ and his church'. He points out that it is the servant of the liturgy and is not to be dependent wholly upon organs, choirs and music groups. Music should be in an idiom and style appropriate to the age, social and ethnic make-up of the particular congregation. Another priest suggests that the Church of England needs to produce music which is 'indigenous to our cultures, founded in the historical styles and traditions of the Anglican church and incorporating the benefits of modern technology'. From an urban area in the North a priest-musician notes that we need to 'worship excellently, using all the varied creative talents God has given us'.

RURAL CONGREGATIONS

Choirs and Organists

201.   Nearly two-thirds of the parishes included in the Survey are rural ones. Just over half of these have a choir. There are a similar number of organists, a third of them being described as 'reluctant'. Only 15% have a director of music with whom the responsibility for organising the music rests. In the remaining 85% of parishes the clergy choose the music and have to arrange for its rehearsal and accompaniment.

202.   One typical submission concerns a scattered rural deanery of thirty-two churches, eight clergy posts (two of them unfilled), nine churches without regular organists and eighteen organists who between them take care of the remaining twenty-three churches. Six parish choirs and a 'group' choir involve 100 people, with regular rehearsals. Standards vary, organists are mostly elderly and of limited ability, and the recruitment of replacements is very difficult.

203.   A submission from the vicar of a group of parishes on behalf of the Archbishops' Commission on Rural Areas (ACORA) suggests that there may be 5,000 village churches with small congregations and no local musician to train the choir or play the organ. At a time when non-stipendiary ministers, Readers and liturgical assistants are emerging to keep small rural churches alive, many such churches will soon be without 'sympathetic music . . . an integral part of worship'.

The Organ and Other Instruments

204.   The maintenance of the organ is often a considerable burden to a congregation which already struggles to meet its financial commitments to the diocese as well as to maintain its building. A piano or an American organ is sometimes used as a substitute. With their increasing popularity, electric keyboards also are finding their way into worship, as are guitars and other instruments when performers are available. Some churches rely on cassette recordings of hymn accompaniments, with some success.

Four Scenarios

205.   Four different pictures, taken from real life, give some impressions of the state of the music in rural churches. In the first, a group of ten villages has three full-time clergy. Because they are within easy reach of the county town, there are four organists among the ranks of

the professional commuters. Of these, two have had some musical training, whilst a retired schoolmaster runs a singing group which assists monthly at the group services, accompanied by two or three instrumentalists. Parishioners have been with the Team Rector to Taizé on liturgical and other courses. Money is spent on music and hymn books, thanks to a large legacy. Three of the churches have small robed choirs.

206.   The second picture is of a small seaside village which depends upon seasonal holiday trade in an otherwise depressed area. There is one church, a choir, and an organ. The organist has little musical training and struggles with the *Wedding March* at the four or five weddings each year. Rite A is used, with a simple modern congregational setting. Occasionally the choir will sing a hymn as an anthem.

207.   Eleven people worship regularly in the church in one of a group of nine scattered hamlets. The organ is badly in need of repair and tuning. The organist is 'reluctant', to the extent of using one chant only for all the canticles and having a very limited repertoire of hymns. Matins or Evensong is 'sung' on three Sundays out of four. On the fourth there is a said Celebration of the Holy Communion from the Book of Common Prayer. Suggestions of using the Alternative Service Book are being resisted.

208.   In the fourth, there is no organist in a village of 240 people. The organ is heard only at the rare funeral or wedding, when a friend of the family or other person is brought in to play. Having four other congregations, the vicar takes services only twice a month. The Reader takes a monthly family service, which he prepares and photocopies for the congregation. For this a local nurse provides guitar accompaniment to worship songs and modern hymns. Of the twenty who come regularly to church about half use their own copies of the ASB for Morning Prayer. The Psalms are said and the hymns are unaccompanied, except when there is the occasional pre-recorded accompaniment.

Signs of Hope

209.   Despite the evident musical poverty in some of these pictures, there is surprising vitality in the worship of many country churches. According to one correspondent, standards of music are generally said to be 'pretty lamentable' but they can on occasion rise to 'rather surprising heights'. The clergy and others who lead services have shown an admirable resilience, even where services have been said

rather than sung. In some cases speaking the Psalms has actually proved to be a real liberation from the 'tyranny' of Anglican chant.

210.   Some dioceses with large rural areas are embarking on lay training in order to help tiny congregations adjust their expectations of worship. For the shortage of priests means fewer Eucharists and a greater reliance on local laity and, not least, on the musical gifts of children. This is a rich resource when it is available.

URBAN CONGREGATIONS

211.   The inner cities present a different kind of challenge. The rural Church struggles for want of people living in its parishes. The Church in urban areas has a large population living all round church buildings which are rarely filled. As one correspondent reminded the Commission, there is 'an increasing failure of the church to break into urban areas or into sections of society other than the relatively middle-class post-war culture. In the light of the fact that over 90% of the British population lives in areas classified as urban, this failure is a great danger to the future of church music and worship. Urban culture is the primary culture in Britain today'.

Choirs

212.   Nevertheless, there is still a flourishing musical tradition in some well-known churches in our cities, often with fine all-male choirs. There are also thriving choirs of this kind in more ordinary churches, for example in the more prosperous towns of Lancashire.

213.   By and large there has been a great decline in the number of boys singing in parish churches, although small numbers of boys sing with girls in many choirs. Most of them will have a predominance of female voices for the upper parts. There are a few choirs consisting of adults only. Sometimes these are excellent, but the general standard of urban church choirs, where they exist, is mediocre.

Music Groups

214.   Many churches in the evangelical tradition have introduced singing and instrumental groups, sometimes alongside the traditional choir but very often replacing it. Very few have abandoned the organ altogether; even where almost all the music is provided by instrumentalists, the organ is retained, maintained and used.

Where Resources are Lacking

215.   There are, however, very many urban churches without resources. Where there is no choir or music group, no organist, and no
organ which is playable, it is hard to know how to provide music for the
worship of what may be anyway a meagre congregation.

216.   Many will therefore sympathise with the incumbent in an
Urban Priority Area who is himself a trained musician. In his submission to the Commission he said that he finds it anomalous for Sunday
School children to pass automatically at the age of eleven-plus into a
robed choir, where there is no further 'teaching about Jesus'. So he had
adjusted the worship 'to count the children in' and there were now a
hundred children attending regularly, with twenty adult helpers.
However, the choir had ceased to exist. Care is taken to provide a
musical diet which relates to the needs of the congregation, in the
belief that it is unrealistic to impose a Radio 3 culture on those whose
normal listening is Radio 1.

Hope in Surprises

217.   It is wrong, however, to suppose that the inner city church is all
musical dereliction. In major cities there may be a struggle to maintain
even the most basic music, but faithful and competent organists are to
be found in the least expected places. Good choirs can flourish in
extremely run-down areas where there is a leader who can inspire.
This is most likely to be true of a city where there is a rich mix of
inhabitants in most neighbourhoods. In many such places the congregation consists largely of people of overseas origin. As a result, the
music is often Afro-Caribbean, and very lively.

218.   There are churches with poor resources, but there are still some
of all traditions where music is taken seriously. Music *is* continuing in
urban Anglican churches, even if the type of music and standards vary
considerably, and excellent things can still be found.

SUBURBAN CONGREGATIONS

219.   Much of the material in this Report reflects the situation in
suburban churches. In general, their musical provision is more satisfactory, even if it gives no ground for complacency. The Anglican
choral tradition finds its strength in many a market town and leafy
suburb. There is also a greater readiness to experiment and much use is
made of music groups of various kinds. The relative affluence of some

suburban churches makes it possible to provide organs and other resources. Because of the number of professional people who live in suburban parishes, the shortage of organists and musical directors is less felt here than in rural or inner-city areas.

Organists

220.   An organists' association in the Greater London area submitted to the Commission some of the information it had gained through a questionnaire to its members. The seventeen organists who replied had held their present posts for around ten years, and their average age was fifty-three. The youngest was thirty and the oldest seventy-eight. Two of them held recognised musical qualifications and seven had passed local graded examinations. Few of them were continuing with any further musical training. Most of them were closely involved in the life of the Church and were not therefore greatly concerned about the usually modest level of their remuneration. Only one had obtained his present post in competition with others; nine had been the only applicant, and the remaining seven had been 'invited' to undertake the organist's duties without even applying.

CONCLUSION

221.   The picture of music in parish churches, emerging from a mixture of fact and opinion, indicates a wide divergence in current practice. The lack of personnel and musical resources, particularly in urban and rural areas, creates a situation which is far from satisfactory. Much encouragement is needed for those who are struggling to maintain music in the face of difficulty and discouragement. That they are doing so is in itself a cause of hope for the future.

10

Music in Cathedrals

222.   At the heart of what is commonly called the Anglican tradition of church music are the cathedrals, collegiate and choral foundations and Royal Peculiars of the Church of England. They represent a continuity of worship and music stretching back to a period well before the Reformation. They have had an enormous influence on the music of this country, both sacred and secular, and this is now perhaps wider than ever, thanks to modern communications. The distinctive contribution which our cathedrals make to Western culture is the more significant because of a world-wide recognition that they represent something unique. This contribution is particularly admired in continental Europe.

223.   In spite of the turmoil of the late twentieth century, cathedrals have shown both resilience and consistency. They have had to face the demands of liturgical change, increasing pressures from tourism, media attention, financial constraints and the expensive upkeep of large and ancient buildings. But they have survived with equanimity and, indeed, with enhanced prestige.

224.   Such a picture has emerged from correspondents and from evidence sought by the Commission. This came from Deans and Provosts, Precentors and other cathedral staff (see Appendix 2.6). Information was also given by the Friends of Cathedral Music, the Cathedral Organists' Association, the Choir Schools' Association and the National Federation of Cathedral Old Choristers' Associations. In addition, the Commission was able to draw on the experience of its membership, which included a current Director of cathedral music, three former cathedral organists and the Head Master of a choir school.

CATHEDRAL AND PARISH

225.   For much of their history and until comparatively recently, cathedrals operated in isolation. There was little relationship between

them and the parishes. Yet a link was sometimes provided by music, where the cathedral organist was involved with diocesan music festivals and other events. Today that link is stronger, as part of a growing recognition that cathedral, parish and diocese all belong together. Consequently many cathedral organists find themselves occupied increasingly with diocesan work.

226.   A combination of history, tradition and resources makes it possible for the cathedral to set high standards, musically as well as liturgically. The best of our cathedral choirs offer excellence of the highest order. Such excellence sometimes has the effect of creating an 'us' and 'them' attitude in parishes, where their parish musicians feel unable or unwilling to settle for more than a mediocre level of performance. At the same time there are local choirs which strive to follow slavishly the cathedral model, even where this is either unsuccessful in terms of quality or inappropriate for their congregation.

227.   Diocesan or regional music festivals are valuable in helping churches find the right musical level and in providing opportunities for cathedral and parochial musicians to work together. The wide variety of music used in these helps churches to maintain and improve standards. In addition, new material is explored which may be suitable for use in the parish and stimulates its musicians to widen their repertoire.

228.   In spite of the quality of their music, however, not all musical activity is from the cathedrals outwards. Many of them welcome parish or other choirs to sing their services. An invitation to sing in the cathedral encourages parishes to see it not only as providing expertise but also as receiving what other musicians can provide. It demands high standards. On the whole invitations are limited as yet to churches with a traditional musical repertoire, using the organ for accompaniment.

REPERTOIRE AND LITURGY

229.   The traditional core of church music is increasingly coming under critical scrutiny by the cathedrals themselves. A broader view than formerly is being taken of music from outside the rich Anglican and English traditions. Editing methods and the standardisation of printing have opened up an immense field of choral music, dating from before the seventeenth century. Thus the selection from which a

modern cathedral can draw its music is considerable. Cathedrals are also, to a small extent, helping to revive the tradition of patronage which produced such riches in the past. There is some evidence that contemporary composers are showing a renewed interest in the Church as a patron of the arts.

230.   One reason why the range of music employed in cathedrals is often fairly narrow is the almost daily singing of Evensong as the choir's main musical offering. This is an important part of the rhythm of a cathedral's worship and it remains enormously popular. Its artistic value was underlined by the support of the country at large when its regular broadcast on BBC Radio 3 came under threat. Liturgically, its significance is shown by the increasing numbers of people who attend as pilgrims and depend upon its availability all over the land for their prayerful refreshment. For many the particular experience of having the Psalms sung 'in course' is the most precious aspect of the service.

231.   Some cathedrals now follow a lectionary which provides for shorter excerpts from the Psalter and have been affected by the liturgical changes of the recent past. After an uncertain start they have responded in different ways to demands for a more active vocal part for the congregation. In many places the schedule includes parish Euchar-ists or family services, in addition to the regular daily services, which may include a hymn for all to sing.

Liturgical Exploration

232.   Implementing change has been easier for parish church cathe-drals, for obvious reasons. Some have wholeheartedly entered into liturgical experiments which have included the re-ordering of space and furniture, new services and music, and the use of musical instru-ments other than the organ. In the worship of some of these cathedrals there are signs of a growing understanding of how to meet the fragmented culture of our age. Others give evidence of thought, but not many practical results so far. Their musicians, in common with everyone else, face undoubted difficulties but also some exciting possibilities.

CHOIR SCHOOLS

233.   The characteristic cathedral sound stems largely from the em-ployment of boys' voices, and one of the most important components in the English cathedral tradition remains the choir school. Its origins are

at least as old as the appointment by St. Paulinus in 627 of James the Deacon to educate the singing boys in York. In other places, such as Gloucester, boys were part of the monastic communities which preceded Deans and Chapters. For many centuries it was primarily through cathedral and church choirs that formal education was available to boys.

234. Today there are forty-one schools attached to our cathedrals, churches and collegiate foundations. Between them they educate more than 800 choristers, as well as 12,000 other boys and girls. Most are preparatory schools, but some keep children to A-level standard. All are independent, except two which are maintained voluntary-aided schools. Three of the schools are Roman Catholic foundations, but most of the others are linked with the Church of England. Almost all of them belong to the Choir Schools' Association, which also has members in Australia, Canada, the Irish Republic, New Zealand and the USA.

235. In England more than £2 million of annual funding for choristers comes from cathedrals or other bodies, given in the form of scholarships awarded to children at the age of seven or eight. Depending upon the size of these scholarships, some parents pay no school fees at all. Those who do, pay on average less than half fees.

236. Not all cathedrals have their own choir schools. A number depend upon special arrangements with one or more local schools, in either the state or the independent sector. Generally this works satisfactorily. The organist's life is probably easier, however, where there is either a choir school or an arrangement with just one school from which choristers are recruited.

Girls and Boys

237. Until recently the all-male tradition of cathedral choirs has continued unaltered, with the exception of St. Mary's Cathedral in Edinburgh, which has had both girls and boys in its choir. However, with changing attitudes in society, questions are being raised about the morality of denying girls the opportunity to sing in a cathedral choir. In being excluded, they are denied the experience of liturgical participation in services as well as a unique form of music education.

238. Opinion is sharply divided on this issue, but it is at present under consideration by some Deans and Chapters, the Choir Schools'

Association and the Cathedral Organists' Association. Meanwhile, Salisbury Cathedral has recently recruited girls as choristers. They will not normally sing with the boys, but are to sing services by themselves on Wednesdays and with the lay vicars both on Mondays and for one of the four services over weekends, by rotation. The boys are to sing with the lay vicars for the other three weekend services and also on Tuesdays, Thursdays and Fridays. The boys-only choir will ensure the continuity of a traditional male choir at a time when the authenticity of musical performance still receives widespread emphasis.

Demands on Children

239.   Because of the demands of the Church's calendar, especially at Christmas and Easter, cathedral choir school holidays tend to be shorter than the norm. Six weeks in the summer and two other holidays of three weeks are probably the average. In the past, longer terms do not seem to have affected applications for places. Choristers sing Evensong generally five or six times a week, as well as services twice or three times on Sundays. In addition there are rehearsals, which account for most of the time spent on music. It is these which, above all, give the children their ability to cope with a large repertoire. Their skill in sight-reading is often astoundingly good.

240.   In spite of so much time being given to singing, many children also learn at least one musical instrument and all of them play their full part in the varied life of the school. Most of them do well, academically and in other ways, amid the heavy demands of the curriculum and the high expectations of parents. This is not only to their credit, but to the credit also of the staff of the choir schools, whose dedication ensures that such schools will surely continue to have a special place in our educational system.

Former Choristers

241.   In reply to an enquiry by the Commission, the Federation of Cathedral Old Choristers' Associations sent a questionnaire to its member associations, in order to gauge the involvement of former cathedral choristers in the life of the Church. From thirty-four returns it would seem that some 5% of cathedral choristers become professional church musicians. By this is meant that they derive an important part of their remuneration from singing, playing or directing in cathedrals and major parish churches. A much greater proportion contribute to worship in churches of all kinds, as organists, singers, servers and

stewards; it was suggested that this could be as high as 80 or even 90%. In reply to a question as to how many cathedral choristers become clergy, the response of 2.5% was consistent across the country.

LAY CLERKS AND ORGANISTS

242.   Many lay clerks are themselves former choristers, and the case is often made for retaining boys' voices in order to ensure a future supply of altos, tenors and basses. Rising musical standards have placed a heavy responsibility upon these singers. Their quality varies from place to place, but the demand is for a comparatively small body of men. Some choirs function with as few as six. Where cathedrals are in or near large centres of population, perhaps with a significant student presence, their ability to pay realistic salaries is an obvious advantage. However, success in recruiting and using lay clerks to best effect depends largely upon the energy and personality of the cathedral organist.

243.   Some cathedrals are able to offer bursaries to lay clerks or choral scholarships within a university setting. An increasing number provide for an organ scholar in addition to a salaried assistant organist. This allows the cathedral organist to devote most of his time to directing the choir, whilst the assistant or scholar provides the organ accompaniment. In terms of skill with the instrument, this arrangement benefits those who play regularly. In creating specialist organists or choir trainers it contributes to the achievement of the highest musical standards, but does not generally offer all-round experience. It should be noted that the remuneration of assistant organists is generally low.

Remuneration

244.   The payment of most cathedral organists is also low, although recent years have seen an improvement. A consequence is that the salary often needs to be supplemented by other work, usually teaching. This brings some benefits through musical cross-fertilisation between the cathedral and the wider community, but the cathedral does not always get the full benefit of one who is employed to do what is commonly regarded as a full-time job, and this at a time when the Church needs from its organists not only the highest musical expertise but also liturgical knowledge and a readiness to take some part in the running of the cathedral. Some cathedral organists have developed considerable liturgical flair and some have a good grasp of theology. Some regularly compose new music for their choirs. All of them

continue to enhance the role of the church musician by their devotion and perseverance. Their job does not always receive the recognition which it deserves.

Conclusion

245.   Success brings its problems. In the case of cathedrals, it makes increasing demands upon their resources, and the cost of their music is very high. It is good to note, therefore, the continuing commitment to their musical foundations of Deans, Provosts and Chapters. The introduction of girls into cathedral choirs and the continuing vitality of choir schools are also hopeful signs for the future. Together with the evident popularity of cathedral music, these are a cause of encouragement for church music in this country.

11

Music in other Christian Traditions

246.   Growing ecumenical co-operation and an increasingly common repertoire demand that any survey of church music today should include some reference to the music used in the worship of traditions other than that of the Church of England. The picture which is offered in this and the next chapter is not fully comprehensive and depends partly upon the knowledge of some of the Commission's members, and partly upon the submissions and correspondence which were received. Help was also given by a number of people whom the Commission consulted. Their names are listed in Appendix 2.8, and the Commission expresses its thanks to all of them, together with an apology for any inaccuracy or misrepresentation of the evidence it has been offered.

THE EASTERN ORTHODOX CHURCH

247.   This heading embraces not only the Greek and Russian Orthodox churches, which are the most numerous, but also Armenian, Bulgarian, Coptic, Ethiopian, Romanian and Ukrainian churches. In Britain there are 172 congregations, to be found in London, Manchester, Liverpool, Bradford and other large towns, with a total in 1987 of 231,000 members. This represents a significant growth in numbers from 193,430 in 1980, although the present membership comes from a community which is probably twice as large. Recently a small choir school has been founded by a Greek Orthodox church in London in order to provide trained singers for churches without them.

248.   Of all Christians, those of the Orthodox family have remained the most conservative. Their cultural roots go back to the Byzantine Empire and there has been no event for them comparable to the Reformation or Vatican II. All the churches have a strong regard for the preservation of tradition and they are still little affected by what happens in other churches. Thus the services and their music have changed hardly at all for hundreds of years.

249.　The Sunday Liturgy is never celebrated without music and large parts of it are sung by the celebrant, the deacon and the people. Traditionally, the people's singing has been delegated to a choir which is generally paid a nominal fee. In some places, and increasingly in these times, the whole assembly is taking a larger musical part. As in the early Christian Church, no musical instruments are used. The singing is flexible and responsorial and all the music is for the words of the Liturgy itself. The repertoire includes traditional chants and much four-part harmony, written by composers within the Orthodox tradition.

250.　In no other tradition of worship is the music so wholly integral to the Liturgy, in the character and style of its performance and in its marriage to actions and words. A comparable example in the West is the Latin liturgy set to plainchant.

THE ROMAN CATHOLIC CHURCH IN ENGLAND

251.　There is little to be said about music in the Roman Catholic Church in this country until the 1960s and the Second Vatican Council. In England for three hundred years after the Reformation there was no official public worship, and even after the Catholic Emancipation Act of 1829 it was some time before the use of music was actively encouraged by the Church. However, the publication in 1903 of a *Motu Proprio* by Pope Pius X provided official recognition of its importance. Gregorian chant and classical polyphony were held up as models for liturgical music, whilst music which was regarded as operatic or theatrical was discouraged.

252.　The revival of Gregorian Chant was greatly helped by the Society of St. Gregory, a small but influential organisation founded in 1929 by Dom Bernard McElligot. Meanwhile, Sir Richard Terry, first at Downside Abbey and then at the newly-built Westminster Cathedral, did important work. In addition to training choirs and editing editions of Tudor polyphony, he persuaded Vaughan Williams and the young Howells, among others, to write for his choir. Another leading contributor from the 1930s was Henry Washington at Brompton Oratory.

253.　In parish churches, however, there was a long period of stagnation, although there were improvements in standards and taste, and until the time of Vatican II there had been few developments in the

Liturgy and its music. There was little vocal participation by the people in the Mass, and such music as they used was generally in the context of other services or 'devotions'. Here they were allowed to sing hymns, mostly from the official *New Westminster Hymnal*, published in 1939 and containing few texts or translations by non-Roman Catholic writers. Any tunes borrowed from other denominations were generally reharmonised.

Vatican II

254.   The Second Vatican Council was an event of huge significance for Roman Catholicism and, indeed, for all the churches. The first of the major considerations by the Council Fathers was given to the Liturgy and its music, as well as sacred art. In the *Constitution on the Sacred Liturgy* there are statements such as: 'In the musical tradition of the Universal Church is contained a treasure of inestimable value. It occupies a place higher than that of other art forms . . .', 'The treasury of music will be maintained and cherished with the greatest care. Choirs will be diligently fostered in their efforts . . .' and 'Bishops . . . will take good care to see that in all sung services the whole congregation may be able to take therein the active part that is theirs . . .'

255.   The *Constitution*'s main concern appeared to be that of conservation. Choirs, pipe organs and the teaching of music in seminaries were all encouraged. In addition to the emphasis on vocal participation by congregations, there was the recognition for the first time of indigenous musical traditions. This led to developments in both music and the Liturgy which were probably more far-reaching than the Council Fathers anticipated. Revision of the Eucharist and its Lectionary was followed by that of the Divine office and of all sacramental rites, and the process continues. There has been unhappiness in some quarters, occasional misunderstandings and ignorance, and a certain amount of unfortunate iconoclasm.

256.   With a new emphasis on the importance of the Word, the trend has been away from hymns, anthems and settings. The restoration of musical priorities means that the *Kyrie* and the *Gloria*, which were key movements in settings of the Mass, have now returned to their former place simply as part of the Introductory Rite. Consequently composers have revived ancient liturgical-musical forms such as responsorial music, acclamations, litanies and processional songs. These call for an increased use of soloists as cantors and for some direction of the congregation, often by means of an *animateur*.

Hymnody

257.   Hymns, nevertheless, retain both significance and popularity. As in other churches, there has been regular production of new hymnals in the Roman Catholic Church in recent years. The collection most used is almost certainly *Hymns Old and New Revised* (Mayhew, 1986), although its presentation, harmonisation and indexes are of the most basic kind and the tunes are not even named. A new standard hymnal might not be welcomed by Roman Catholics. But there is no doubt of the acceptability of new resource books containing eucharistic acclamations, psalm-settings, songs for entrance and communion processions, and music for wedding and funeral rites. A typical compilation of this kind of material is to be found in *New Songs of Celebration* which is the latest volume of the *Celebration Hymnal* (Mayhew-McCrimmon, 1978).

258.   For many churches there is a problem of expense. Books like these contain much music which is transitory but include insufficient hymnody from the traditional repertoire. The maintenance of this repertoire is made more difficult, in that the majority of children in Roman Catholic schools seem to be taught contemporary hymns and other religious music by religious education teachers, rather than by the music staff.

Composition and Publishing

259.   When the use of the vernacular was introduced a good deal of new music was demanded. Much of it was needed for texts from the International Commission on English in the Liturgy (ICEL), many of which were provisional and required frequent revision. This is one of the reasons for the reluctance of many 'serious' Roman Catholic composers to write for the new Liturgy, thus leaving it to others, especially those in the folk tradition. Consequently, when the definitive form of the Revised Order of Mass was published in 1970, the larger publishing houses had invested fully in the popular and flourishing field of folk music. Some composers, therefore, set up their own publishing enterprises which did well for some years, especially during the visit of Pope John Paul II to Britain in 1982. The largest of them, Magnificat Music (under the auspices of the Westminster Diocesan Liturgy Centre), has become the most important publisher of music for the reformed Roman Catholic rites.

260.   Left to themselves, folk musicians did what they could without

the guidance which might have come from experienced musicians. The result was not always music of good quality, but many worshippers were attracted by it and folk music made much headway, particularly in those parishes which had no working church musicians to compose for their own communities and resources. Religious congregations of monks and nuns also used home-written music for the Office, and the Panel of Monastic Musicians was founded so that they could share their efforts and talents.

261.   Perhaps the most satisfactory music in recent years has come from writers involved in the liturgy of a particular community, effectively as composers-in-residence. Among those in Britain writing for the Roman Catholic Church may be mentioned Stephen Dean, Philip Duffy, Bernadette Farrell, Paul Inwood, Alan Rees, Bill Tamblyn and Christopher Walker.

262.   Most of these composers have participated in the annual meetings of Universa Laus, a group of mainly European liturgists and musicians formed in 1969. Its purpose is to consider the more philosophical aspects of the new liturgical provisions, with an input from disciplines such as linguistics, psychology, anthropology, and the social sciences. So far, discussion at Conferences has ranged around questions such as the form and function of music and rite; what distinguishes liturgical music in respect of its use, function and significance; and music as the servant of the Word, the liturgical action and the congregation.

Organisations and Structures

263.   In spite of such conferences and the dedication of a number of musicians, little or no provision is made for the liturgical and musical formation of Roman Catholic musicians and clergy. Many of the cathedrals are former parish churches and they retain an attitude to music which is more appropriate to a parish than to a cathedral. There are only three Roman Catholic choir schools in England and one in Wales. Music is generally accorded a low priority and is underfunded, and standards of performance are unsatisfactory in many places.

264.   In order to help Roman Catholic musicians, there are organisations such as the Society of St. Gregory, the Schola Gregoriana of Cambridge and the Spode Music Weeks. There is also a national advisory body, without executive powers, the Bishops' Committee on Church Music. This is one of three sister committees, the other two

97

being for Pastoral Rites and for Art and Architecture. In many dioceses there are comparable structures and some of the diocesan music commissions have been very active. Those with a professional approach have provided structured courses for church musicians lasting a year or more.

A Hopeful Future

265.   Some dioceses have appointed Parish Music Advisers. This is a positive step which promises to improve standards and taste, and gives cause for some optimism. Experimentation has begun to yield results, instrumental groups flourish in some churches, and the standards of playing and performance are certainly higher than they were even five years ago. There is also a heightened awareness of music's proper place in the liturgy. In addition, there have been tremendous advances in ecumenical co-operation, locally and nationally, in the music that is used and in the church music organisations.

THE LUTHERAN CHURCH

266.   The Lutheran family of churches constitutes the largest Protestant denomination in the world, with some 60 million members. In Britain, its 20,000 people belong to small local congregations, whose services are generally simple and rely for their music chiefly upon hymns and chorales.

267.   Its most prominent church is in London, with a fine musical tradition. In addition to an extensive use of music from the baroque period, chorale preludes are often played or extemporised to precede the hymns. The worship is led by a voluntary choir under the direction of the organist, except on one Sunday evening a month when the service incorporates a Bach cantata sung by a professional choir. Services are held regularly in English, German, Swedish, Norwegian, Danish, Finnish, Icelandic, Latvian, Estonian, Polish, Hungarian, Chinese and Swahili.

METHODIST AND UNITED REFORMED CHURCHES

268.   Contrary to the popular myth of largely extempore worship, there is a more or less set liturgical pattern for most of the services of the former Congregationalists and Presbyterians, who, together with the Churches of Christ, form the United Reformed Church. The pattern derives, through *A Directory for the Public Worship of God*

(1644), from the order of service used by the Protestant exiles in Geneva approved by 'that famous and godly learned man', John Calvin. Although Methodists later developed a freer Nonconformist style, their services originated in the Book of Common Prayer.

The Priority of Scripture

269.   The most important element in Free Church worship has traditionally been the reading of long passages of Holy Scripture and their exposition by a learned minister. Closely associated with the proclamation and preaching of the Word was scriptural hymnody, in the form of metrical psalms. Today's worship contains the same basic ingredients in most Nonconformist churches, although there are usually some modifications to the accepted pattern. Heart-religion, too, has always been highly prized, with its emphasis on individual commitment and inspiration; everyone with faith becomes a temple of the Holy Spirit and a vessel for the expression of God's power and love. A firm belief in the priesthood of all believers means that singing belongs to the whole congregation as well as to the choir.

The Ecumenical Influence

270.   In recent years, the separation of church and chapel has lessened considerably. The ecumenical movement has reversed three centuries of division which began with the failure of the Savoy Conference in 1661 and the imposition of the Act of Uniformity. Today, Holy Communion is celebrated more frequently and with a set liturgy, often in an 'Anglican' way; set prayers are common and sometimes take a responsory form; the increasing use of a lectionary means that the choice of readings depends less upon the whim of the preacher and more upon an ordered scheme. Many of the Free Churches now mark the seasons of the year and the major feasts in the Church's calendar, in addition to the observance of their traditional days such as a Church Anniversary and the annual Covenant Service. There is generally a much greater liturgical awareness and a willingness to experiment. These are encouraged, perhaps, both by the experience of united services and by worship televised from churches of differing traditions.

Psalms and Hymns

271.   The musical tradition of Free Churches originated in the singing of metrical psalms by the whole congregation, and psalm-singing still plays an important part in their worship. The Church of Scotland sets great store by metrical psalms, whilst the Free Church of Scotland

sings its psalms unaccompanied by instruments. In some parts of that country there is a remarkable tradition of Gaelic Psalmody, with elaborate variations on a melodic line. The new URC hymn book, *Rejoice and Sing* (Oxford University Press, 1991), has a substantial section of psalms and canticles in various styles. These include metrical psalms, those pointed for Anglican chant or Psalm Tones (involving fewer note-changes to the line) and Gelineau or Gregory Murray settings of prose psalms. Suggestions are also made for antiphonal singing.

272. The Methodist *Hymns and Psalms* (Methodist Publishing House, 1983) also includes a good number of psalms, pointed for Anglican chant, and a few metrical psalms are included in the body of the book. In both books mentioned, however, the principal emphasis is upon hymns. To the works of major Nonconformist writers like Isaac Watts, Charles Wesley and James Montgomery have been added hymns from many other traditions. These include the Church of England and the Roman Catholic Church, the Churches of Christ, the *Wild Goose Songs* of the Iona Community and the 'charismatic' hymns and songs to be found in all denominations. The Free Churches have made much use of the explosion of hymn writing which has occurred during the last thirty years and which crosses the boundaries of all denominations.

The Musicians

273. Many churches have choirs, and a place is given in most services to an anthem or other piece sung by the choir alone. Settings of the Holy Communion and of canticles are rarely used, however, and the emphasis remains firmly congregational. Nevertheless, the organ has an important place and this is indicated by its prominent position in most buildings, often behind the central pulpit. In addition to its use for accompaniment and for playing before and after a service, it is commonly used as a solo instrument during the course of worship. For example, there may be a voluntary during the taking up of the collection. In less conservative congregations, and where they are available, other instruments have their place on occasions. Worship songs are also beginning to find widespread acceptance.

BAPTIST CHURCHES

274. In the very early days of the Baptist churches a typical service consisted of prayer, the reading of one or two chapters from the Bible, a

series of expositions on the readings and a collection for the poor. In some places metrical psalms were also included, and in the 1670s Benjamin Keach introduced some congregational hymn-singing into his services in Hackney. This met with some opposition, for there were those who regarded music with suspicion because of its 'human' origins and its consequent unworthiness for the offering of pure worship. Nevertheless, hymns grew in favour in succeeding years and especially in the first part of the eighteenth century. John Bunyan portrayed his pilgrims as singing, and Joseph Stennett was a fine hymn-writer in the early Baptist tradition.

Hymnody

275.   Metrical psalms are still occasionally used in Baptist churches, but hymns are the main musical items in their services. A new hymn book, *Baptist Praise and Worship* (Oxford University Press) was published in 1991, including many newer hymns, together with a good number of worship songs which are becoming increasingly popular.

Instruments

276.   The organ is at the heart of the musical life of most churches, although other instruments, including the piano and electric keyboards, are increasingly being used. Much thinking has been given in recent years to the use of instruments as well as voices in worship. The formation of the Baptist Music Society in 1962 was an indication of the mounting importance attached to the place of music in church services.

277.   There are basic elements common to the services of all Baptist churches, but there is a great variety in the styles of worship and of music. No two churches are the same and there is no centralised authority. Congregations may belong to a Union of Baptist Churches, but each has considerable autonomy. In recent years much has been drawn from other denominations and a much wider choice of hymns and music is one of the fruits of ecumenism.

THE SALVATION ARMY

278.   To many people the Salvation Army is best known for its band and this certainly holds an important place in its life and worship. The band is used not only for worship in the citadel, but also for evangelism in public places. A typical service includes an item by the band, as well as a choir item and several hymns and choruses sung by all. Many of these are chosen from the common repertoire, but there is also much

music written by Army members. Music is frequently commissioned from professional composers.

279. The training of musicians, both instrumental and vocal, is organised systematically through local and residential courses. These are designed particularly for the young and contain a strong spiritual element in them. All musicians have to be committed members of the Army, and their dedication and discipline, as well as the investment of their time and money, are impressive. They are normally responsible for purchasing their own uniform and music, and often their own instrument too.

Publishing

280. There is a highly organised publishing enterprise which exercises control over the music used by bands and choirs. Only that which has been officially authorised is permitted for use in services. A new edition of *The Song Book of the Salvation Army 1986* (Salvationist Publishing and Supplies, 1986) contains words alone, but is supplemented by *The Tune Book* which is published both as a set of band parts and for keyboard. The repertoire is extended by the publication of new music each quarter.

CONCLUSION

281. It is encouraging to note both the variety of musical resources and practice within the Christian denominations in England, and also an increasing convergence. This augurs well for the future and underlines the truth that music as a universal language is an important resource for ecumenism.

12

Music in some Ecumenical
Congregations in England

282.   In addition to those churches which are organised along denominational lines there are many congregations in England which are
best described as ecumenical, for they generally contain members
from a variety of churches, or from none. This chapter does not include
Local Ecumenical Projects (LEPs), which normally reflect a combination of the worship and music of their constituent denominations.
It does, however, deal with those congregations which are loosely
termed chaplaincies, where worship is provided chiefly for members of
an institution or organisation of some kind. The Commission has not
given particular consideration to the use of music in the services of
schools, colleges, hospitals or to every kind of institution. Its gratitude
to a number of people for their advice is recorded in Appendix 2.8.

HOUSE CHURCHES

283.   The term 'house churches' is applied to a variety of congregations. Some of them belong to organised groupings, but all are
characterised by a common emphasis on the dynamic activity of the
Holy Spirit in the lives of their members. A typical house church is
marked by the exercise of some or all of the gifts of the Spirit listed in
1 Corinthians 12 and by a belief that scriptural prophecy is being
fulfilled today. Often there is a strong sense of warfare being waged
against Satan, in which God's people participate through prayer,
healings and exorcisms. A house church congregation may gather for
worship in the home of one of its members, but commonly it assembles
in a hall or other large meeting-place.

Variety
284.   A range of styles of worship is to be found in house churches. A
very relaxed and spontaneous service stresses the individual's intimacy
with God, whilst fairly formal liturgical worship, led by an elder,
emphasises the corporate responsibility of the congregation to witness

103

to Christ. There may be a gathering of two or three people to wait in quiet expectancy on the Holy Spirit, or an organised 'Praise March' through the streets. Whatever the style, congregations show few inhibitions in facial expression and in their use of the body to express devotion. The raising of arms and hands in the air conveys praise and thanksgiving, whilst prostration on the floor speaks of repentance and openness to God. There is much vocal participation by all who are present, in singing and in giving testimonies or prophecies, as well as in speaking or singing in tongues.

Musicians, Instruments and Repertoire

285.   The pipe organ is almost unknown in the worship of house churches, not least because they seldom use church buildings. Rarely is there a choir as such. Instead the music is usually led by a music group or band which may consist of almost any combination of instruments, together with a piano or other kind of keyboard and one or more singers. It is common for the music group, through its leader or one of its members, to take responsibility for leading a substantial part of the service. This usually consists of worship and praise and comprises the singing of a number of songs, with a good deal of repetition in which one song succeeds another without a break. There may follow a period of spontaneous singing in tongues by the congregation, after which the whole assembly might lapse into a profound corporate silence and a still waiting upon God.

286.   Much of the set-piece music used by house churches has a common feel to it, although the styles differ considerably from congregation to congregation. So one may experience variously what may be called 'Radio 2-1970s-disco-feel' music, or heavy rock, or traditional hymnody, or 1960s jazz-band music. Within a chosen style it is possible to create a full range of moods. For example, slow and meditative songs convey the depth of God's love for the individual; majestic ones centre on the exalted Christ; and those which are up-tempo express the joy of being a Christian. Where there is traditional hymnody, it is often used selectively with perhaps only one or two verses of a well-known hymn being repeated several times.

Wider Influence

287.   The influence of the house church movement on the life and worship of the established denominations has been considerable, not least in the field of music. For some ten years now, house church

musicians have arranged training opportunities, with seminars and annual gatherings such as those at Spring Harvest and Greenbelt propagating new music, and with the regular publication of self-help music books and song material. In developing styles of music to make worship accessible to as many people as possible, the primary aim of music in the house church movement is understood to be to glorify God.

'ETHNIC' CONGREGATIONS

288.   There is an obvious problem of terminology here. Many of those who worship in Orthodox, Catholic, Lutheran, Free Church or Anglican churches belong to 'ethnic minorities'. They include those who are visiting this land for a week or two, or students and professionals from other parts of the world, temporarily resident in this country. For most of these the use of English presents no problem and the Church does not assume the cultural importance that it has for some of those from ethnic minority cultures who live permanently in Britain.

Cultural Roots

289.   Many from ethnic minorities belong to the main-line churches, but there are many others who are unfamiliar with the English language and culture and may find that Western ways of worship do not meet their needs. So there is a steady blossoming of congregations (such as the Chinese Christian Churches in London, Birmingham and Oxford) initiated by and for a particular ethnic minority group. Their emphasis is usually 'Christian' rather than 'denominational' and they are to be found almost wholly in large conurbations. In addition to being a gathering of worshippers, such congregations may be at the centre of the life of a community in 'alien' surroundings. To them the maintenance of cultural roots, folk festivals and the ways of the Church 'back home' are important. If a church is large enough it may support artistic performing groups and there is often a sense of responsibility for the education of that community's children in language, traditional customs, crafts, music and dance.

290.   This is not to suggest that no efforts are being made by the main-line churches in this country to care for and accommodate the traditions of those in their congregations who have come from overseas. There are in London, for example, Cantonese, Ethiopian, Portuguese and Spanish congregations which have come into being through church planting by a strong congregation from one of the

denominations. In the Roman Catholic Church priests are sometimes appointed to look after the needs of a particular ethnic group. Special celebratory services with ethnic bands and music are arranged, and in some areas parts of the Mass are celebrated in languages other than English. A Black Catholic conference is planned for the future, in order to look at ways of making white middle-class worship relevant to those from another culture.

Joint Ventures and Training

291.   In other denominations, as well as seeking to meet the social needs of those who are disadvantaged, there have been experiments with weekly joint services with the Asian community. These have contained a mixture of languages and music, and have often employed an interpreter. Because of problems with disparate styles of music, however, an occasional Sunday afternoon service is held at a time when white people who are committed to this kind of outreach are free to attend.

292.   In this and other ways some attempts have been made to integrate the differing traditions of music and worship. A 'Worship in Harmony' think-tank was initiated in 1989 in order to bring black and white musical styles together. Other requirements are more mundane, and include money in order to provide hymn and song books, instruments and music stands for churches in which such necessities are not taken for granted. There is a need, too, for the training of musicians. Several Asian churches have found difficulties in finding instrumental tuition for their youngsters. In the West Midlands one Local Education Authority provides a class on Saturday mornings for young Asian musicians to learn traditional instruments, whilst in Islington and Southall two Asian churches organise an annual festival for soloists, choirs and instrumentalists from a wide area.

Asian and Afro-Caribbean Repertoire

293.   Many older Asian Christians still enjoy long traditional hymns with tenuous melodies, accompanied by harmonium and tabla, not least because of the limitations of language (Gujurati, Hindi, Punjabi or Urdu). For most Afro-Caribbean people English is a *lingua franca*. Even if it is not their native tongue, Western songs, choruses and hymns are readily accessible to them and they relate fairly easily to the established churches in England. Many of them contribute much to the musical life of those congregations whose members enjoy singing to

the accompaniment of steel bands and a variety of other musical instruments, with their distinctive rhythms and harmonies. As one Anglican incumbent noted, the liturgy 'came to life in a new way' with such music and the recent publication of *Gospel Praise* reflects the growing interest in it.

294.   In some places the Afro-Caribbean community has composed Mass settings and produced its own hymn books. There has also been a significant growth in the number and size of black-led Pentecostal churches during the last two or three decades. These are marked by lusty singing and strong rhythms and reflect very much the extrovert nature of the worshippers.

295.   The enthusiasm, the energy and the sheer endurance of many ethnic congregations are in strong contrast to the more restrained worship to which the average British Christian is accustomed. The exuberance of their music and sincerity of their worship readily compensate for flaws in performance or thin theological content. From this tradition have emerged a number of notable black Gospel choirs, some of them performing to a very high standard. Not surprisingly, the range of musical styles among ethnic minority cultures is considerable.

HER MAJESTY'S FORCES

296.   In the British Forces there are more than ninety Royal Marine, Regimental and Royal Air Force bands, and the investment in music by the Ministry of Defence exceeds the public subsidy of the arts generally in Great Britain. An important, if small, part of this investment relates to parade services, such as Remembrance Day and Regimental Sunday, and other ceremonial occasions which include an act of worship. But the musical resources available for the weekly services in the churches and chapels of the Armed Forces are slender indeed.

Organists and Choirs

297.   Some of the RAF churches have competent and well-trained organists, but these are generally difficult to come by and, as in many parishes, it is a pianist who is pressed into service. All three Services depend a good deal upon civilian help, and naval chaplains, who are appointed for two-year terms of duty, are inclined to leave the running of church music ashore to those whose ties with a church are more permanent. The Ministry of Defence pays £12 per service to an organist who is not a serving member of the Forces.

298.   The frequent changes resulting from postings and the demands of the duty roster make it difficult to ensure the continuity not only of a 'uniformed' organist, but also of a choir. Nevertheless, three-quarters of RAF churches have robed choirs, half of them made up entirely of adults and averaging eight to ten members. Most of their churches in Germany are affiliated to the RSCM, and some use its Choristers' Training Scheme. Such choirs as the Navy has in its on-shore establishments consist largely of former naval personnel who have rather more conservative musical tastes than those still serving, eighteen being the average age of those at sea. Of the dozen or so choirs in the Navy, including two in Gibraltar and Hong Kong, the one in Greenwich has sufficient expertise to record hymns for use in ships at sea. Many Army garrisons have no choir and rely a good deal on local resources, especially overseas. Army schools in Germany provide a useful source of singers.

Instruments

299.   Where there is no pipe organ, the churches, chapels and ships of the Forces are equipped with a small electric keyboard. This has replaced the old portable harmonium so familiar to former generations of service personnel. In addition, there is the growing use of other instruments, either singly or in groups. Over half the RAF churches consulted use either a piano or a guitar, or both, to accompany worship songs, especially at family services. In ships at sea chaplains or commanding officers have pre-recorded tapes containing organ accompaniments and a compilation of hymns. At present this comprises twenty favourites, but is shortly to be enlarged by another twenty.

Repertoire and Services

300.   Almost all of the music used in the Forces consists of hymns, generally drawn from *Hymns Ancient and Modern New Standard*. With fewer of those serving having been to Sunday school and with the small number of hymns learnt at school, the repertoire is very limited. The use of Anglican chant for psalms and canticles has almost entirely ceased, but in the Eucharist the better known settings by Appleford, Rutter and Shephard are used. Where there is an adult choir, an anthem may be sung.

301.   For Anglicans most of the main services take the form of a Eucharist and the ASB Rite A is almost universal. Matins has almost wholly disappeared and its substitute in Anglican worship is often some

kind of family service, common also in the Free Churches, and generally of the 'hymn-sandwich' variety.

302.   Except in large garrisons or establishments, there is usually only one church and the situation in the Armed Forces obviously encourages partnership between the Churches. There is a good deal of ecumenical co-operation, particularly between Methodists and Anglicans in the Army. Service congregations are familiar with joint services.

Training

303.   The RAF holds an annual five-day course for church musicians at Andover, led in recent years by the organist of Coventry Cathedral. However, little seems to be done in the Navy and the Army to provide musical training for either chaplains or musicians.

HER MAJESTY'S PRISONS

304.   In prison chapels the abandonment in the early 1960s of compulsory worship for all prisoners has meant the demise of Matins and its lusty singing. In its place there are more flexible forms of worship and much smaller attendances. Nevertheless in some of the larger prisons such as those at Liverpool, Durham and Leeds, congregations remain large. Strangeways in Manchester, before recent riots, had between three and four hundred people present at the Church of England service, some two hundred at the Roman Catholic Mass and a good number of others at the Methodist service. In such establishments the emphasis is usually strongly evangelistic, with worship songs, visiting choirs, pop groups and challenging preaching. By contrast, Parkhurst, with long-term high-security prisoners, a badly-sited chapel and a long tradition of low attendance, has between ten and twenty men at the Eucharist. Even so, a simple musical setting is used.

305.   There are not many prison choirs, and the organs provided are usually electronic instruments. Many organists are recruited from outside, some of them playing for all the denominations which use the one chapel. Although the fees they receive are small, most of them are faithful and often long-serving. They do not, perhaps, receive the recognition which they deserve.

306.   Generally speaking, the present scene is a varied one and a number of factors contribute to the way in which a missionary situation

is tackled by the Church. These include the size of the prison, the nature of its population, the availability and attitudes of the staff, the number of competing activities, the effectiveness of the chaplain and the tradition of the place.

CONCLUSION

307.   There are clearly immense riches in the different musical traditions of Christian congregations, and great benefit could result from their being even more widely shared. The more traditional churches could often do with some of the energy and spontaneity of the newer fellowships. These in their turn might derive something from the order and timelessness of the mainstream tradition.

13

Music in the World-wide Church

308.   Little more than a general impression can be given of the state of music in the churches outside Great Britain. Most of the following information was obtained from replies to a letter from the Chairman to more than fifty correspondents in various parts of the world (see Appendix 2.9). Although there are some gaps, there is no reason to think that the overall picture would have been significantly different with contributions from all parts of the globe. Most of those consulted by the Commission are Anglican and they were asked to give their views on ten specific points. It was recognised that these would be subjective and impressionistic, to some extent at least, and this chapter quotes *verbatim* from many of the letters it has received.

The Past Twenty-five Years

309.   The introduction of new services has occurred everywhere, and the Parish Communion has almost universally become the main Sunday service, with the consequent disappearance of Matins and Evensong and their choral opportunities. The growth in vocal partici-pation by congregations has lessened the significance of the choir, and it is even viewed in some places as élitist.

310.   Often this has resulted either in a loss of heart by both choirs and organists, leading to the demise of choral singing and organ-playing, or in these services being no longer required. A South African cor-respondent noted that the choir is not now seen as 'a binding organisa-tion within the structure of the church'. In Zimbabwe there are now eight 'traditional' choirs, all in Harare, as compared with twenty a few years ago.

311.   As against that, some of the American churches have evidently continued to value their musical personnel. The 'Crystal Cathedral' in California, for instance, has 700 people involved in its music. It is but one of several dozen churches in that country promoting impressive

musical programmes. Although these are mostly non-Anglican in a
land where only 2.5% of Christians are Episcopalian, they are highly
significant. Much emphasis is laid by very many churches on high
musical standards in selection and presentation. The Director (or
'Minister') of Music is an important member of the church's management team.

312.   A lowering of standards is generally noted, however, in the last
quarter century. In Australia, the growth of Pentecostal-type churches
with their highly-charged musical professionalism makes the average
choir seem very inadequate. The use of music in worship in New
Zealand has grown in quantity as a result of greater congregational
singing, but its quality is said by a correspondent to have declined
greatly. Many note that the 'traditional' has been largely replaced by
'informal' music which plays on the emotions, with 'joy' being given
great prominence.

Recruitment of Church Musicians

313.   People seem to prefer that which is informal, spontaneous and
unrehearsed, and the lack of stimulus presented by much of the 'new
look' music makes it difficult to persuade musicians to be committed on
a regular basis. From Canada comes the comment that 'because
musical demands are now far less challenging, it is difficult to recruit
serious musicians'. In Australia 'recruitment is at a very low ebb', not
least because few parishes actively encourage the training of organists.
A contributory factor in Canada, in common with other places, is the
sometimes problematic relationship between organists and clergy.

314.   Robed choirs are in decline in New Zealand, although smartly
dressed secular choirs are to be seen on television. In Hong Kong, as in
many African countries and Europe as well, the disappearance of the
more settled residents of a generation ago makes it difficult to recruit
for the church choir. (Choirs have always thrived best in well-rooted
provincial communities.) Today's mobility, the five-day week, the
range of leisure pursuits, sport and predictable weather all militate
against recruitment, especially of the young. Nevertheless, in America
considerable use is made of junior choirs in addition to those consisting
of adults.

315.   One response to a difficult situation, which is not without its
merits, is the growth of *ad hoc* choirs and groups, singing on special
occasions. These may consist of able musicians who are unwilling or

unable to commit themselves on a regular basis. Another response is the formation of music groups which sometimes include all who want to play or sing in them, regardless of their ability. Because they are heavily dependent upon the quality of their leadership special music groups tend to come and go.

Encouragement, Training and Employment of Church Musicians

316.   On the whole, correspondents did not believe that church musicians receive as much encouragement as they deserve. There may be grounds for dissatisfaction with some church musicians, but many have suffered from high-handed treatment, sometimes leading to dismissal. 'Lukewarm toleration' is the description given by some New Zealand correspondents who believe that clergy sometimes feel that 'traditions are inhibiting parish development'. It is clear that few theological colleges anywhere do much to instruct and encourage ordinands in matters musical.

317.   In spite of some clergy who are 'not appreciative of art or excellence', the Church in the United States still sees the need to train musicians as a pastoral priority. Elsewhere, as in Australia, 'the half-trained pianist is often accepted as sufficient for the task'. Artistic and musical skills are not always highly prized, and those who are qualified musically may find themselves at a disadvantage because they 'have not been trained to serve the Church', and so do not 'speak the language of theology'. Moreover, some of the best qualified people in South Africa, Australia and elsewhere have sought openings for training in Europe or America because of lack of opportunities or resources at home. Consequently there are few new musicians in many areas who might have been able to train others to follow them.

318.   There are many more unpaid Church musicians overseas than in Britain and the 'reluctant organist' is in great demand. A recent survey in Sydney showed that only 3% of the organists in that city are remunerated at a realistic level for the hours and work involved. In New Zealand the Church generally pays only its cathedral musicians. By contrast, the salaries paid to church musicians in North America are generally high. There are some instances where 'extravagant wages' are paid, and some musicians are also 'parish managers with the duties of an office administrator'. Even so, the American Guild of Organists is seeking a rise in salary scales, for many a highly qualified Church musician is 'paid at a level far below what his or her competence and training should expect'.

Relationships

319.   Mention has been made already of difficulties in the area of relationships, and it would seem that this is a widespread problem. Lack of communication and the inability to see a differing point of view are cited as being the main causes. The result is that the key leaders of worship fail to relate properly and their dealings with one another are inhibited by suspicion and threat. One American correspondent suggested that 'the music department is the war department of the church'.

320.   Other factors which create or add to problems in relationships are quoted as: interference rather than encouragement by musical clergy; jealousy; vagueness about who chooses what; last-minute alterations; incompetence of the organist; insufficient musical knowledge in the clergy and insufficient liturgical and theological knowledge in the musician, so that neither fully understands what the other is about; and suspicion by the clergy of musical 'professionalism'.

321.   Because both the congregation and the worship suffer when clergy and musicians are at loggerheads, an Australian correspondent recommends more overall planning meetings. These are especially important where there is 'the potential for discord when anything beyond the conventional or ordinary begins to surface'. In New Zealand, music groups seem to get on better with the incumbent than many an organist. But, as a consequence, musical decisions may be made by people with little or no real musical knowledge, sometimes without proper consultation.

Instruments

322.   There is a growing use of instrumental groups, but the organ holds its own in 'traditional' situations. Where a new instrument is required, it is now common to install a small tracker-action pipe organ rather than an over-large romantic one which is costly to maintain. There is surprisingly little use in African countries of indigenous instruments in the worship of indigenous people. In many situations it is felt to be inappropriate to worship God without an organ. The majority of African congregations, however, still sing lustily without any accompaniment. For this reason there is an exciting variety of improvised harmonies in their worship.

New Music

323. The new liturgical texts of recent years have generally lacked music to accompany them. But now composers are writing 'Alleluia' refrains and music for Holy Communion, as well as psalm settings. In America *The Hymnal 1980* contains no fewer than 288 examples of service music and it is permissible to reproduce some of it for congregational use.

324. The use of today's worship songs is much in evidence and they are described in the United States as 'songs important to pilgrim people'. One correspondent notes that, having gone through a period of using much folk music and guitar accompaniment, 'this phase seems to be declining in some places'.

Hymn Books

325. In former British colonies, *Hymns Ancient and Modern* and *The English Hymnal* are still widely used. But the boom in hymn publishing has made available a great variety of material, from Roman Catholic, Free Church and Lutheran sources amongst many others. In New Zealand five new hymn books were published in 1989. In South Africa, Zimbabwe and some other places the high cost of foreign imports, local taxes and unfavourable exchange rates militate against the use of new books from abroad. Steps are therefore being taken to permit some legitimate reproduction of copyright material.

326. An interesting development has been the emergence of national hymnals, such as *The Australian Hymn Book* in 1977 (subsequently published elsewhere as *With One Voice*). This includes some 'interesting examples of truly indigenous music of the Australian aborigines and of Papua New Guinea'. It is also the result of ecumenical co-operation between the major denominations. A less formal supplement, *Sing Alleluia*, followed in 1988 and contains a number of psalm settings. In the Episcopal Church of the United States, *The Hymnal 1980* is used virtually everywhere. Its publication was preceded by years of painstaking preparation, with nation-wide workshops and promotional material. These were evidently very successful.

Hope

327. Correspondents were asked to identify that which is positive in their situations. Many of them expressed appreciation of local cathedral organists and parish musicians who provide a lead and incentive to

others. They also mentioned the value of the RSCM, particularly in respect of its teaching role in annual summer schools. These are regularly held in Australia, New Zealand, South Africa and the United States. In Canada the work of the Royal Canadian College of Organists was commended, especially for its work with theological colleges. Joint programmes are arranged for learning in theology, liturgy and music.

328.   In Australia there is now more variety generally in church music. More people are involved in its selection and performance, even if levels of skill, experience and interest vary widely. Although the average age of choirs is high, younger people are being attracted to music groups and some simple music of good quality is emerging. 'The trite music of the 1970s' is being replaced in New Zealand by 'more musical' songs, as the Church learns to accommodate divergent tastes. There is still an element of polarisation, however, which proclaims 'belief in the old and distrust in the new'. The music of the Roman Catholic Church in New Zealand is very strong, and generally in that country there is great awareness of what is happening world-wide. Both Australia and New Zealand suggest the need for a cross-fertilisation of resources and for a measure of compromise between those of differing views.

Anxiety

329.   The fact that music is allowed to become divisive is a particular concern in New Zealand. Polarisation is encouraged by bickering between 'charismatic' and traditional churches and hardened attitudes. But by far the most common complaint the world over is of low standards and lack of training. Although the new forms of service are not necessarily responsible, it is felt that the whole ethos of worship has changed. According to some, it has reached 'an all-time low'. Spontaneous and unrehearsed music seems to be acceptable to clergy who do not know about music. They evidently 'enjoy the inartistic, un-beautiful, and the superficial emotional appeal of much that they foster'. Much money in Australia is being expended on Christian rock music, with the suggestion that anything traditional is *passé*. In the same country there is some regret at the abandonment of Latin masses, psalmody and Evensong. But there is suspicion of 'the domination of one person (usually the organist) standing in the way of developing other considerable talent reserves'.

330.   Although correspondents from the United States are optimistic, the musical resources of the average Episcopalian church are some-

what slender. In addition to people with musical qualifications, there is 'a big need for persons with pastoral and teaching gifts. By and large, this broader concept of training persons as pastoral musicians is missing, and sorely needed'. In South Africa children are no longer being taught the traditional hymns in schools. There, as elsewhere, 'perhaps the most depressing thing is the lack of interest shown by so many towards the beauty and power of the arts in enriching worship'. Much quality music is being lost and many people are being alienated as a result.

The Future

331. The most positive view comes from the United States: 'The fact that much is being done, and that there are few areas of stagnation, makes one believe that better and more fruitful days are ahead'. In spite of the 'failure of the seminaries and theological colleges to give the clergy the background to be in full charge of the music in the parish . . . people are thinking and talking about liturgy and music in new ways, and reassessing everything'.

332. By contrast, Zimbabwe is pessimistic because there are fewer people available to train choirs and play the organ. Secular university choirs are said to be much better than church groups. New Zealand notes that because many of its young professionals are disenchanted and disillusioned, there is a gradual disappearance of 'traditional choirs'. On the other hand, it is in the 'Renewal' churches that there is growth. That is said to be no longer true in South Africa where a general feeling of 'tiredness' in the Church is alleged. Many had pinned their hopes on the Renewal Movement and found it wanting.

333. More positively, from South Africa comes the observation that music's power to unite must give it a role in a country where at least twelve languages are spoken. Although Africans generally read tonic sol-fa and Europeans use staff notation, RSCM committees consist of Blacks, 'Coloureds' and Whites together.

334. It is clear that in both Australia and New Zealand there is a continuing ferment arising from conflicting support for the old or the new. Both sides, however, agree that 'while poor standards prevail, competent musicians will not be interested in working for the Church, and standards will consequently continue to remain low'.

335.   In Canada, although there are few opportunities for training outside the big city, high standards of worship and music are still to be found in places. A positive response comes from North-West Europe where relationships between clergy and organists seem to present few problems, and where there is a general improvement and growth in matters musical.

Conclusion

336.   In spite of widely different histories and circumstances, many of the joys and sorrows of church music all over the world are familiar to us in this country. There is a sad tally of declining standards; the divide between traditional and modern; the lack of encouragement and training of church musicians; low pay and low levels of commitment; and unhappy human and professional relationships. These and other problems seem to be common everywhere. Solutions in one place may not be successful in other contexts, but the Church everywhere also offers some positive signs of hope. Among them are the burgeoning of musical writing; the involvement of an increasing number of people in making music; in some places the improvement of quality, and the dedication of many choirs, organists, directors, instrumentalists, composers and clergy to the cause of music in worship.

14

Music in Religious Communities

337. No survey of the current state of church music would be complete without some consideration of the music of religious communities, with which plainsong is particularly associated. In a report such as this it is possible to attempt only a limited review, and the concern of the present chapter is chiefly with communities in the Anglican tradition. It will be evident that these are greatly influenced by Roman Catholic religious congregations, and some of what is said here applies to monks and nuns of both Communions. The Commission is grateful for information and evidence from many communities and from a number of people whose names are listed in Appendix 2.10.

Anglican Religious Communities and their Worship

338. It is not commonly known that within the Church of England there are some fifty recognised communities of monks or nuns. These embrace the Benedictine, Augustinian, Franciscan and other main traditions of the religious life. Some communities have a number of branch houses, containing perhaps only three or four members, and some are reduced to a handful of elderly professed members. In all there are between six and seven hundred men and women living communally under vows. The sum total of their daily offering of music in worship far exceeds that of the cathedrals. In addition to the (usually) daily celebration of the Eucharist there is the rhythm of the Divine Office. This comprises chiefly the recitation of the Psalter, traditionally to chant, and takes place in some communities seven times a day, from Vigils or Lauds in the early morning to Compline at night. In others there are three or four offices consisting of Morning and Evening Prayer (often from the ASB), with prayers at midday and/or Compline.

339. However, not all communities sing the Office. Those which say all or part of it, with perhaps the addition of a hymn, do so either because their numbers are small and their voices ageing, or as a result of a deliberate choice. This may be out of a desire for absolute

119

simplicity and ready accessibility for visitors, or because other commitments do not allow time and people to be available for the preparation and practice of music. Or it may be because 'more and more we find we have people who say they "can't sing"'. Nevertheless, in spite of a much less universal use of music than formerly, the monastic musical tradition remains a vital one. It increasingly interacts with the music of the wider Church.

The Recovery and Adaptation of Plainsong

340.   The re-establishment of religious communities within Anglicanism has taken place only since the middle of the last century, and the tradition upon which their founders drew was mainly that of the Roman Catholic Church. Latin was adopted by some communities. Although a few continued with it until recently, it is used today only occasionally. From the beginning Gregorian chant was used by almost all communities, usually adapted for English texts. This followed the rediscovery of the Sarum Use, which had been a local medieval modification of the Roman rite, used in nearly every place in Britain by the end of the fifteenth century. In addition to the influence of Solesmes Abbey, there was the scholarship of men such as Briggs, Frere, Palmer and Arnold, reflected in the publications of the Community of St. Mary the Virgin at Wantage which made possible the recovery of plainsong for English congregations, parochial as well as religious. Today Dr. Mary Berry, as champion of the English tradition, continues the tradition of scholarship in the promotion of Gregorian chant, and Dr. Nick Sandon has done invaluable work on the musical text of the Sarum Use.

Modern Reforms

341.   There have been immense changes in recent times. These have come partly through the influence of Vatican II, but also because of the availability and use of a wide variety of biblical and liturgical texts in modern English. Unlike Roman Catholics, who had to come to terms with the use of the vernacular, Anglicans had used English for four hundred years. For them the difficulty was not to change from Latin but to move from the language of the Prayer Book to that of the ASB.

342.   One correspondent, however, sees little evidence today of an agreed understanding of what constitutes monastic music or even that the music of the monastic tradition is above all the vehicle for its prayer. He acknowledges that liturgy is not a museum piece but needs

to evolve as part of a living tradition. Nevertheless, he says that it has been difficult to avoid the wholesale abandonment of a fascinating liturgical and musical tradition which had sound scholarly foundations. 'A flurry of well-meant, but largely insubstantial, activity' has been scornful of scholarship, discipline and a proper kind of sacramentalism. It has resulted in some cases in 'banality rather than simplicity'. It should be noted, though, that as yet there has not been a long enough period for what is banal and insubstantial to be dropped in favour of what is an enduring renewal of the tradition.

343.   Some form of chant continues to be used in most communities at some time, not only because of historic associations, but also because of its fundamental simplicity. It enables all to partake in vocal recitation and yet demands sufficient practice and attention to ensure the full involvement of those using it. There is obvious importance in having music, as well as words, in order to create and express the unity of those who offer regularly and frequently the daily common prayer of an ecclesial community.

344.   Chanting can be made immensely complex, with syllables expanded in long neums and a substantial 'jubilus' element. It can also be as elementary as the monotone with either few or no inflections. This is the way in which, it seems, an increasing number of communities are using it. For some it is all the singing they do, other than the occasional hymn or Mass setting. Others introduce Gregorian or modal material on high days and special occasions. Many sing Psalms on a monotone for one or more of their daily Offices and employ a more elaborate chant for Morning and Evening Prayer. Invitatories, responses and responsories, as well as antiphons, are still commonly chanted.

Office Books and the Psalter

345.   Few communities now use the Coverdale or old English plainsong Psalters. They have been largely replaced by the American Psalter, the Grail Psalms and the Frost/MacIntosh Psalter of the ASB. Antiphons are still widely used and are frequently written by one or more members of the community, using modal formulae. Both in music and in text, the variety of offices and office books is considerable. As one sister put it, 'our office needed to be an expression of who we were'. Some communities have successfully completed revisions and some are still in the process of doing so. The Society of St. Francis is engaged in revising its very successful office book published in 1980.

346.   Those undertaking revisions have been helped by the publication in 1980 by the Anglican Communities Consultative Council of the *Anglican Office Book*. Few communities adopted it *in toto*, but it provided a useful source of material, even if those responsible for it fell into the common trap of producing texts which were not necessarily appropriate for musical setting.

The Eucharist and Hymn Books

347.   If there is a wide range of office books in use by religious in the Church of England, almost all of them now use the ASB rite for the Eucharist. This is sung at least sometimes by most communities and simple settings composed by their members are often used. Some are common to more than one community. Also used are settings familiar to parishes, such as those by Patrick Appleford, Gregory Murray and Richard Shephard. A few communities use vernacular plainchant settings, usually with one of the older rites. A large collection of modern texts set to traditional chants is to be found in the recent *An English Kyriale*. This ecumenical publication has its origins in the experimental work of the Community of St. John the Baptist at Clewer.

348.   For hymnody the main source of those with a traditional approach to the office hymn is *The English Hymnal* (or *The New English Hymnal*). However, all the standard books are used, from *Hymns Ancient and Modern Revised*, and its supplements, to *Mission Praise* (Marshall Pickering, 1986) and *Sound of Living Waters* (Hodder & Stoughton, 1974). One sister reports that her community uses four or five books. Others, such as West Malling and the SSF, have compiled their own collection of hymns. Most modern hymn books contain few office hymns. There is also the difficulty of obtaining good modern translations of hymns appropriate for use in monastic worship, which avoid the use of exclusive language which is particularly difficult for women's communities. Hopes are therefore being pinned upon the forthcoming production of a new monastic hymnal under the auspices of the Panel of Monastic Musicians.

Meetings and Resources

349.   The Panel of Monastic Musicians was formed in 1971, following the reforms of Vatican II. It seeks to provide a forum in which ideas, principles and the understanding of monastic worship can be shared particularly by those responsible for the music of a community. Its concerns are primarily those of the Roman Catholic Church, but

Anglicans also belong to it and there have been some useful ecumenical conferences over the years. In addition to 'monitoring' new music, the Panel remains committed to promoting the study and use of Gregorian chant. It has been helpful for many in showing that complex medieval Latin plainchant can be simplified and adapted to modern English texts, whilst retaining the basic musical principles of the eight Gregorian modes. There have also been gatherings in recent years of Anglican monastic musicians. These have taken place so far at Ditchingham, Mirfield and Whitby.

350.   While considering help and resources for Church of England communities, mention must be made of Stanbrook, a Roman Catholic abbey whose Dame Laurentia McLachlan and Dame Hildelith Cumming were amongst the pioneers of the modern use of plainchant. Hymns and modal chants are still regularly published by this community and are very widely used by Anglicans. St. Mary's Abbey, West Malling, has also been influential in helping other Anglican communities to attempt new musical expression whilst remaining within a monastic ethos. The St. Thomas More Centre in London has been a much-appreciated source of experimental music of an 'occasional' nature.

Musicians and Instruments within Communities

351.   Many convents and monasteries use music composed by their own members, partly because of the understandable wish to use what is tailor-made for a community and partly out of necessity. The quality of the music obviously varies, but many communities have had (and a few still have) distinguished musicians and liturgists among their number. The overall picture today, however, is of a decreasing number of musically-skilled people. There is sometimes a pull to a 'lowest common denominator' approach, lest any feel excluded. This is in part a reaction against a past striving for excellence in the plainsong tradition and, in some places, against the hierarchical division between 'choir' and 'lay' members. Today, however, the amount and quality of monastic music depends chiefly upon commitment and the personnel and time available to practise. In some monastic traditions the Office is only one of a number of priorities. Time and resources spent on music, therefore, may be considered to be disproportionate to its importance in the life of the community.

352.   Most chanting is unaccompanied, often because no one is available with the required skill, especially to accompany plainsong.

Increasing use is being made of guitars, flutes and other instruments, as well as of electric keyboards, for hymns and eucharistic settings. Not surprisingly there is a greater readiness to experiment where there are more, and perhaps younger, people than where the few elderly remaining members of an order cling to what is familiar.

Value to Parishes

353.   The maintenance of the plainsong tradition and the commitment of religious communities to the rhythm of worship is valuable to the wider Church. Parishes can learn much from the qualities of discipline and prayerfulness and a proper other-worldliness which mark the daily recitation of the Office, often in unaccompanied singing. There is, too, a sense of timelessness, stillness and silence which leaves a deep impression on visitors. This quality could bring great benefit to the clatter and chatter of much parochial worship.

Communities at Taizé and Iona

354.   Although it is neither in England nor Anglican, the ecumenical community at Taizé in France has become well known in recent years as a place of pilgrimage, especially by young people, and its music has a profound and growing influence in our churches. The chants of Jacques Berthier and others from Taizé are occasionally used in Anglican religious communities, and are becoming an increasingly common ingredient of parish worship.

355.   These chants combine the traditions of West and East. The simplicity of their melodic lines invoke the melismas of plainchant, whilst the harmonies which accompany the melody suggest the depths of Orthodox chanting. Consequently the chants seldom seem banal or trivial, in spite of being repeated over and over again. There is a mantra-like quality about them which creates an atmosphere of stillness and contemplation, and even those who are not used to prayer or formal liturgy are readily moved by them to devotion.

356.   Because the music is simple, repetitive and easily accessible to all, no great musical ability and no books are required. Thus much of the 'business' is taken out of worship, without numbers to be announced, places to be found, rustling of papers and shutting of books when the music is finished. Instead, the chant often returns to the profound silence from which it began, even with two or three thousand people in the congregation.

357.   Most of the chants are set to simple Latin texts, which perhaps heightens the sense of their 'traditional' feel. The reason for this is the pragmatic one that the Taizé community comprises people from many Christian traditions living together under vows. Very many different languages are spoken, both by the community and by their visitors who come from all over the world, and Latin provides a *lingua franca*. Most 'living' languages are also used in worship.

358.   In spite of its simplicity, the music at Taizé is always rehearsed before each of the three daily liturgies. Usually a volunteer choir of singers and instrumentalists from young visitors is formed. Their role is not so much to perform on their own as to lead and embellish the chants. Indeed, much musical interest is provided by the descants by instruments and, sometimes, voices as well.

359.   The music of Taizé has grown out of a particular context, culture and spirituality and it effectively serves the need of the ecumenical community for which it is composed. Taizé has become the focus of religious renewal for thousands of people and its music is their chief way of entering into the Community's worship. It has therefore been brought out of its original setting and is used widely in the churches to which the pilgrims return. Some concern has been expressed that in its transposition the idiom of Taizé may seem musically and liturgically slight, because it has been separated from the particular spirituality of which it is part. Certainly too much of it in a service (and there are Mass settings, songs and hymns as well as chants) can wear thin. But English congregations generally find its simplicity, accessibility and memorability a valuable aid to worship.

360.   Another non-English and non-Anglican community is that founded by Dr. George Macleod before World War II at Iona. It, too, is an important place of pilgrimage and its music is increasingly finding its way into parishes. More like folksong than chant, it reflects the Community's concern to relate worship and prayer to social issues. It generally uses English words, but has a Celtic feel to it and reminds British churches of an important element in their tradition. In Celtic spirituality the Holy Spirit is represented by a wild goose and this symbol gives the songs from the Iona Community their name.

Conclusion

361.   One monk noted in reply to the Commission's enquiries that religious communities probably owe to music more of their spirituality

than they will ever know. We might go on to say that not only in the medieval period with its plainsong, but also today, the Church owes more to the prayer and music of the religious orders than it will ever appreciate.

15

The Training of Musicians

362.   An examination of the training received by, and available to, those chiefly responsible for music in church presents a varied picture. In compiling this chapter, the Commission has drawn both on submissions made by music colleges and organisations, in particular a very full and helpful one from the Royal Academy of Music, and on the evidence received from individuals and derived from parish questionnaires (see Appendices 2.2–2.5). The picture includes the provision made for amateur and professional, part-time and full-time church musicians.

Professionals and Amateurs

363.   About one-fifth of parochial directors of music earn their livelihood through music. By a process of extrapolation and arithmetic, it can be estimated that there are about 3,500 professionals and 13,000 amateurs who take a leading role in church music in the parishes. In addition, there are perhaps another 200 professional musicians who work for a substantial part of their time in cathedrals, collegiate and choral foundations, and Royal Peculiars.

364.   These figures suggest that slightly fewer than a quarter of our most influential church musicians are professionals, in the sense that they derive the major part of their income from music. This is significant for any analysis of the training of church musicians. More than three-quarters of those who are currently in post, even where they receive some remuneration, are amateurs in status, and in many cases in training as well. The extent and quality of their musical education is therefore extremely varied. Many amateur musicians will have been influenced by the training undertaken by the professionals by whom they were, or are, themselves taught.

Learning on the Job

365.   The most long-standing method of training church musicians has been through apprenticeship. Many have learnt musical skills and

earned an income by singing in a church choir. Like J. S. Bach, the choirmaster or cantor of the past usually taught his choristers and pupils harmony and counterpoint, as well as instrumental skills. In this way they could continue their musical careers after their voices had changed. This system was confined mainly to boys, although a few orphaned girls had limited opportunities in such institutions as the *Conservatorio della Pietà* in the Venice of Vivaldi. Purcell, Haydn and Schubert were among the many who derived most of their basic musical training from being apprenticed as choristers.

366.   Originating in Renaissance times, this pattern of training persisted in this country almost to the present day. Within living memory there have been cathedral organists who have taught their skills to articled pupils. By first observing, then imitating their teacher, and then gaining direct experience of their craft under expert supervision these pupils learnt in the most practical of all ways. During the last fifty years the church musician as a kind of freelance 'general practitioner' has been increasingly replaced by those who derive their livelihood more as school music teachers than from their appointment as parish organists. Many organists nevertheless continue to fulfil the additional and varied roles of performing or conducting, and of private teaching.

Qualifications

367.   School musicians are likely to have taken either a graduate course at university or music college, or a specialist music course during their teacher training. During or after such courses they may have acquired some additional external diplomas in organ-playing, conducting, harmony and counterpoint. Their teaching qualifications are of obvious benefit to the church; the ability of a musical director to teach is as important as his or her mastery of musical skills.

368.   Until a generation ago it was not uncommon for a successful parish church organist to be appointed to a cathedral post. Today, however, the cathedral organist is more likely to be one who has been successively an organ scholar, a university graduate and a sub-organist at a cathedral. The system of organ scholarships provides young musicians with opportunities to learn on the job as an apprentice, but a degree in music is also increasingly required.

Universities and Colleges

369.   Academic studies in university music faculties often pay considerable attention to sacred music from the Early and Renaissance

periods. In the older universities, especially, there are likely to be opportunities of hearing or performing such music. However, the growing number of students with instrumental proficiency in recent years has meant an increasing concentration on orchestral work. Consequently, there is a trend towards a wider and rather more secular choice of repertoire.

370.   Several polytechnics and colleges of higher education offer degree courses with a substantial practical element. In these institutions the budding church musician has the opportunity to develop skills in conducting, performing and composing. The Colchester Institute offers a two-year course in church music, as does Hull University. Goldsmiths' College has a special second year option on 'Music and Religion'. A particularly interesting new development is a project for the training of musicians, chiefly for parishes, which is being set up jointly by Anglia Polytechnic and Chelmsford Cathedral.

371.   In spite of a long-standing tradition of appointing former cathedral and university musicians as principals of music colleges, the amount of time given in these institutions to the study of church music is limited. Trinity College of Music, for example, was founded in 1872 as a 'School for the Study and Practice of Music for the Church'. Whilst some small provision is still made for such study, the College's aim today is 'to train young musicians for careers as performers and teachers of music' (Gowrie: *Review of the London Music Conservatories*, 1980). The Royal Academy of Music inaugurated a Church Music Studies programme in 1987. In spite of promising prospects for the future, it has so far been a complementary course, to be undertaken in addition to the main course of study.

372.   Keyboard studies remain paramount for about a third of music college undergraduates although opportunities are provided for the learning of a second instrument or singing. This emphasis is true also of most of their graduate diploma courses. In all the music colleges, particular stress is placed upon the acquisition of high standards of general musicianship.

373.   In 1980 the Royal Academy of Music, the Royal College of Music, Trinity College of Music, the Royal Northern College of Music and the Birmingham School of Music between them had a total of 1688 students. Of these sixty-nine (4.1%) took the organ as their first study.

However, specialisation in the organ is no indication of a student's intention to work in the field of church music, for in recent years the organ has become increasingly recognised as a solo instrument in its own right. It is therefore possible that in 1980 no more than 2% of students at five major colleges intended to make a significant career in church music. Twelve years later, there are no signs that the situation has changed.

Organisations for Church Musicians

374.   The Royal College of Organists was founded in 1864, in order to represent and promote the organist's profession. It is mainly an examining body and awards the prestigious diplomas of ARCO, FRCO, CHM and (jointly with the Royal School of Church Music) ADCM. Most of its 3,000 members are Anglicans and many of them work in the field of church music.

375.   Another body concerned with qualifications in church music is the Guild of Church Musicians. Since 1961 it has offered preparatory courses and annual examinations for a Certificate in Church Music. Until 1988 it was known as the Archbishop of Canterbury's Certificate, but as it is now open to Roman Catholics has been renamed the Archbishops' Certificate (ACertCM). The Guild also awards a Fellowship Diploma (FGCM) in conjunction with a four-year full-time course in church music at Goldsmiths' College, London.

376.   The School of Church Music was founded in 1927 in order to improve the standards of church choirs, and to establish a college for the study of church music and the training of church musicians. In 1945 it was given the royal accolade and since 1954 it has had its headquarters in Croydon, although the College of St. Nicolas (latterly at Addington Palace) closed in 1974. Both before and since that closure residential and non-residential courses have been held, both at Addington and throughout this country and overseas. Affiliated choirs are spread throughout Britain and the English-speaking world, and since 1967 it has been fully ecumenical. The Director and Commissioners regularly visit parishes and arrange choir festivals, so that help is given 'in the field'. A significant part of its work is its extensive publishing operation. Although the RSCM is not primarily concerned with examinations and awards, it administers (with the RCO) the ADCM.

Provision for Amateurs

377.   All three of these organisations make provision for non-professional as well as professional church musicians. The use that is made of it, however, depends more upon the decision of the individual than upon the expectations of the Church. Equally, local training events for church musicians or workshops in the use of 'renewal music' are likely to receive their support from people who have an interest in them, rather than as part of a co-ordinated pattern of training for parish organists or directors of music. These are often described as amateur, but certainly in no derogatory sense. For, as in other spheres, the contribution of amateurs is often at least as significant and valuable as that of professionals.

378.   At one end of the scale are those competent enthusiasts who could probably have qualified as professionals had their careers taken a different course. Some have, indeed, achieved standards of excellence in performance and direction as high as those reached by some professionals. These musicians take pride in keeping abreast of new developments by attending courses and obtaining certificates or external diplomas from musical institutions. They continue to learn and to work at their skills.

379.   By contrast, there are those who are commonly called 'reluctant organists'. These are usually pianists of modest ability who have been persuaded to help out where there is no organist. It would seem that some 38% of the parishes surveyed by the Commission depend upon the goodwill of such people, and there are fewer of them in rural than in urban areas. Such ability as they may acquire depends more upon the situation in their parish than upon any systematic education or training.

380.   However, not all blame for an unsatisfactory situation should be attributed to the musicians and their training. A number of those giving evidence to the Commission discern a lack of clear diocesan initiatives and guidance in the field of church music. One correspondent suggests that there has been 'a progressive debasement . . . of the quality of worship as well as a diminution in the prestige and credit-worthiness of those responsible for directing it'. Some of those offering evidence point to the lack of a satisfactory career structure, inadequate remuneration and the absence of proper conditions of service for parish church musicians. One correspondent asserts that whilst there is no shortage of organists, there is a dearth of those who

131

are prepared to take on the regular commitment of parish church music.

Sacred and Secular

381.   From numerous comments made to the Commission it is evident that the limitations of the training offered to, and undertaken by, many church musicians is a cause for considerable concern. A major anxiety is the apparent dichotomy (as expressed in the submission by the Royal Academy of Music) between giving church musicians 'essential musical skills' and training them 'specifically in Church music'. Furthermore, preparation of students to work as church musicians without regard to their religious convictions can lead to confusion or insincerity. The Panel of Monastic Musicians, for example, believes that the church musician 'must be a deeply committed worshipper'. Otherwise the result can be as described by the Head of BBC religious broadcasting; in summarising the impressions gained by his producers of broadcast services, he quotes examples of choirs and music directors 'for whom worship was an excuse to parade their skills'. He suggests the need to recapture 'the nature of true worship'. That many of today's church musicians seem to be unfamiliar with developments in hymnody over the last thirty years is noted as significant by the Hymn Society of Great Britain and Ireland.

Conclusion

382.   Most of the institutions involved in the training of future church musicians seem to be largely unaware of the changing character of worship today. They would appear also to overlook the widening gap between the more traditional 'cathedral' ethos and the comparative informality of many parish church services. This is understandable, for the paucity of full-time, or nearly full-time, church music posts for professional musicians (as compared with those available for teachers and performers) is likely to dissuade any college from making radical changes to the content of its courses.

383.   There are, nevertheless, a small number of organisations, as well as music colleges, universities and institutions of higher education, who are doing what they can to improve the situation. In seeking to equip and help both amateurs and professionals in their work as church musicians, they offer a ray of hope in what is, overall, a fairly sombre picture.

16

Music at School

384.   The training of church musicians begins with their basic music education. For most of them all else, whether it be playing the organ or other instruments, or singing in the choir, is laid upon the foundation of what is learnt at school. The Commission therefore believes it is important to assess the place of music in the primary and secondary education offered to children in this country, chiefly in the public sector. For this purpose it has drawn on the knowledge and experience of its Secretary, a former HM Staff Inspector for Music.

Individualism and Instruments

385.   In the past four decades teaching has become increasingly child-centred. No longer passive recipients of instruction, pupils are encouraged to be active collaborators in the learning process. The most effective lessons are those where the child is given the opportunity, either as an individual or as a member of a small group, to explore and to create something original. The skilful teacher sets up a learning situation in which pupils can solve their own problems and draw their own conclusions.

386.   In music, as with other subjects, the trend has been away from regimentation towards an individual approach and small group work. As an 'emblem of belonging', therefore, massed singing has become less popular in schools, especially amongst pupils of secondary age.

387.   Another significant factor has been the instrumental 'explosion' which has affected all schools during the last forty years. The possession and mastery of one's own instrument, and the opportunity to contribute to an ensemble have given an exciting new dimension to music-making. The more accomplished players gain additional encouragement from their membership of, and loyalty to, one of the many music centres which have sprung up in every part of the country. The ablest of these young instrumentalists go on to become members of an area, borough, county or even national youth orchestra or band.

Consequently, many young people now see choral singing as less glamorous and challenging than playing in an ensemble. There are nevertheless still some school, borough and county choirs which flourish and some music centres which also promote choral singing.

Composition and Experiment

388.   The final report of the working party considering the content of music courses in the National Curriculum strongly affirms the centrality of performing, composing and listening in the new syllabus. Thus, performing remains part of every music course and is duly acknowledged in the National Criteria of the GCSE. Composing and arranging are already recognised as appropriate pupil activities. Closely allied to these are the opportunities given for pupils to appreciate the actual *sound* that music makes and to appraise its character, its dynamics, its associations and its wider emotional significance. The approach to listening to music has changed, with less emphasis upon analysis and the acquisition of facts about composers' lives.

389.   Not surprisingly, electronics are almost as common in the classroom as they are in the high street. The advent of electric keyboards, synthesisers, sequencers, samplers, amplifiers and multi-track recording facilities has opened up an exciting new world of sound for young people, at the touch of a key.

390.   Whether it be in listening, composing or performing, the range of music has widened dramatically. Familiarity with many different styles and genres is now encouraged. Jazz, Rock, Folk and Ethnic Music rub shoulders with Early, Baroque, Rococo, Romantic and Avant Garde pieces. If a high proportion of compositions submitted for GCSE employ the language of 'popular' rather than 'classical' music, this does not imply that creative standards are being compromised. For many young people now are confidently writing real music, using the idioms that come most naturally to them. The tapes and scores which they produce come across with real sincerity, and display surprisingly high levels of competence.

The Eclipse of Singing

391.   All these developments have given fresh stimulus and increased scope to music in schools, notwithstanding the current limitations in staff and resources. However, one area which has inevitably suffered in the process is that of choral singing. Not only do few children enter

school with a wide repertoire of nursery or religious songs learnt at their parents' knees, but many primary schools lack a full-time music specialist. Some class teachers are reluctant to become involved with this subject. Schools are often obliged, therefore, to amalgamate two or more classes for massed singing, or to rely heavily upon BBC Schools' broadcasts. These are excellent, but their exclusive use robs the subject of a personal and local dimension and inevitably leads to a measure of stereotyping. Even when school assemblies provide opportunities for singing, the quality of hymns and songs is variable, in both religious and musical content.

392. Many schools are unlikely, therefore, to be able to offer their pupils as rich an experience of choral singing or as wide a repertoire of religious vocal music, as once they did. Singing, the most natural way in which young children acquire a first-hand experience of music and an important means of expression for them, is being seriously curtailed.

393. Many teenagers feel embarrassed when asked to sing, and few adults are heard singing around the house or whistling on street corners. Other than at football matches or on coach journeys, people sing less spontaneously than in previous generations. Even the great tradition of Welsh male-voice singing has declined, with fewer choirs and ageing membership. In part this has been caused by the closures of collieries and factories, but the sharp drop in chapel or church attendance also means that fewer people are singing.

394. What is true of schools in the public sector is true also, to a lesser extent, of independent schools. Some of them, however, maintain the fine choral tradition which has produced many church musicians and the recent admission of girls into those which were formerly all-male establishments could well encourage the development of careers for women in church music.

Conclusion

395. It would be most unwise for the Church to ignore or discount the far-reaching changes which have taken place in school music since World War II. The implications of the present situation are serious and present a threat to the future of a great British choral tradition. All the evidence suggests that early involvement in choral singing can awaken an interest which lasts for a lifetime, and church musicians have always seen school singing as a natural preliminary to the distinctive tradition

of Anglican music. However, some encouragement may be derived from the enormous instrumental potential among the younger members of the Church's congregations. As yet, this is largely untapped by the Church.

17

Training for Ordained Ministry

396. In correspondence and submissions to the Commission repeated reference is made to the training received by clergy before ordination, and to the place of music in that training. A simple questionnaire was therefore addressed to theological colleges and ministerial training courses in England, Scotland and Wales (see Appendix 2.11). Its purpose was to survey the quantity and quality of training in church music currently being given to ordinands in Britain. The response to that questionnaire, together with other correspondence and submissions, forms the basis of what follows.

397. A common strand in comments coming to the Commission from many quarters emphasises the vital role played by the clergy in the leading of worship, and the need for them to receive proper training in the selection and use of music in church. Where that is lacking, the result may be the exercise of power without sensitivity, poor relationships with church musicians, little sense of occasion in worship, and frustrated worshippers.

Length and Content of Training

398. All who are prepared for the ordained ministry are trained under considerable pressure of time and with an overcrowded curriculum. Those who are under thirty normally complete thirty-three months in residential training. Those who are over thirty, and not fifty or over (for whom nine months is the norm), or who have a theology degree, undertake twenty-one months. For those on non-residential courses three years' part-time training is normally demanded. For all alike the training has to include studies in the traditional fields of theology and biblical studies, pastoral studies and practical placements. Continuing demands by the Church of the colleges and courses for ever more subjects, without any increase in the time of training, means that priorities have to be set. In most cases music comes low on the list.

399.   The first responsibility of colleges and courses is commonly understood to be that of educating their students to think theologically, and nurturing their personal and spiritual formation. Training in practical and particular ministerial skills is a secondary task. In any case, ministerial training continues on a less formal and standardised basis for at least the first three years after ordination, in the context of one or more curacies. The assumption is commonly made that instruction in the use of music in church is given (and many would say best given) during this period. It has the advantage of being in the context of a 'normal' worshipping congregation, where it is possible to develop and maintain the vital art of good relationships between clergy, organist and choir.

Teaching about Music

400.   All colleges and courses offer at least some training in the use of music in worship. But the quality, quantity and content of that training differ very considerably. Provision consists variously of regular seminars and lectures, occasional workshops, visiting speakers, parish placements, and student involvement in the planning, leading and reviewing of worship. Where there are ordinands or members of staff with professional musical skills, they are used for teaching. One college involves the local cathedral organist on a regular basis. Another college calls on local parish organists and music group leaders to help with occasional workshops. Many colleges and courses invite a representative of the RSCM to speak to students on an annual or biennial basis.

401.   The overall picture, however, is of a lack of systematic training in church music for ordinands. In particular, there appears to be a paucity of effective teaching on the theology of music and its significance in worship. An exception is in those curricula where it is an integral part of a course of liturgical studies. Then it takes its place over a period of time within the wider teaching of the principles, planning and practice of worship, enabling the ordinand to explore the theological and practical importance of music in an appropriate context. The one-off session on 'Music in Worship', offered by several colleges and courses, can hardly provide the same opportunity.

Music in the Worship of the Community

402.   An important element in the educational process is the participation by students in the corporate worship of college courses. In all the colleges there are regular services in which ordinands and staff

alike are worshippers. Experience of being in the pew naturally plays an important part in forming perceptions of how to plan and conduct worship, and the place of music within it.

403.   At the level of practical skills and of selecting music, all colleges and courses give students at least some training. Its intensity, however, is directly related to the degree of active student involvement in the planning and leading of acts of worship. In many places of full-time residential training the organisation of worship is largely a student responsibility and some supervision and guidance in the choice of music appears to be given. Those who are studying on a part-time basis as members of a regional course do so as non-residential students, with regular residential weekends and summer schools. For them there are fewer opportunities for planning and leading worship, and they receive correspondingly less guidance.

Use of the Voice

404.   Among the practical skills offered by all colleges and courses is voice training. There is some variation between its being compulsory for all students and its being only for those who need help in reading or preaching in public. Sessions with professional speech therapists or voice specialists are common and video or tape recordings are sometimes used.

405.   Training in singing appears to be less systematised than training in voice production. Two respondents indicated that all ordinands in their college have their singing voices assessed during their training, and then receive instruction as necessary. Others offer training in singing only at the request of the ordinand, or the tutor or parish placement supervisor.

406.   The lack of priority given to teaching singing to ordinands is explained by one respondent who wrote, 'Part of the problem with the teaching of singing has to do with the relative infrequency with which the Sunday Offices are now sung . . . Few placement churches have anything like a *regular* sung Book of Common Prayer or Alternative Service Book Evensong; and many of the churches [from which ordinands come and] to which ordinands go as curates follow a similar pattern. Under these circumstances, [the college] can aim to do little more than build some confidence in a student . . . More effort . . . needs to be put into in-service clergy training in this area – with refresher courses for those appointed to parishes where the Offices are

sung regularly'. This observation is borne out by the Commission's statistical Parish Survey in which it appears that only 43% of Anglican churches have one or more Evensongs with a choir each month (see Appendix 2.5).

Away from College or Course

407.   An important element in training for ordination is provided by one or more parish placements. These vary widely in their duration and organisation. There may be a four-week residential block in a parish during a summer vacation or a four-week block followed by Sunday and two days each week for two and a half terms. The former provides an involvement in the parish almost wholly at the level of observation, normally in the company of the incumbent. The latter is likely to provide some scope for active involvement in the worshipping and musical life of the parish. Placements in parishes are complemented by one or two three-week residential community placements in which life in a non-church institution, like a hospital, is observed. This is unlikely to provide much in the way of musical experience or opportunity, but its requirement demands an investment of precious time.

After Ordination

408.   Colleges and courses can offer relatively limited training for the ordained ministry. All, therefore, look to post-ordination training (POT), the training incumbent, and in-service clergy training (or CME), to build on what has already been learnt. The RSCM has found involvement in POT and CME to be valuable. It has generally been much more effective in forming the musical sensibilities of clergy than hit-and-run visits to theological colleges.

Conclusion

409.   The training of ordinands and others in the use of music in worship is recognised as important by colleges and courses alike. But, as has been seen, time is precious. Relatively little thought appears to have been given to developing systematic forms of training in the area of music in worship, and little assessment of the quality of training seems to take place. Its effectiveness is revealed only after the ordinand has been ordained. Let one such ordinand have the last word: 'If a student leaves college as a musical novice (both in terms of their own singing ability and their ability to select music for worship) then the worship of the churches in which they serve is going to be severely

disadvantaged . . . The more that can be done to help students to develop their own musical abilities and understanding, and thus see the immense potential of music in worship, the better'.

PART 4

RESOURCES

18

Musical Instruments and Equipment

410.   The most important and most frequently used musical instrument in worship is the human voice. Monastic communities often sing unaccompanied, and churches in Africa and the Third World commonly rely upon the congregation's ability and enthusiasm in singing even polyphonic music without instrumental help. Many churches in the West, however, have come to depend upon an organ or other instrument to lead, support, or even dominate, the use of voices. This reliance can be an inducement to laziness of vocal effort, and people are often more capable of good unaccompanied singing than they realise. The provision of musical instruments in church should not be seen as solely for the accompaniment and embellishment of singing, but also for solo and ensemble playing before, during or after a service.

411.   For the material in this chapter the Commission is grateful to one of its members with wide experience of writing for, and using, various instruments in worship. It also acknowledges its debt in what is said about electronic instruments to *Repair or Replace?* (Council for the Care of Churches, 1990); to *Organs in Churches*, (an unpublished paper for the Department of Art and Architecture in the Archdiocese of Liverpool) by Mr. Terence Duffy; and to a memorandum from Dr. John Webb.

PIPE ORGANS

412.   A long tradition associates the organ with Christian worship and it is commonly assumed that every church has one. This expectation is so strong that most congregations are prepared to spend huge sums for the provision and maintenance of an instrument which is, in many cases, the single most valuable asset in the building. The organ is described by its devotees as the King of Instruments, and it is certainly very versatile when properly designed. For the accompaniment of a large congregation there is no substitute, and the sustained and undergirding tone of the organ's pedal department makes it

particularly suitable for bold, harmonic music such as stately hymn tunes or processional marches.

413.   Depending upon its design, the organ has a wide variety of tone, from pungent reeds to mellow flutes, and a great range of volume, from *pianissimo* to *fortissimo*. This makes it a most useful instrument not only for solo pieces but also for the support of voices. For example, the imaginative use of stop changes can greatly enrich the singing of the Psalms. Where there is compatibility of pitch, the organ can be used very effectively with melodic solo instruments, or as part of an ensemble, or as a continuo instrument to fill in harmonic gaps and add weight of tone and sustaining power. With the solo use of its stops, it can also offer light-weight, high delicate playing of running scales or arpeggios in a detached style, with other instruments providing sustained harmony.

414.   Sadly, many an organist falls prey to the ponderous and unrhythmic playing which is invited by the instrument's ability to sustain a note for as long as the key is depressed, with results which may be sentimental or lugubrious. Under the hands and feet of an expert the organ can sound more rhythmical than many people imagine, although it does not usually match the rhythmic or percussive elements of a piano or modern keyboard. These are demanded particularly by contemporary rock and folk styles of music.

ELECTRONIC ORGANS

415.   The term 'electronic organ' covers a wide range of instruments, some of which are clearly inappropriate for music in church. The earliest instruments were the electro-mechanical organs of the Hammond and Compton 'electrone' type. These used rotating discs to initiate a quasi-musical sound which was then filtered, processed and reproduced at different pitches. Although long-lasting and generally reliable, their musical shortcomings were obvious and none have been manufactured since 1980, although they are still in use in a few churches.

416.   The 'analogue' organs which followed came closer to an imitation of true organ sound by using valves, but these displayed increasing unreliability. The use of transistors has brought an improvement in this respect, but the quality of sound remains poor, especially in the cheaper instruments which some would deem to be more appropriate for the cocktail bar than for playing in church.

417.　Present-day computer or digital organs incorporate new and complex technology, and this has led to some impressive developments. Single stops are either synthesised by the manufacturer, or sampled from actual organ pipes. The final sound is determined by the skill of the manufacturer, the time given to programming the computer and the extent of its memory.

418.　These instruments offer a wide range and large numbers of stops, and some provide an extra selection by means of computer cards which are fed into a slot. They often include a coupler which simulates the use of the pedals by isolating the lowest note being played on the manual and doubling it to the pedal register, using whichever pedal stops have been selected. They may also incorporate a transposition device. Thus they are less daunting than a large pipe organ to the 'reluctant organist'. An electronic memory can be fitted, so that a performance can be recorded and later played back. This facility is available on some modern pipe organs and can be used as a tool for students, and for the recording of pieces or hymn accompaniments by a competent organist, to be reproduced later when the player cannot be present. Electronic organs can also be fine-tuned to match other instruments, and because they always remain in tune there are no tuning costs to be incurred. Moreover, there are continuous advances in tonal and technical design and production.

419.　At present, however, even with the 'top resistance' touch fitted to some electronic instruments, they cannot match the ability of a good pipe organ to exercise effective control of rhythm and phrasing. This in turn may influence the singing of a congregation, and make it flabby and dull. Lifelessness can also result from the less than satisfactory effect of the full ensemble of most electronic instruments. This is caused largely because their sound is synthetic. In a pipe organ of quality each pipe is a carefully-designed and individually-voiced musical instrument which produces only one frequency of sound. Tone generators and loudspeakers, however, have to cope with a multitude of frequencies and cannot hope to move the same amount of air as the equivalent number of pipes. Nevertheless, for softer tones and individual colours an electronic instrument can be most effective, particularly in a large building with good resonance.

420.　Until recently loudspeakers had to be large to be effective. Today, however, the size of a speaker does not dictate its efficiency and it is possible to use relatively small output units to good effect. A disused pipe organ case is sometimes employed as a screen and certainly a more accurate impression of a pipe organ is gained if the speakers are positioned in one place, rather than dispersed around the building. They should not be too far from the console if the organist is to avoid playing too loudly for those people seated near them. There is no reason why they should not be visible, provided their design is in keeping with their surroundings. Architectural considerations apply also to the design and placing of the console. One of the advantages of an electronic instrument is that there is considerable flexibility for its positioning.

Financial Considerations

421.   Cost is one of the major factors for churches in deciding between an electronic and a pipe instrument. If there is an existing pipe organ and it is of good quality, it may prove to be more economical in the long run to restore rather than replace it. For new instruments, both electronic and pipe, it is possible to give here only very rough figures, relating to the situation in the latter half of 1991.

422.   A small, middle-of-the-range electronic organ would cost about £7,000 and churches would be unwise to consider anything less than this. A more versatile one could be obtained for about £10,000 and one with a comprehensive specification for about £20,000. A 'cathedral-size' model would cost at least £30,000. Extra speaker units, which are necessary for all but the smallest instruments, cost about £700 each. It is usual to buy electronic organs 'off the shelf', but larger instruments are designed to a customer's specification and to suit particular buildings.

423.   Pipe organs are usually individually designed, but it is quite common to purchase at lesser cost one of the standard models offered by many organ builders. A very basic instrument consisting of five ranks of pipes on one manual and pedals would cost about £15,000. A comprehensive instrument with two manuals and pedals, and between eighteen and twenty ranks of pipes would cost upwards of £70,000. For an organ larger than this, there is no limit except that imposed by the customer's ability to pay. Second-hand pipe organs are sometimes worth considering when they are fine instruments and when the total cost of their purchase, removal and rebuilding in a place suitable for them makes economic sense.

424.   Those making a decision need also to have in mind that, whilst an electronic instrument requires no tuning and very little main-

tenance, its life expectancy is at present shorter than that of a pipe organ. Modern electronic organs may last for between twenty and fifty years, but there is a question as to whether spare parts will be available for that long. A pipe organ may be expected to last for between fifty and one hundred years, but at least one major overhaul will be necessary during this period. It also needs regular maintenance and tuning. It has the advantage, however, that new parts can be made for it as required, because it is not mass-produced. With regard to second-hand values, a good pipe organ is a better investment than an electronic instrument.

OTHER KEYBOARD INSTRUMENTS

The Piano, Acoustic and Electric

425.   A piano can be used to good effect with the organ, provided its pitch is compatible. Its special force of percussive tone helps to define musical entries and mark changes of tempo. By means of added rhythmic patterns in chords and arpeggios it can fill out the music to enhance the singing of a congregation. It is not, however, a wholly satisfactory substitute for an organ, because of its lack both of volume and of sustaining power. It may nevertheless be better than even a reasonable harmonium or American organ. Moreover, it has the advantage of familiarity for pianists who may be nervous of an organ, and pianists are more numerous than organists in our congregations.

426.   However, many of the pianos to be found in our churches have seen much better days. If they cannot be replaced by more adequate instruments, an electric keyboard can be appropriate. This instrument offers a variety of sounds, including that of the classical piano, the pop-based electric piano which is useful for effects and atmosphere and for accompanying solo singing, and the harpsichord or clavichord for older music. Even fairly inexpensive keyboards make pleasing sounds. They can be fine-tuned to match other instruments and have the advantage of remaining in tune once they are set. They are little affected by changes in temperature and humidity and are easily portable. However, unless they include well-amplified organ tones, they are a useful addition to the organ rather than a substitute for it.

The Synthesiser

427.   The synthesiser can be used either as a melodic or as a chorus instrument. Melodic lines may vary from synthesised or sampled sounds which reproduce classical instruments, to more obviously

electronic tones. Melodies can be reproduced as counter-subjects or descants in the treble, or as horn or cello sounds in the tenor, or as bass guitar or organ pedal in the bass. When used for playing full chordal accompaniments they can reproduce the sound of a full pipe organ, or of the string, brass or percussion section of an orchestra. They have much in common with the best of today's electronic organs.

OTHER POLYTONAL OR HARMONIC INSTRUMENTS

The Harp

428.   The harp is an instrument of considerable versatility which is not commonly associated with use in church services. It can, however, be employed for simple piano parts, or its occasional rolled chords are an effective accompaniment to choral work. Its possibilities are best exploited in partnership with a single instrument, such as the flute or oboe, using rippling arpeggios, tremolos, cascades and glissando effects, or with the human voice. It can be particularly effective in providing an instrumental background to the spoken word, in drama, readings or prayers. The harp is, however, susceptible to fluctuations of heat and humidity, and keeping it in tune may require its re-tuning even during a service.

The Harpsichord

429.   The tuning problems mentioned above may also apply to the harpsichord. This is sometimes used as a complement to the organ in accompanying Early, Renaissance, Tudor and Baroque music. It is also useful for some contemporary music where a light, jazz-style accompaniment is required.

The Guitar, Acoustic and Electric

430.   Much contemporary music, in its dance-style, ballad, folk and gentle rock forms, relies on the strumming rhythm of the guitar. Both acoustic and electric instruments can be forceful and strident. They can also convey an intimacy in providing gentle, 'finger-picking' backing for soft or solo singing and playing, inducing a mood of vulnerability or timelessness. In anything other than in a small space, the acoustic guitar needs electric amplification to be heard. Although a number together may overcome this, there can be problems of intonation and ensemble. The electric guitar demands particular sensitivity on the part of those who play it since, by its very nature, its sound is somewhat aggressive. Because it has no sound box of its own, what comes through a loudspeaker can be varied enormously. It is commonly associated

with 'heavy-rock' sounds which include ringing, 'buzzy' chords, obtrusive rhythmic bite and a harsh, penetrating solo melody line. A common fault is over-amplification of the instrument.

SINGLE NOTE OR MELODIC INSTRUMENTS

431.   All of the instruments so far mentioned can be used to play a melody as well as chords. The other instruments in this chapter are confined to the playing of one note at a time, other than the stringed instruments where it is possible to employ double, triple or quadruple stopping effects.

Recorders and Flutes

432.   Of the woodwind family the recorder, often made of plastic, is the easiest instrument to play. But it is not by any means just for children and can be used as a solo instrument or in bands. The cheapest and most generally in use is the descant recorder, although the other members of the family are equally useful, if harder to play. The sopranino has a pure, bright tone, whilst the treble gives a mellow sound in the mezzo-soprano range. Recorders are most comfortable in sharp keys and simple key signatures like G or D major. The flute can be very useful in public worship, and is relatively easy to learn, although the piccolo is more of a specialist instrument. Equally at home with Bach or jazz, the flute is capable of rapid notes and exciting dashes in busy upper register counter-subjects. It provides an effective descant over voices, and can sound languid and restful, especially when unaccompanied in its bottom octave, rising from middle C. In its middle register it is useful for teaching new tunes or doubling the melody line.

Oboes, Clarinets and Bassoons

433.   The oboe is much harder to play, but gives a clear, incisive lead and offers a range of effects from the Oriental and haunting to the gently pastoral. Its lowest note is the B^b below middle C, and from the G above that it begins to rise and soar expressively. Effective use can be made of two oboes playing in thirds. Clarinets also blend well together and they have a wide range, both of dynamic and of pitch. The B^b instrument encompasses the tenor, alto and soprano ranges, with a rich sound at the bottom. There is a trumpet-like incisiveness in the middle and upper registers and a positively ringing sound at the top. Its speciality is rapid and repeated upward scales or arpeggios. Like the B^b trumpet, for which it is sometimes substituted, the B^b clarinet's part

151

is written one tone higher than the pitch required. The bassoon is less common. Its range extends from bass to alto but it is most happy in the tenor register, where it is effective in sustaining or filling in the harmony. It is tiring for the player constantly to double a bass line.

Brass Instruments

434.　Brass instruments generally are best used occasionally and sparingly, being saved for climaxes or dramatic moments. Open Bᵇ trumpets, soaring high and doubling melodies or playing descants, can produce the most sublime and majestic sound. When muted and playing close intervals, they produce an effect which is jazzy, or even sinister. For reproducing or doubling alto and tenor lines the French horn is splendid in its ability to sustain a velvet tone. Its part is written a perfect fifth higher than it plays and as long as its notes are on the stave it sounds well. However, the player needs to rest periodically. Where available, trombones and a tuba complete the brass ensemble.

String Instruments

435.　A solo violin and solo cello can be a most useful addition to a small ensemble. Even very simple parts, consisting of a few long notes, are effective. Violins may double a significant melody, or play rapid semiquaver counter-melodies in fine eighteenth-century style, to add brilliance and excitement to a piece. The violin covers both the alto and soprano ranges, the viola those of the tenor and alto, and the cello all four vocal parts. The cello has a rich, penetrating sound throughout its range and is the most versatile of the stringed instruments. The double bass, too, is more versatile than is commonly recognised (as is the bass guitar). Pizzicato playing injects rhythmic lightness and clarity and this is useful especially for music in a modern dance-like or folk idiom. Bowed long notes make good additions to organ pedal parts or timpani rolls. All strings should be especially carefully tuned to the rest of the musical ensemble.

Percussion

436.　Like brass instruments, percussion is best used sparingly and occasionally. All percussion has a pervasive sound and even when played quietly the effect of one instrument does not go unnoticed. A relentless beat can be extremely tedious, but powerful dramatic or martial effects can be gained by the careful use of side-drums and cymbals, especially in conjunction with brass instruments. Tambourines add sparkle and rhythmic life to cheerful, dance-like pieces and glockenspiels, playing single or double notes, can highlight portions of a melody with good effect. The combination of timpani and organ greatly enhances spacious, majestic music.

437.   In contemporary music with a jazz, rock or 'ethnic' feel, drum kits and other collections like bongos and tom-toms reinforce the beat and articulate rhythmic patterns. The 'kick' drum, the 'ride' cymbal and the 'high-hat' implied in Psalm 150 usually need some dampening or restraining when used in church.

Handbells

438.   Handbells, although very common in the United States, are to be found in few churches in this country, except where they are used by bellringers in connection with change-ringing. They are popularly associated with Christmas, but have great value for musicians in all kinds of music. They have a range of many octaves and their richness of tone allows them to be used as an ensemble. Their percussiveness makes them suitable as an accompaniment to congregational singing. Handbell ringing has potential as a social as well as a musical activity in church. It also fits well into any situation from the shopping mall to the living room. As one correspondent notes, handbells provide 'as good a practical and possible evangelistic tool as a church can have'.

Co-ordination of an Ensemble

439.   Where an instrumental ensemble is employed, with or without singers, it is necessary that there be at least a leader, if not a conductor. If that person has the ability to make instrumental arrangements, then that is an additional bonus. Orchestration does, however, demand some skill and a great deal of time. There are few arrangements for instruments on the commercial market, not least because different churches have different combinations of players available to them.

440.   The physical disposition of the musicians can be problematic in many church buildings, especially where the organist is hidden away. Happily, the advent of closed-circuit television has largely overcome the difficulty of an invisible console, even if the pipes themselves are still in an inconvenient place in relation to other instruments. In simpler situations the system of mirrors still works well, and is, of course, much cheaper than a television camera and monitor.

SOUND SYSTEMS

441.   Modern technology is also valuable for the reinforcement of instruments and voices. Amplification is not necessarily a bad or inartistic phenomenon. It is often necessary where a distinctive and valuable sound made by an instrument or small group of voices cannot be heard over the singing of a congregation. Not all such performances are inspiring, however, and a plenitude of decibels does not compensate for lack of quality. Those operating an amplification system need to ensure that there is a proper balance between the sound of the musicians using it and those who speak on the church's public address system, where there is one.

442.   All electric instruments depend upon good amplifiers and speakers. Some have their own built into them, although in large buildings further amplification and speakers may be required. But the use of microphones, amplifiers and speakers can entail unsightly ironmongery, technical clutter and hazardous cables which can provide visual distraction and even physical danger in church. A direct injection (DI) box can sometimes feed the sound from electric keyboards and guitars straight into the PA system. In this case, some kind of monitor or 'fold-back' speaker may be necessary for the musicians to hear the results of their playing. It should always be remembered that amplification is there to serve, not to dominate the congregation, and to enhance and not simply to magnify the artistry of musicians.

CONCLUSION

443.   The use of instruments of various kinds, in addition to the organ, is not widespread in our churches. Yet it is clear that there are enormous possibilities for offering a rich mixture of sounds and players which can only enhance public worship.

19

Radio, Television and Recordings

444.   The electronic media make a significant contribution to the popular perception of religious music. Television and radio in particular have an influence upon the attitudes and preferences of worshippers and their power is not to be ignored. So the Commission has thought it appropriate to include some consideration of these forms of communication in its Report.

445.   In doing so it has had the benefit of conversations with the Revd. Roger Hutchings, a BBC producer, and with Mr. Graham Kendrick, who is an experienced recording artist. It has also drawn upon the experience of two of its members in broadcasting and recording. In addition, the Commission conducted an informal survey of the Christian music used on broadcasting outlets, consulted producers about their editorial policy, and made use of written submissions and correspondence.

National Radio

446.   As might be expected, the greatest spread of Christian music comes from the BBC's national networks. Their policy is 'to reflect the best religious music that is around. Traditional music/hymns will dominate, though we aim to introduce listeners to new compositions and stimulate new music and music-makers, e.g. through the Choirboy and Choirgirl of the Year Competition and the Festivals of Gospel Music.'

447.   A considerable amount of varied religious music of the more traditional kind is offered by BBC Radio 3. This appeals to a faithful minority of listeners. Their loyalty was powerfully demonstrated recently in the storm of protest which greeted, and reversed, the decision of the BBC to take the weekly broadcast of Choral Evensong off the air. It remains one of the few 'constants' in the changing world of broadcasting.

448. So, too, does the 'Daily Service' on BBC Radio 4. Until recently this offered traditional hymns and Anglican psalmody sung by the BBC Singers. Now the Singers contribute once a week, alternating with other musicians, and there is a much wider selection of music. The daily broadcast has a uniform structure except on one day a week when it is described as 'an act of worship'. On this day the presenter is asked to create a special format, with music employed to amplify or illustrate the theme of the service. The changes of recent years have brought a small but measurable increase in the size of the audience, now at just under half a million listeners, in spite of its transmission being confined to AM at an off-peak time. Many evidently value a 'still window' each day.

449. A much greater number of the public listen on Sunday, both to BBC Radio 4's 'Sunday' programme which presents occasional music features, and to 'Good Morning Sunday' on Radio 2 which is music-based. On an average Sunday, more people hear these two programmes than go to church in the whole of Britain. More popular than either of them is Radio 2's 'Sunday Half Hour' which has presented well-loved hymns for fifty years. In addition, there are very significant audiences for the more than one hundred Independent Local Radio and BBC local stations, and new independent network, community radio and satellite services.

Local Radio

450. The sharpest judgments by listeners are made about local radio, perhaps because the audience identifies easily with a nearby station. Its religious music is likely to fit that particular station's music policy in aiming at its target age-range. In most areas this consists of people roughly between ten and forty-five years old. Contemporary Christian music holds an audience of this kind, although it may be necessary to mix it with chart music to make it generally acceptable.

451. Traditional music and hymnody are seen to be for an older audience. Hymnody might be used more if the production of most recordings were better and the words could be heard more clearly. The variable quality of both production and music in outside broadcasts from churches, together with budgetary limitations, means that they are almost wholly precluded.

452. Those in local radio believe that the Church should put more resources into encouraging and developing modern music and musi-

cians. They suggest that 'contemporary music is a means that God uses today to reach out to people who otherwise would not consider the truths of Christianity for themselves'. Although 'in our age music is . . . an important way of imparting an important message . . . the standard of contemporary religious music is not very high in the UK'. Producers do not want 'third-rate numbers that are instantly forgettable, all sounding the same'.

Television

453.   There is much less scope for religious music on television, but the BBC's 'Songs of Praise' and ITV's 'Highway' are popular programmes with a wide influence on church and non-church people alike. On a high-rating Sunday, they will draw up to a third of the population of Britain. In 'Songs of Praise' Christian music is used increasingly to reinforce a powerful testimony or trenchant editorial comment. There are also the regular live television relays of church services.

454.   The survey *Godwatching* (IBA and John Libbey, 1988) showed that 62% of adults sometimes watch religious programmes. This challenges the assumption that such programmes are of interest only to a specialist few:

> What is particularly noteworthy is the fact that, despite the relative paucity of religious output compared to, say, news or drama, many people do choose to encounter religious programming. It is unlikely, judging from this analysis, that very many viewers are loyal or watch particularly frequently, rather that a large number of people dip in on a relatively occasional basis. This is clear evidence that religious output, despite some criticisms of its style and approach, is by no means the anathema for viewers that it is supposed from the purely commercial viewpoint of some broadcasters.

455.   It remains to be seen what effect the Government's deregulation will have on the dissemination of Christian music through radio and television. At present, a very large number of people are exposed to it in one way or another. The Church is perhaps largely unaware of its influence and its potential.

The Recording Industry

456.   For some years the recordings of well-known choirs, such as King's College, Cambridge, have had a steady and growing market. Sales of traditional church music records are boosted annually before Christmas, with a wide variety of recordings of carols. Many cathedral and other choirs spend a good deal of time on making recordings, and derive from them a modest but useful income.

457.   Much more money is to be made, however, from the sale of recordings produced by Contemporary Christian Music (CCM). In the United States, for example they account for 7% of all record sales (compared with 1% in 1975), thus exceeding sales of jazz and classical music.

458.   CCM has its roots in Negro culture, but the genesis of much of what we have now lies in the Jesus Movement. In Britain it came to the fore in the 1970s through *Buzz* magazine and the Greenbelt festival. Consequently, the idea began to spread that it was perfectly proper for Christians to be involved with pop and rock music. Although the charge could be laid that CCM depends upon the imitation of other forms, so great is its variety and so gifted its musicians that it can hardly be accused of lacking originality.

459.   In Britain CCM is not much more than a cottage industry, largely because of lack of radio exposure. Excluding the Cliff Richard phenomenon, sales of twenty or thirty thousand are regarded as a 'hit' in this country. Put beside 'gold' and 'platinum' standards such sales are minute, but not insignificant. They are, in fact, comparable to those of traditional jazz recordings.

460.   In Britain a large share of the market is held by Word (UK) Ltd., which usually sells directly to the customer. Christian bookshops are also an important outlet. The market is a distinctively evangelical one and the lyrics are addressed to Christians, particularly those who are commonly described as 'charismatic'.

461.   There are signs in the USA of more aggressive, sharper music which is directed to the listener rather than to the worshipper. This suggests that the situation may change, and CCM in this country is in a state of flux. If the new forms of 'Christian' music can find financial backing, substantial inroads could be made into the music industry in Europe.

Conclusion

462.   The potential of radio, television and recordings is plainly enormous, both for business and for the Church. The accessibility of audio-visual media, and their pervasiveness, means that very few people are unaffected by them. They play a large part in moulding the musical tastes of all members of society, including those who go to church. This presents an important challenge to composers and performers, and church musicians dare not disregard or dismiss so potent an influence for evangelism.

20

Composing, Publishing, Copyright and Insurance

463.   The provision of music and other books in church is often taken for granted. But before anything can be put into the hands of the worshipper, many people are involved in its production. The composer and the writer of the text (where one is used) mediate and transcribe the words and music which are their particular inspiration from God. The printer and publisher are responsible for making the printed piece available to all who will perform it. Those who make and operate the laws of copyright seek both to safeguard the integrity of a work and to ensure an income for its writer.

464.   The Commission is indebted to Heather Rosenblatt (formerly a Senior Administrator for the Incorporated Society of Musicians) for a summary of the provisions relating to copyright, and to Bernard Braley of the Pratt Green Trust for some helpful information. Also included in this chapter is a description of those areas of insurance which apply to church musicians and their instruments.

COMPOSERS

465.   A large proportion of the music used in church is an inheritance from the past, containing contributions from almost all major composers. Although the Christian faith is no longer at the heart of the culture of this land, and the Church is peripheral to the lives of many people, mid-twentieth-century British composers such as Vaughan Williams, Walton, Britten, Berkeley, Mathias and Leighton have all contributed to the choral repertoire. They have done so as part of a widely comprehensive output, ranging from chamber music to symphonies and opera. This indicates not only their wealth of invention but also the artistry and professionalism of their approach.

Commissions

466.   Much newly-composed music is commissioned for festivals, royal occasions or events of local significance, such as choir festivals and church anniversaries. Composers are also commissioned to write anthems and settings of the Eucharist for the regular round of worship. Some of our cathedrals regularly add to their repertoire in this way.

467.   Patronage by the Church has been part of the musical world for centuries, and in the past many of the greatest composers have depended upon it for their livelihood. It is on a much-reduced scale today, as the Church can no longer afford to be the foremost en- courager of the arts. There is a need for sensitivity on the part of those from whom music is commissioned. Performers and listeners do not generally warm to music which is written in discordant or arid style. Nevertheless, sponsors of commissioned works are committed to accepting the finished product, even if the composer fails to produce exactly what was envisaged or specified. Consequently, some first performances also prove to be the last.

New Music for New Texts

468.   There are still reputable composers who are reluctant to write music for new liturgical texts, as they find the quality of their language unacceptable. However, recent publications such as *Lent, Holy Week and Easter, Patterns for Worship* and *The Promise of His Glory* (all Church House Publishing) offer many new resources for today's musicians. A recognition of the prominence being given to psalmody outside Morning and Evening Prayer has led to the provision of simpler substitutes for Anglican chant. Both responsorial psalms of various kinds and Taizé refrains have become widespread.

Settings for the Eucharist

469.   Some composers have written eucharistic settings in traditional vein providing for the needs of choirs with limited resources and expertise. Among them, Peter Aston, Martin How, John Rutter and Richard Shephard may be mentioned. Their music is simple enough to be within the competence of an average choir, yet has the melodic, harmonic and rhythmic interest which gives satisfaction and enjoy- ment both to singers and to congregations. Alternatives to the tradi- tional writing for four parts (SATB) are increasingly being produced. These take account of the limitations of depleted choirs, in two-part writing for high and low voices or three-part music for sopranos, altos and men's voices.

470.   New music being written for the ASB Holy Communion has the needs of the congregation very much in mind. But more complex writing is also available to meet the requirements of skilled choirs. Every type of situation, from village church to cathedral, is embraced in a wide range of settings and styles. Relatively few cathedral organists today are also composers. Among those who are, there are those who follow in the fine tradition of writers such as Bairstow, Bullock, Darke, Harris, Stanford, Sumsion and Charles Wood.

More Popular Writing

471.   There is a significant burgeoning in the composition of music in a more popular genre. This is used mainly in churches where informality marks much of the worship. In the 1950s Patrick Appleford, Geoffrey Beaumont and the Twentieth Century Church Light Music Group laid the foundation for composers today. Their writing has wide appeal and provides material for many publications. Only a small proportion of this music demands more than one voice part, making it highly suitable for congregational singing, and it is easily accompanied by instruments other than the organ. The guitar and the piano are perhaps the most common alternatives, but instruments of all kinds can be used and this gives encouragement to the formation of music groups.

Locally Composed Music

472.   Encouraged by the acceptability of more popular styles of composition, willing but inexperienced composers are turning their hand to the production of 'home-grown' music. Many a parish is proud to have a setting of the Eucharist by its own organist. Some writing is of undoubtedly high quality and may well find a place in the permanent repertoire of a wider public. However, many pieces are unworthy and ungrammatical, and are likely to join the dusty piles of discarded music in vestry cupboards, produced in great quantities in the nineteenth century because of the relative ease of finding publishers. The photocopier has made reliance on a publisher less necessary than it was, but the future of the material coming from parish musicians will nevertheless be determined by the passage of time and the growing musical literacy of the public. There are undoubtedly 'amateur' composers with real potential, and the availability of teachers with experience could do much to encourage and help them.

PUBLICATION

473.   Publishing has been revolutionised by new technology. The photocopier, for example, not only reduces pressure and demand upon publishing houses, but also allows newly-composed music to be tried out in manuscript before seeking the permanency which publishing provides. Improvements can be made in the light of performance and composers may discard or destroy compositions which are found wanting. Those who do this follow a precedent set by all great composers.

474.   Resort to the photocopier is often determined by economic factors. These also dictate the systematic deletion from publishers' catalogues of slow-selling items. However, major publishers will usually supply photocopies of items which are out of print. Some publishing houses are also beginning to recognise the need for cheap, expendable publications.

475.   Today there are far fewer music publishers than previously in Britain. Their catalogues contain fewer items, but the range of publications is wider than at the turn of the century. Rather than imitate the blanket policy operated by other publishing houses, a few publishers cater for more specialised needs, such as Taizé chants or responsorial psalmody. The Royal School of Church Music concentrates to a great extent on essentially simple music for small choirs with restricted resources.

Hymns and Songs

476.   The provision of hymns and worship songs today makes the most work and revenue for publishers. The production of hymn books, supplements and small collections is so prolific that it is almost impossible to keep abreast of all that is in circulation, whether in traditional or in more popular vein. In recent years this 'hymn explosion' has been detonated more by new words than by new music. In good, relevant poetry, writers such as Timothy Dudley-Smith, Fred Kaan, Fred Pratt Green and Brian Wren have filled the gaps left by more established hymnals. The valuable musical contribution of Betty Pulkingham, Graham Kendrick and others in this field should not be overlooked.

477.   During the past twenty years, many hymns and songs have had their first circulation in large annual gatherings for events like Spring

Harvest. Pieces which have proved to be of enduring worth have passed from special conference song books into collections with a wider circulation.

478.   Given the variety of published material, both 'good' and 'bad', a church musician may find it difficult to choose music which is appropriate for a particular choir and congregation and which possesses style, invention and staying power. Out of necessity, publishers have an eye to their profits and neither a work's inclusion in a catalogue or collection, nor instant popularity, guarantees its suitability.

COPYRIGHT

479.   The purpose of the provisions relating to copyright is to ensure that both composer and publisher receive the reward which is due to them for their work. Put another way, 'The protection given by the law of copyright is against copying, the basis of the protection being that one man must not be permitted to appropriate the result of another's labour' (LB [Plastics] v. Swish). It is only at the end of the term of copyright that what has been protected passes into the public domain. At this point, it is not necessary to seek permission for the reproduction, performance or recording of pieces. In the case of choral works both words and music must be out of copyright.

480.   Copyright in a work lasts for fifty years from the end of the calendar year in which its author or composer dies. Typographical copyright continues until the end of the calendar year twenty-five years after the date of the first publication of a particular edition. Reprints of that edition do not extend this period. In sound recordings copyright exists until fifty years from the end of the calendar year in which the recording was made.

Printed Works

481.   It is an infringement of copyright to reproduce a work by photocopying it, other than for the purposes of research and private study. Whilst the Copyright, Designs and Patents Act 1988 contains many fair-dealing provisions, no exceptions are made for copying music for use in church services. The production of multiple copies of the same material, such as parts for a church choir, is specifically banned by the Act. However, permission may be given by the publisher for the reproduction of part of a work or the whole of one

from a collected edition, such as an anthology of carols. A fee may be demanded.

482.   The Music Publishers' Association has produced a Code of Fair Practice which offers helpful advice as to when church musicians may be permitted to copy without application to the publisher. For example, a single page may be reproduced where there is a difficult page turn for an organist. The whole movement of a work may not.

483.   If a work is out of print, reference needs to be made to the publisher. If it is not possible to supply the work, its reproduction may be allowed on payment of a fee, in order that the composer should receive the appropriate royalty. If permission for copying is refused by the publisher, it may be that the work has been withdrawn at the request of its composer. Whatever the reason for a refusal, the church musician has to abide by the publisher's decision.

484.   Publishers are often willing to grant permission for the reproduction of music upon written application, or even by a telephone call, supported by a subsequent letter. Time can be saved by using a standard letter of application. Church Music Copyright Ltd. (formerly the Christian Music Association) sponsors a licence to allow the reproduction of the words, but not the music, of worship songs published by its members. This covers a wide range of worship songs, but only a small amount of hymnody.

485.   Attempts to establish a comprehensive scheme to include more hymns and to cover all publishers have so far been unsuccessful. The Pratt Green Trust seeks to represent the interests of the churches in this area, but needs wider support from the Church if it is to make much progress. In the meantime, the Trust has compiled a directory, to be published in 1992, containing information about the copyright of texts included in some two hundred collections of hymns and songs. The Trust also operates an information service in reply to written enquiries about copyright.

Performance and Recording

486.   In return for the licensing of a venue for public performance of copyright works, the Performing Right Society is entitled to charge a fee. This is in order that copyright holders may receive proper benefit from the performance of their material. Divine service is legally a public performance, and the singing and playing of music in church

constitute a 'qualifying performance'. They therefore come under the protection of the Copyright, Designs and Patents Act. However, the Performing Right Society waives its right to a fee for 'performances' during services in churches or other places of worship. Permission for the use of copyright musical works in worship is not therefore required. This provision does not extend to concerts or other non-liturgical performances in a church building.

487.   If part or the whole of a service, for example a marriage, is to be recorded in sound or video, care needs to be taken not to infringe a performer's rights. This may happen where someone makes a recording for anything other than private and domestic use without consent. But in addition to gaining the permission of the participants where necessary, the person responsible for making the recording must also obtain the licence of the copyright holder or the appropriate body. In this case, it would be the Mechanical Copyright Protection Society. It is in the interest of church musicians to ensure that the necessary licence is obtained, or their playing or singing of copyright music in such circumstances could constitute an infringement of copyright through being an unauthorised 'performance'.

488.   To a small parish church with few resources, the laws of copyright may seem somewhat overbearing. It is important, however, that the interests of those copyright owners whose publications are sold be protected, and that the composers to whom the Church owes so much can be remunerated. Without them, and without record companies and publishers to disseminate their work, Britain's rich heritage of church music would be considerably diminished.

INSURANCE

489.   Proper stewardship of resources demands that churches and their contents be insured against damage. Most churches have policies issued by the Ecclesiastical Insurance Group (EIG) which normally cover buildings, contents, liabilities, money and personal accident. Advice is available without cost from regional surveyors of the EIG, and a useful guide has been published (*It Won't Happen To Us*, CIO, now Church House Publishing, 1981). Church musicians are well advised to ensure that church policies, whether with EIG or another company, are adequate to cover both their own needs and the instruments and equipment which they use.

Instruments

490.   Organs are usually insured for their full replacement value against the risks of fire and special perils. There is often a 'first loss amount' of up to £10,000 to cover accidental damage and theft. Portable instruments are generally insured automatically as part of the contents of a building. It may be prudent to have them specified, particularly with regard to theft and accidental damage, and certainly if they are to be covered for use in other places.

491.   Insurance companies understandably expect proper precautions to be taken for the security and safe storage of musical instruments. An organ, for example, should be locked and the power turned off when not in use. It is important that only competent and recognised organ builders or their staff undertake tuning and other work on the instrument, and no unauthorised person should be given access to it. Few insurers place any restrictions on young people using an organ. Reasonable competence is expected of players of any age. It is for the organist, or some other responsible person, to exercise control over the use of the organ by other people, and to specify any conditions attached.

Personnel

492.   Parochial clergy are normally covered comprehensively against personal accidents, but other church employees are usually covered only whilst actually working for the Church. In the case of voluntary workers, such as choristers and members of music groups, insurance against personal accident is provided whilst they are on duty on church premises. It is possible for a standard church insurance policy to be extended to cover them and their equipment for other locations and for travel. In certain circumstances, and especially where foreign travel is entailed, it is sensible to obtain separate travel insurance for church personnel. Provision should be made for medical treatment to be included in the cover. Day and residential courses attended by choirs are usually insured by the RSCM or other organisations responsible for organising them.

CONCLUSION

493.   The cost of a policy premium is a small price to pay for peace of mind. Although there is a temptation to save scarce money by cutting down on insurance, the Church's human and material resources are too important to be exposed to needless risk or loss. Equally, money has to

be found not only for the payment of church musicians, but also for the composers and publishers upon whom church musicians depend. Such expenditure is a necessary investment, but it is one which yields high dividends. Unlike many other organisations, the Church usually gets much more than it pays for, thanks to the generosity of those who provide for its music.

PART 5

INTO THE FUTURE
Reflections and Comments by the Commission

21

Music in the Church's Worship and Mission

494.   The preceding chapters of this Report suggest that the outlook for music in the Church of England is an uncertain and, in many ways, disturbing one. Although there is much that is positive and encouraging, a sad picture emerges of a dwindling supply of musicians, a reduced use of other than congregational music, a considerable lowering of standards, and a lack of both resources and expectations. The overall impression gained by the Commission is that the Church in general either takes for granted the contribution of music to its worship, or places little value upon it.

495.   The Commission does not seek to deny the validity and value of services without music, such as those held early in the morning or on a weekday. But these should occur as a result of tradition or of conscious choice rather than of necessity. Music has always had a vital role in Christian worship, and the main services on a Sunday naturally and necessarily include it. If they do not, they risk being seriously deficient, with congregations deprived of an important element in their worship.

Music as Revelation and Communication

496.   Music's place in our services may be seen as a gift of God which he uses to reveal something of himself to us. It can communicate with unsurpassed effect the majesty of the Almighty, the gentleness of his love or the challenge of his righteousness. This power to 'speak' to the worshipper at a deep level is sufficient to justify its use alongside the reading of Scripture and the preaching of the Word of God.

497.   An equally important reason for God's giving music to us is that it forms part of our response to him. In the praise, penitence and prayer we address to God, music underlines and complements our speech. It enables us to express what we feel but cannot fully articulate in words alone.

498. One of the most powerful, though imprecise, ways in which music communicates is by its setting and sustaining a mood. With or without words, it has the ability to create an atmosphere, to evoke memories, and to enable worshippers to receive from God and to respond to him.

499. The Commission affirms, therefore, that music in worship is not an extravagance but a necessity if people are to receive the special blessings which God gives through it, and if they are to offer to him their best and their most. Where they are denied this opportunity, their worship is likely to be uninspired and lacking in energy. Consequently, the life and vigour of the Church in that place will be attenuated and its efforts in mission enfeebled. The Commission believes that effective mission depends upon inspired worship, and that inspired worship usually demands the contribution of good music.

500. But services often become sheer routine, with the result that not much effort is put into preparation, either by congregations or by their leaders. Members of the congregation need the foundation of a solid personal spirituality of which public worship is but an ingredient. Clergy and musicians need to use their imagination as well as their professional skills. Each service should be approached as a fresh encounter, with the eager expectation of glimpsing the glory of God. For this, the preparation of prayer is essential.

Worship and Mission

501. The Commission believes that the life and witness of the Church depend first and last upon the quality and vitality of its worship, and is convinced of its importance for the future. A recognition of this truth doubtless underlies much of the attention given in recent years to matters liturgical. However, consideration of music's place in worship has often been left until other decisions have been made. Church buildings have been re-ordered, dress and ritual have been simplified, leadership in worship has been widely shared, liturgies have been restructured and texts have been rewritten. In all these, especially in the production of new words, reform has often taken place without a recognition of the implications for music in worship. Nor has the potential and positive contribution of musicians been widely acknowledged in the process of reform.

502. The Church should now recognise the priority which needs to be given to music if the impoverishment of services is not going to

continue. The Commission states this emphatically not only because the offering of music should be itself an act of worship, but because there are other important benefits arising from its use which have particular relevance today.

Unity and Ecumenism

503. It has already been argued in this Report that music is not appropriately used in worship primarily in order to instil or increase fellowship. Nevertheless, this is one of its important functions. Fellowship is not to be confined to congregations, but is essential within and between denominations, and in a time of growing ecumenical cooperation we rejoice that churches are beginning to share their liturgical and musical riches with each other. Local Ecumenical Projects (LEPs) naturally produce their own kind of mix, but in the looser association of different churches and denominations there is the continuing need to share, as well as to preserve, our treasures.

504. There has always been a sharing of hymnody across the denominations, and anthems and songs are increasingly being regarded as part of our common musical currency. Whilst the Church of England has become less rigid in its liturgy, some Free Churches have come to recognise the value of formal worship patterns. In parts of the Roman Catholic Church there is a wide-ranging exploration of new forms of worship and liturgical expression. In all this, music has a significant role to play in enabling and fostering closer relationships between the denominations.

Church and Society

505. Music may also provide a common bond and language between the Church and the wider world. As this Report has noted, people of other faiths or of no faith, as well as Christians, are used by God to mediate his gift of music, and those who are not believers are as capable as those who are of responding to the power of religious music. In continuing to provide good and appropriate music in different styles the Church has something important to offer to the world, and as part of its mission it has the responsibility to do so.

506. This responsibility is fulfilled not only in the context of services but also in the use of church buildings for musical events. Local schools, for example, might be involved in more than an annual carol service. The building itself and its atmosphere as a place of worship can

speak powerfully to those who do not normally use it, and brings them into contact with the church community.

507.   The Church's music can also be taken into the street and market-place, as the Salvation Army has been doing successfully for years. Sensitive planning and careful organisation are required, but marches and processions, perhaps with dance and drama, can contribute to a powerful musical witness to the faith of the Church.

Evangelism

508.   Music can also be used as an effective aid to evangelism. Again, this should not be the prime reason for having it in our services. However, the Commission believes strongly that music has a significant contribution to make to the Decade of Evangelism. Where it is good, it has a great ability to draw people into church. Even if some of them come for what others hold to be a wrong reason, they should not be discouraged or their motives despised. The Commission affirms the value of music for attracting potential believers to acts of worship and to the Church's fellowship. Music itself possesses the power (under God) to convert. Conversely, music that is ill-chosen or ill-performed can actually be a hindrance to commitment, as can a service or preaching which is poor. Together with holiness in the individual and various forms of testimony to Christ, the Church's worship can be powerfully effective in evangelism. The Commission therefore reiterates the absolute priority which needs to be given by the Church to its worship, and to the place of music within it.

Public Relations and the Media

509.   Good opportunities for the dissemination of the Church's worship are afforded by the electronic media, both in the conversational setting of the radio and through the more proclamatory medium of television. The transmission of religious services, in addition to being a blessing to those who cannot go to church and a substitute for those who choose not to, offers considerable potential for evangelism through worship. Usually a broadcast is an 'eavesdropping' on a normal service by the listener or viewer. For the congregation, musicians and clergy involved, it provides an incentive to their best efforts which may not be so marked at other times. Only the highest standards in church broadcasts are acceptable, and they require much careful planning and rehearsal. What we are prepared to do when thousands of people are watching or listening we ought to strive to do for God week by week.

510.   In addition to broadcasts of services there may be other musical events in which to involve the local or regional media. Full advantage should be taken of the interest and availability of the press, as well as of radio and television. Whether for special occasions, concerts or visits by distinguished people, there may be the chance for the Church's music to reach and influence a wider public. When it comes to advertising, more use could be made of diocesan newspapers in addition to parish magazines and the local press.

Pleasure and Creativity

511.   Any consideration of music's place in the life of the Church must not ignore the fact that for most people music is a source of pleasure. Very few are so unmusical as to have no music at all within them, and all of us are surrounded by it for much of the time. Since it is one of the most natural of all pleasures, the Church should not be afraid to provide opportunities for enjoyment of it in worship. We should be doing all that we can to promote the revival of singing, and we should encourage rather than stifle the musical creativity of those who write and perform. Since God is the source of our ability to make and enjoy music, we risk ingratitude if we spurn so rich a blessing.

Healing or Harmful?

512.   Music has the power to help and to heal. The Commission has noted its use by therapists and believes that this is an area which should be explored further by the Church. It is obviously relevant to those engaged in pastoral care and counselling, and music could be a valuable resource in the Church's ministry of healing. But it's power also of concern to those who are responsible for the planning and leading of worship. They need to be aware of the effect which music has upon people, for good and for ill.

513.   The hurtful effects of a piece of music do not necessarily stem from anything intrinsically harmful within itself, or even from its being used for manipulation. They can be produced as a result of the mood of the performer, or the manner of performance, or of the mood or personality of the listener. As has been mentioned in this Report, recent research on the relationship of psychology and spirituality has shown how different personality types have different needs and preferences. This is another area largely unexplored by the Church, and the Commission believes that more work needs to be done here, for the implication of the research completed so far is that the average

parish congregation demands a variety of musical styles if the needs of all its members are to be met.

514. We can no longer assume that the only proper music in church is that which is commonly called 'traditional'. Nor is it appropriate to exclude all that is so described. Even if it is almost impossible in worship to accept that which we dislike, we should not be dismissive of those who do not share our preferences. Most of our congregations contain a multiplicity of people who react differently to different kinds of musical expression. This demands a rich diversity of repertoire and great versatility on the part of our musicians. It also demands the Christian virtue of tolerance.

Differing Styles

515. Different doctrinal and liturgical emphases have their influence upon the kind of music used in churches of different traditions. There are also occasions when it is fitting for everything in a service to be either purist and 'traditional' or 'modern'. But the Commission believes that in the average parish church on an average Sunday, especially where no other is within easy reach of parishioners, a blend of different styles of worship and music is desirable. For the Church of England is essentially a national church. It has the responsibility of offering regular worship which is accessible to everyone in the land, in addition to providing for great local and national occasions, which it generally does well.

516. For this reason the Eucharist and Morning Prayer are being complemented, or replaced in some places, by the family service. This is growing in popularity and provides an opportunity for sensitive and careful experimentation in order to embrace a wide range of local people, of all ages and with different musical preferences. However, it requires some skill to devise a service which is relevant to a varied congregation and yet remains first and foremost an act of worship. Those who seek to do so need to be guided by sound liturgical principles, such as those found in the Liturgical Commission's *Patterns for Worship* (Church House Publishing, 1989).

Non-Vocal Participation

517. 'Relevant worship' does not necessarily require all present to participate vocally all the time. The popular misconception which holds that unless one is able to sing one is not able to take part in a

musical item needs to be dispelled once and for all. The Commission strongly affirms the value of silent as well as vocal participation, and it believes that worshippers need to be taught how to listen to music no less attentively than they do to the reading of Scripture, or to preaching, or to the recitation of prayers. The acceptance of this principle would do much to dispel the 'us' and 'them' attitude sometimes found where there are choirs, and it would counter the idea that an offering by skilled singers and players is merely a performance and an exercise in self-advertisement, unless by their attitude musicians invite such criticism.

518.   Listening to others in worship should not be seen as passive. Indeed, it requires some effort to keep the attention focused on the music and its words and on God. Most of us find it easier to use our mouths without our minds, than our minds without our mouths. There is no guarantee that by singing the words of a hymn we have participated any more fully than by giving silent attention to someone else doing so.

Silence

519.   The use of silence by the whole body of worshippers during a service does not imply that they are not participating. The value of corporate silence is considerable, both for its own sake and as a foil to the busyness which marks most of our worship. Some parts of the Church are coming to recognise this. But the Commission would nevertheless urge that greater place be given to silence in our services, so that all present can be still before God in silent reflection and prayer. Our silence offers God an opportunity to speak to the soul and it can provide blessed relief from over-activity and the torrent of speech and song with which we assail both his ears and our own.

Said and Sung

520.   Words are generally as much over-used within worship as they are outside it. Because they are a more common form of communication than music, they usually play the major part in our services, with music in a supporting role. This Report has argued that music can have a life of its own and an ability to communicate without the support of words. However, it is the combination of words and music which constitutes what most people understand as church music. This is particularly true of hymnody where words and music should be related

177

and where the text is enriched by song. Nevertheless, the words of a hymn are generally the determining factor for its inclusion in a service.

521.   There is also a need to recognise the importance of the spoken word and its relationship to the musical parts of the service. The ideal is a combination of the said and the sung. The one sets off and contrasts with the other, and a choir should give a lead as much to the spoken as to the sung parts.

522.   At all times the language of worship needs to be clear, but not banal. It should speak to the condition of the worshipper. The reading of Scripture, preaching and prayers can take place in a variety of idioms, depending upon the circumstances. For some congregations and occasions an informal, relaxed language is appropriate, whilst others will require one which has more formality and dignity. What is true of speech is true also of music.

523.   In seeking to make the Church's worship widely accessible, however, people's capacity should not be underrated. Most will respond to good language or to good music of whatever style. A congregation must not be baffled by obscurity, but it must not be patronised by too much informality either. It takes both sensitivity and experience to strike the right balance, especially for special occasions when the right language and music for a particular situation or mood are crucial.

Conclusion

524.   The musical needs of parishes and congregations differ from place to place, and the way in which they are met is determined largely by the resources available. What is possible for a large suburban congregation is out of the question for a tiny congregation in a rural situation. Where there is a skilled director with commitment and an attractive personality in an inner-city parish, it may be possible to produce excellent musical results. The village church without either organist or choir may limp along with three half-hearted hymns and two fingers on a harmonium. In a situation such as this much of what this Report contains may seem to be irrelevant.

525.   However, the Commission hopes that at least some of its reflections and recommendations may bring hope, encouragement and new ideas to those who are struggling. Whilst recognising that the worship of a small, dispirited congregation is of importance to God, it

does not believe that we can acquiesce in despair or even discouragement. Above all the Commission hopes that the Church of England as a whole will take a fresh look at, and a renewed interest in, the music of worship which is an essential part of its rich inheritance. A greater commitment to this music will ensure its continuing to enrich the worship of the people of God.

RECOMMENDATIONS

That clergy, musicians and congregations alike give fresh consideration to the place and value of music in the services of the Church (494–499, 501–502, 511).

That those responsible for planning and leading worship make as thorough a preparation for each service as is possible, including the preparation of prayer (500).

That the potential of music for fostering ecumenical relationships be utilised to the full by the Church at all levels (503–504).

That clergy and musicians recognise the value of music as an ingredient in evangelism, both in worship and outside it, and take opportunities afforded by the media (505–510).

That the therapeutic use of music in the Church's ministry of healing be further investigated, perhaps under the auspices of the Churches' Council for Health and Healing (512–513).

That clergy and musicians be prepared to plan and lead worship imaginatively, to blend different styles, and to allow themselves to be guided both by the needs of the congregation and by sound liturgical principles in devising church services (514–516, 522–523).

That congregations be taught to use opportunities of silence and the value of listening, and that those responsible for planning services ensure a proper balance between the spoken and the sung (517–521).

22

The Repertoire

526.   Where there is musical apathy, quality of performance suffers, and the range of music used can become limited. Without stimulation and vision, church musicians, clergy and congregations easily settle into the rut of the familiar. Hymn lists differ little from year to year and music programmes remain unadventurous. If the previous chapter of this Report is taken seriously, however, there is a challenge which faces us all. The Commission does not advocate change for its own sake. But it does urge all who are responsible for ordering the worship of parish churches to be sensitive to the variety of people who constitute our congregations.

527.   Responsibility for the musical repertoire is shared between the musicians and the clergy, together with the worship group if there is one. All who have that responsibility need to be aware of their own musical and liturgical preferences. Within a congregation there will be different preferences, based upon age and temperament, and upon the varying stages reached by individuals in their spiritual pilgrimage. It is usually impossible to meet the needs of every person at every service, but some congregational input into the choice of music is nevertheless valuable, for the people provide the best indication of what is appropriate and they have an important part in creating and maintaining the tradition of their church.

The Familiar and the New

528.   Much of the tradition of Anglican church music has been built up in cathedrals and in the cathedral-style worship of some parish churches. But the Commission considers that the role played by music in the worship of parish and cathedral ought not to be confused. It affirms strongly its belief in the importance of congregational music in the average parish. It also believes that the repertoire of music should be a varied one, but with a familiar core of material in order to provide stability for the worshippers. From a secure base parish musicians can

be adventurous in exploring new music and in experimenting with differing styles. This initiative is perhaps most needed in those very small congregations where there are few musical resources, and where the inability to maintain the 'traditional' style of music has led to near-despair.

529.   Unaccompanied congregational singing can be beautiful and satisfying. It requires only a little training and someone to lead it. It should also find a place in the repertoire of those churches with good musical resources. There is a simplicity in plainsong or Taizé chants, for example, which is well suited to certain seasons of the year and to some parts of a service. It provides a good contrast to more elaborate music. Equally, strong unison singing to an accompaniment is always effective and is to be encouraged.

Hymnody

530.   The selection of hymns is the most important choice that has to be made by those responsible for worship. This is not only because there is such a wide range from which to choose, but also because worshippers have strong views and deep feelings. These relate perhaps as much to the tunes as they do to the text. Because those planning a service probably give greater weight to the words than to the music, the Commission believes that those texts which promote ancient truths in a readily-understood manner and in good, or at least passable, poetry are the ones which ought to be used. Some of the modern hymns have a very shallow doctrinal content and may need to be rejected for that reason, whatever their other virtues.

531.   There is still an important place for traditional hymns, many of which have a timeless quality about them, even if some of their language raises problems. It is usually desirable to leave old words as they are, since hymnody is governed by the number of syllables in the line as well as by rhyming verse. In the case of the exclusive language of traditional hymns, it is better that congregations be helped to respect and accept such hymns as coming from a former age than that they be either inappropriately altered or abandoned altogether.

532.   Sometimes a small sensitive alteration can save a hymn from going out of use. But there is no excuse for modern hymns to contain gender-based or sexist language. They will be rightly rejected by most congregations. Happily, there are many fine new hymns and hymn books now available, including those compiled by the Jubilate Group.

In addition to a wide choice of contemporary writing, both literary and musical, these offer a good number of traditional hymns from which unnecessary archaisms have been removed. In this way they ensure the perpetuation of one of the great traditions of the Christian Church.

533.   Hymns are the most accessible of all music for a congregation and they are the main musical ingredient in the worship of most churches. They are also of ecumenical significance, being common to almost all denominations. Hymns offer varieties of mood, style, origin, length, metre and key. In a service there should be a mix of these and not a concentration on one metre or one key, for example.

534.   It is helpful to worshippers if they have editions with at least the melody line printed with the words. We are a more musically literate nation than formerly and if some members of the congregation can read music, their lead will be important in the singing of an unfamiliar tune.

Psalmody and Songs

535.   The Psalms offer a rich mixture of spiritual, literary and musical expression and they have been at the heart of the Church's daily worship since biblical times. The Commission believes that this is a tradition which must be maintained. In addition to other considerations, there is again an ecumenical one, for psalmody is common to all the churches and is acceptable in those few churches where hymns are not.

536.   According to the Parish Survey some 74% of parishes use Anglican chant at least occasionally. It is to be hoped that their congregations have copies of psalms and canticles which are pointed for singing. The Methodist *Hymns and Psalms* (Methodist Publishing House, 1983) and the United Reformed Church *Rejoice and Sing* (Oxford University Press, 1991) include a number of psalms in their pages. Anglican chant is a distinctive way of singing the Psalms and it would be a pity if it were lost altogether in the parishes. It does nevertheless require some expertise and the melody line is often set too high for congregations. The Commission recommends that parishes explore alternative ways of singing the Psalms. These include plainsong and the responsorial or antiphonal methods of Gelineau, Taizé and Dom Gregory Murray. *Psalms for Today* and *Songs from the Psalms* (Hodder and Stoughton, 1990) offer a useful collection of psalmody.

537.   Where a musical setting is not feasible, the rhythmic and dignified speaking of psalms and canticles is an acceptable and traditional substitute. In the Commission's view, this is best done either antiphonally, between two sides of a congregation, or responsorially between the leader and the people. The widespread practice of saying a whole psalm or canticle together (unless it is a short one) is tedious, inartistic and spiritually unhelpful.

538.   Another form in which psalms may be sung is when they provide the basis of the words of worship songs, frequently but inaccurately called choruses. Most of these are paraphrases of biblical texts, and like hymns they vary in theological emphasis and musical appropriateness. In some respects today's songs have something of the character of the Psalms, in their expression from the heart without the cerebral and linguistic demands of hymnody. As yet there is usually a reluctance to follow the Psalmist in including the negative aspects of human emotion, but songs have considerable potential for the expression of anger and sadness. Many of the new hymn books include worship songs and they find widespread acceptance.

539.   The contemporary style of worship songs generally makes them easily sung by a congregation and they lend themselves to a variety of arrangements for voices and instruments. Accompaniments are often provided by instruments other than, or in addition to, the organ. They should be used together with hymns, rather than as replacements for them. Chosen with discrimination, they make a welcome addition to parish church music.

Settings of Liturgical Texts

540.   The Commission encourages the continuing use of musical settings of liturgical texts, both in the Eucharist and in the Offices. It may be appropriate on occasions, or in certain traditions, for these to be sung by the choir alone. But in most places, and particularly in the parish Eucharist, the congregation ought to be enabled to sing more than hymns. The Commission therefore welcomes the availability of some of the new settings which provide parts for congregation as well as choir.

541.   The revision of liturgical texts over the last thirty years has brought both problems and opportunities. Problems have arisen because of the belief that none of the well-known and loved musical settings could be used in the new rites. But these rites have also

brought opportunities for composers to provide new settings. This Report has already mentioned both the composers who have taken these opportunities with happy results for the Church, and the production of much locally written music. Jesus likens those who have been instructed about the Kingdom of Heaven to householders who bring out of their treasures things both new and old (Matthew 13:52). It is now being recognised that it can be appropriate to use musical settings of the 'traditional' words in the 'new' services. The rubrics of The Alternative Service Book allow this, and a mixture of styles of language and music in worship is perfectly proper.

Anthems and Solos

542.   The principle of including words of a former age in a modern rite is well established through the use of anthems. Well-chosen and properly performed, these neither interrupt the flow nor intrude into the service and can be a powerful means of proclaiming the Faith. Much has already been said here about the activity of listening by the congregation. The singing of an anthem provides, above all, the opportunity for this. So too does the use of solos or worship songs and instrumental pieces.

Organ and other Instrumental Music

543.   The most common form of instrumental performance is the organ voluntary. However, its use before a service needs to be reviewed in many of our churches. It often has to compete against church bells or, increasingly, the chatter of the congregation. The Commission does not wish to discourage the friendly greeting before the service, or the fellowship after it. But it does not believe that music should be used to cover up, or encourage, worshippers to talk. They will do so ever more loudly as the organ attempts to drown their noise. In some traditions worship songs are used for some five or ten minutes before a service to prepare people for worship, often followed by silence. Alternatively, there is the example of some churches overseas, where an instrumental prelude sets the mood and is the beginning of the service. This takes the form of organ or instrumental music, or of a recording. People listen quietly, and it is often balanced by a concluding piece at the end of the service during which the congregation remains quietly seated.

544.   This presupposes that pieces are not too long and that they are properly rehearsed set-pieces rather than the meaningless meander-

ings which too often pass for improvisation. Silence is generally better than this, as it may be during a service. It is not always necessary to plug a gap or fill every pause with music and there are points at which silence has significance. These might include the preparation of the bread and wine for Communion or the time of Communion itself. Nevertheless, extemporisation by a competent player at the end of a hymn can be thrilling, as it can during a procession before or during the service.

545.   The Commission would like to suggest the revival of the custom in some churches of an occasional short voluntary during the service. This can set a mood or enhance a period of reflection. A central voluntary is used in some of the Free Churches for the taking of the collection and a hymn may not always be appropriate for this, if people are to think of what they are singing. Indeed, it is a mistake to use hymns simply to fill spaces or to cover movements of ministers and musicians, except in the case of a liturgical procession. A hymn should be an act of worship in its own right and not something to dispel a silence.

Composers and Commissions

546.   The amount of new music being published might suggest that commissioning people to write music for worship is unnecessary, particularly given the expense which may be involved. However, the Commission believes that the Church ought to invite composers to write pieces, particularly for special occasions. This is in line with a long tradition and there may be more established composers willing to accept such commissions than is realised. An up-and-coming composer would probably welcome the opportunity to write music in a religious idiom. The gifted local amateur occasionally writes a piece of enduring worth, and not all commissions involve an expensive financial transaction. For example, something may be written for the wedding of a friend, or for the local organist to play.

547.   A good way of encouraging composers is by means of a competition. The BBC's 'Songs of Praise' runs a hymn- and song-writing competition and some cathedral festivals, such as that at Norwich, invite the submission of choral pieces. Composers of new hymn tunes should be discouraged from writing for a traditional text which is either wedded to a well-loved tune or has more than one good tune to which it may be sung. On the whole, the Commission urges that new hymn tunes should be composed for new words, and vice versa. There is

185

already an over-exposure of well-known tunes upon which some new texts have come to rely.

548.   The suggestion of commissioning composers probably applies more to cathedrals and large parish churches with a strong musical tradition, than to the average local church. Nevertheless, distinguished musicians might be pleased to tackle the challenge of simplicity required by a church with few musical resources, and congregations are not often taken into account in commissioned music. It is important that those who commission a work give the composer a brief of what is required and information about the resources available. Otherwise there is a greater risk of the result being unacceptable and unrealistic. In commissioning music the Church has an opportunity of affirming the importance for society of musical creativity.

Conclusion

549.   In seeking to be innovative and adventurous, church musicians will need to be careful not to abandon the traditional repertoire or to relegate it to second place. Stewardship of our resources, as well as respect for the preferences of many of our people, demands that it be maintained at a high level. Nevertheless, a fresh outlook and the readiness to explore and experiment will do much to put new life into the Church's music.

RECOMMENDATIONS

That those responsible for the choice of music in our churches take account of the varying tastes and preferences of their congregations and set up a system for congregational feedback (526–527).

That congregations be given ample opportunity to sing in services, even where they have to be unaccompanied (528–529, 540).

That those responsible for the choice of hymns and worship songs be guided by the quality of their doctrinal content, language and musical idiom, and that both the new and the old be included in the repertoire (530–533, 538–539, 541).

That parishes provide melody line editions of hymn and song books for their congregation (534).

The Repertoire

That clergy and musicians ensure the continuing place of psalmody in Anglican worship, whether it be sung or said (535–537).

That congregations be taught to regard solo anthems, songs, and organ and other instrumental pieces, as integral parts of a service (542–545).

That parishes find ways of encouraging composers to write music for their particular needs and resources (546–548).

23

The Congregation and the
Leaders of Worship

550.   Any attempt to revitalise the music of the Church of England
must also involve its people. Given that the most important and readily
available musical instrument is the human voice, even the smallest
congregation has the ability to make music in its worship. Most of those
who come to church expect and want to be able to sing, and the
Commission believes that the music in parish churches ought to be
substantially congregational. Both the choir (if there is one) and the
organist form part of the congregation, as do the clergy and other
ministers. With or without musical gifts or ministerial skills, all are
called to serve each other, as belonging equally to the gathered people
of God.

Holding on to the Familiar

551.   People in church do not usually sing when they either dislike or
do not know a piece. But what is familiar is generally popular, and most
people look to music to provide an enjoyable way of expressing their
faith and aspirations. They expect to feel comfortable, secure and
unselfconscious as they do so. This is one of the reasons for the choice of
hymns and other music being so often limited to a few old war-horses.
But opportunities for both religious and musical development are lost
where the repertoire remains narrow and static.

552.   People reluctant to learn new music tend to take a similar
attitude to new forms of service or variations within it. However, it is
not commonly recognised that the Anglican liturgy has been evolving
continuously since the sixteenth century. Staying with the familiar may
well result in spiritual stagnation, particularly if this is because some
people have become inflexible. There has to be, by congregations,
clergy, and musicians alike, the recognition of other people's needs
and preferences. None of us must expect to have what we like all the
time, whether musically or in any other way, and personal sacrifice is
part of the Christian way.

553.   A reluctance to change may present an especial difficulty in respect of the younger members of society, so few of whom belong to our congregations. For those of them who do come to church, particular sensitivity and encouragement are needed and they should never be patronised. Like others, young people respond to high standards, whatever the style of worship or music. Often their involvement is gained through membership of a choir or music group.

Introducing Change

554.   It is by no means impossible to introduce people to music that is unfamiliar. Congregational practices are not generally liked. But much can be done to teach new music by one person using voice and gesture alone. A 'ginger group' within a congregation, specially formed for the learning of new material, can be a useful way to introduce and give a lead in singing it. There is also value in having it sung or played in advance, perhaps on several occasions, by the choir, music group or organist.

Responsibility Shared with a Worship Committee

555.   Because changes in church services arouse strong emotions and can lead to serious divisions, the Commission believes that it is sensible for a parish to have a worship committee or group. In Canon law the decision as to which services are to be used rests jointly with the incumbent and the Parochial Church Council (Canon B.3). The ultimate responsibility for the ordering of music in worship rests with the incumbent (see Appendix 3.1). It is difficult, and possibly unwise, for one person to attempt omnicompetence in an area of the Church's life in which there have been so many recent changes in rapid succession. Responsibility could be shared with a body made up of certain ex officio members (the clergy, the director of music, others with particular responsibilities in worship), and representatives of the PCC, the congregation and particular constituencies such as the youth group. Its task would be to advise on the devising or altering of services and their planning and execution, and it would undertake a regular review of the parish's worship.

556.   Committees can become as tyrannical and authoritarian as individuals, and therefore the members of a worship committee need to take particular care to listen to comments or complaints from the congregation, and to take note of the varying temperaments and requirements of worshippers. The committee should be ready to

attend lectures, courses and events devoted to the principles of worship, and to visit other churches in order to exchange ideas. It would also be in touch with any diocesan or other body or person responsible for giving advice on music and the liturgy. Such a committee might also help to satisfy those who are given to complaining about the choice of hymns. It would need to delegate attention to this task to one or more of its members and to support them in it.

CLERGY AND MUSICIANS

557.   With or without such a committee, both clergy and church musicians need to be valued and respected for their skills and responsibilities, as well as for themselves. Only 3% of the incumbents completing the Parish Survey questionnaire indicated an unsatisfactory relationship with their director of music. But there is a widespread impression that breakdowns in the relationship between clergy and musicians are common. Not only are these harmful to the people directly involved and to their congregation, but they often receive publicity and may also bring the Church into disrepute.

The Resolution of Conflict

558.   It is rare for the responsibility for causing conflict to rest solely on one side, and this may involve more than the organist and the minister. However, as leaders of the Christian community the clergy should be the first to foster good relationships through effective communication. Where these break down, clergy should take the initiative for their restoration and the resolution of conflict. The observance of procedures agreed with the PCC in the appointment of a musical director and the provision of a proper Job Specification and Agreement (see Appendices 3.1–3.3) should help to prevent trouble. But even with formalities, the day to day working relationship between two people depends upon goodwill, sensitivity, tact, humility and a whole range of virtues on both sides.

559.   Where a conflict cannot be resolved, it may be necessary to call in an arbitrator from beyond the parish. This might be the Rural Dean, or Lay Chairman of Deanery Synod, or the Archdeacon. It would be sensible for dioceses to establish procedures for arbitration in case these are needed to settle disputes. It might also be desirable to use the services of a consultant, either from the Church or from a secular agency, in order to help parish leaders to develop inter-personal skills. Certainly in these days of ever-greater sharing of roles and delegation

of responsibilities, clergy need to acquire management skills as well as the ability to run meetings.

CLERGY AND OTHER MINISTERS

560.   The ability to manage people is the more necessary at a time when a number of different lay ministries are being encouraged and developed for the conduct of worship. Readers, worship leaders, lesson readers, intercessors and musicians of various kinds are all involved. Thus more of the laity, who already have a say in synodical affairs and carry an ever greater financial responsibility, are being encouraged to use their gifts in the Church's most important activity. Many of these may already be recognised in their local community but are being lost to the Church, with consequent resentment, frustration and impoverishment of the parish.

561.   A source of potential talent such as this is particularly important for rural areas. A parish may have no Reader and its clergy may be overstretched because of having to care for a number of churches. Here, as elsewhere, simple training of the laity in the conduct of services and the dynamics of communication could help beginners in the effective use of position, body, voice and words. Sometimes in a country parish there is no organ or other instrument, let alone some-one to play it. Somebody, therefore, has to lead the singing, either unaccompanied or to the accompaniment of a pre-recorded tape, and training is needed for this as well. The responsibility for organising the training and co-ordination of ministries, including that of musicians, is likely to fall upon the clergy.

562.   Opinion is divided as to whether it is preferable to have an incumbent who is wholly unmusical or one who is at least as well qualified as the musical director. Unmusical clergy may leave every-thing to the organist. But they may not appreciate the difficulties of recruiting, and may not understand the inappropriateness or imprac-ticality of a particular piece of music which has been requested. Musical clergy, on the other hand, may find it hard to accept standards of choice and performance which are lower than they believe they could achieve themselves. This is to portray extremes; most clergy have at least some musical skill, and a good proportion of church musicians have some theological knowledge. Happily, in most of those parishes which have an official organist or director there is mutual respect and good co-operation. It is the exceptions which make the headlines.

CLERGY TRAINING

563.   Most clergy have received some instruction in voice production and singing during their theological training. In spite of this, there are those who really cannot sing. They should not undertake the sung parts traditionally assigned to them in the Offices and in the Eucharist. When it is permissible, according to the rubrics, these parts may be delegated to others. When it is not, it is better than both clergy and congregation resort to speech. Clergy who intone their parts in the service should nevertheless be open to receive tuition from the musical director, where this is needed. Neither an operatic performance nor an unattractive preciousness of style is acceptable in the context of worship.

564.   The ability to sing a service is not, however, as important as having the skills required to lead worship. Ordinands do not necessarily have more imagination than others. But they do need to learn to understand the effect which different styles of communication and presentation have on a congregation.

565.   It is clear from the evidence received from theological colleges and courses, that the training given to ordinands for their responsibilities in leading worship is seriously inadequate. Little appears to be done to help them understand the place and use of music within it. The Commission is well aware of the pressures upon curricula of theological training and understands the dilemma faced by those responsible for it. But if worship is the foundation of all the Church's other activities, greater priority must be given to matters liturgical and musical, even at the expense of some subjects which at present form part of the syllabus. Many skills can be learnt in the parish in which a person serves after ordination. But there is no guarantee that the quality of the worship and music in that parish will provide adequate formation in what is arguably the most crucial area of the ministry of the clergy.

566.   A first parish may prove to be perfectly satisfactory, or the formation of the ordinand's understanding and attitudes in respect of worship may have taken place before theological training. But the worship of the college or course is obviously very influential. It needs to be of the highest possible standard, and the music which is used within it should represent a variety of styles and traditions, as a preparation for leading worship in the wider Church. Students are not necessarily less conservative in such matters than many congregations.

567.   Given that many ordinands have musical gifts, it should not be too difficult to explore a wide variety of music for worship. But there needs to be a commitment on the part of the college or course to give more time and greater attention to music's role in worship. If finance allowed, the creation of a college bursary for a church musician to spend a period in residence would bestow great enrichment upon both the community and upon the individual.

568.   Once ordained, clergy usually undergo some continuing train- ing for a year or two. Thereafter there are various in-service courses. The opportunities offered by Post Ordination Training and in-service clergy training (CME) should be used much more than they are by most dioceses, perhaps in collaboration with music colleges or diocesan music advisers. Valuable help could be given in areas such as the choice of music, examples of different musical styles, introducing new music, the resources available, and making the most of a limited budget. Church musicians might be encouraged to attend such courses together with the clergy.

569.   The Commission feels strongly that the training received by the clergy is crucial to the future of Church music. It believes that theological colleges and courses must take a new look at the quantity and quality of the preparation given to ordinands for their respon- sibilities in leading public worship. The parishioner's ability to worship depends not only upon the personal spirituality of a relationship with God in Christ, but also upon relationships with fellow worshippers, the atmosphere of the building and the vitality of the services. The person with the greatest influence over these is the priest or presiding minister. The task of ordering the Church's worship is too awesome to be left to chance, either in the hope that the person responsible for it will pick up the necessary skills or in the belief that it can be done by anyone.

CHURCH MUSICIANS

570.   Second to the influence of the priest or presiding minister is that of the person responsible for the music, for music can make or mar a service as powerfully as anything else. It is not, therefore, unreason- able for the Church to expect its musicians to have natural musical talents, some training and an adequate technique. If the congregation is distracted by an inappropriate piece, and technical shortcomings or insensitivity in its performance, the worship will not get off the ground.

571. Recognition of the contribution made by leading musicians is shown in their being described increasingly as 'ministers of music'. This is common in many denominations in the United States of America. Although there are those who cavil at using the term 'minister' for anyone other than those who are ordained, there is no doubt of the significance of the musician's role. It is as much pastoral as it is liturgical.

572. Those churches which are blessed with good human and material resources may have a number of music leaders and musicians. An overall director of music may supervise an organist, a choir conductor and the leader of a music group. More common is a two-person team, consisting of an organist and a choir director. Most common of all is one person who is responsible for both the direction of the choir and the playing of the organ.

Worship Leaders

573. There are a substantial number of churches, particularly in either rural or inner-city areas, where there is not even one trained musician. Sometimes a largely self-taught pianist or 'reluctant organist' can be found to help, or a rota of local organists might be compiled. Often, however, the person taking the service has to lead the music as well. In this situation the Commission believes that consideration should be given to the use of a cantor, or animateur. This is a person who, amongst other things, gives a vocal lead, with or without accompaniment, in singing phrases which the congregation repeats, or to which it responds.

574. This method can be used effectively with responsorial Psalms and some settings of the Eucharist. Plainsong also offers wide possibilities for unaccompanied singing. With a little training both the congregation and the soloist can produce good results, and thus provide a welcome supplement to the singing of hymns. Where there is adequate equipment, consideration should be given to the use of pre-recorded hymn accompaniments and voluntaries. An increasing number of these are being produced commercially.

575. Cantors or animateurs could also have a place in those churches with a thriving musical tradition and they should not be regarded simply as emergency personnel. Nevertheless, they may be needed more widely yet. For there is evidently a growing shortage everywhere of people who are both musically qualified and prepared to invest a

significant amount of time, energy and expertise in the Church's music. To those who do make a commitment of this kind the Commission expresses its admiration and appreciation, particularly in the light of the small salaries paid to most church musicians.

The Musical Director

576.   A director of music holds a position of great responsibility and a number of special qualities are required. Musical competence and proper professionalism are obviously needed, but personality, teaching and managerial ability are no less important. In addition to working with other musicians, whether singers or players, the director is likely to have dealings with people who are not regular churchgoers, but come to choose music for weddings or funerals. For them this meeting may be one of the few contacts they have with the Church. A director will also be expected to undertake at least some administrative duties.

577.   It is not easy to find people with both musical and personal skills in perfect balance. One side without the other is likely to create problems and it may be better not to make an appointment than to settle for someone who is seriously inadequate either as a musician or as a leader. It is also unwise to overlook all else because of a person's Christian commitment. The well-meaning piety of one who is neither leader nor musician ought to be used elsewhere than in the direction of the Church's music.

578.   Having said this, and conscious of the arguments advanced in this Report against excluding non-believers, the Commission believes that the musical director needs to have some Christian commitment. Experience has too often shown that problems arise where there is a lack of sympathy with the Church and its worshippers. Damage can be done, particularly to young people in a choir or music group, if their director does not support the clergy and join in the worship, or does not receive Communion, for example.

579.   The wisdom of having a contract and job description for the church's organist or director has already been mentioned. Some protection of the position is afforded by the Church's legislation (see Appendix 3.1) and an intelligent job description will help employee and employer alike to avoid misunderstandings. However, as has been said, relationships depend upon more than legal provisions. Personal support, guidance and encouragement for the musical director are rightly to be expected from the clergy, parish leaders and

congregation. In addition to the occasional attendance at rehearsals by the incumbent, positive words of appreciation can go a long way in making the musician feel that the job is worthwhile. They also make any necessary criticisms and suggestions more easily acceptable when they are offered.

580.   A worship committee should be able to offer support as well as advice to the director. It needs to be emphasised, however, that just as the clergy's specialist knowledge of theology, spirituality, worship and pastoral care is to be respected, so too are the musician's particular skills and qualifications. Healthy relations between all involved in the leading of worship are at the heart of the matter. Both individually and corporately they should be nourished by their relationship with God.

Remuneration

581.   Part of the problem which has created a shortage of church organists or directors is the level of remuneration which is offered to them. Comparisons are sometimes made with the growing number of laity who give freely of their time and skills to the Church. But many organists have undertaken some years of an expensive musical training and still give many hours a week to practising. Evidence received by the Commission shows that cathedral and other professional church musicians receive salaries which are a fraction of the remuneration they could command on the basis of their qualifications, outside the Church. Equally, what many parishes pay their musicians is barely sufficient to cover their expenses.

582.   The Commission recognises that church musicians generally offer their skills as part of their Christian commitment and primarily *pro Deo*. It also believes that if the Church wants better music and musicians, it will have to be prepared to pay more at least for its music leaders. Where it employs professional musicians full- or part-time it should ensure that their salaries take account of their training and qualifications as well as of the time and contribution which they are expected to give to the worship. The latter considerations apply to the majority of the Church's amateur directors of music. A higher degree of commitment is demanded of church musicians than of any other leader of worship. For all but a few weeks in the year there is the demand of regular attendances and rehearsals, often at unsocial hours, as well as regular private practice.

583.   The General Synod could consider laying down salary scales for church musicians, as it does in respect of parochial fees. Nevertheless, parishes should recognise their responsibility. Guidance is offered by the salary scales suggested by the Royal School of Church Music for amateur organists (see Appendix 3.4), and by the Incorporated Society of Musicians for professional musicians.

Learning on the Job

584.   With or without more realistic salaries, opportunities for further training could act as an incentive to serious musicians. They could be encouraged to attend appropriate courses or continue with lessons. Parishes ought to pay the costs of these, as they often do for their clergy or other personnel to receive in-service training. In spite of its financial implications, this could be a good investment in helping organists and choir directors to develop their skills and expand their horizons. This is particularly important if a 'traditional' training has kept them to a limited understanding and repertoire. A greater difficulty than finding the finance may lie in persuading old hands of the value of such opportunities for learning. Training events arranged by the RSCM and other organisations seldom attract those who need them most, perhaps for fear that their inadequacies might be revealed.

CONCLUSION

585.   Whether or not budgets can run to making provisions such as have been suggested, it is important that the Church affirm and encourage its leading musicians. It is important, too, that both during their theological training and throughout their subsequent ministry, the clergy be encouraged to give a high priority to their role in the planning and leading of worship. To this end, there needs to be greater provision for training in liturgy and the use of music within it.

RECOMMENDATIONS

That congregations be helped to explore and experiment with new music (550–554).

That parishes set up a worship committee, where there is none, in order to advise the incumbent and Parochial Church Council, and to support their organist or director of music (555–556, 579–580).

That clergy and musicians do all in their power to ensure close and amicable working relationships (557–559, 562).

That, where it is appropriate, clergy seek out and train others for the leading of worship (560–561, 573–575).

That theological colleges and courses, as well as those responsible for post-ordination training and continuing ministerial training, review their provision for the training of ordinands and clergy in the art of preparing for and conducting public worship, and the use of music within it (563–569).

That parishes aim to have an organist or director of music with Christian commitment, together with personal and leadership skills, as well as musical ability (570–572, 576–578).

That parishes work towards a realistic level of remuneration for their organist or director of music and make provision for their continuing training (581–584).

24

Choirs, Music Groups and Recruitment

586.   One of the major responsibilities, and a cause of much anxiety, for the director of music is the recruitment of people for choirs and music groups. Without the status and obligations of a church organist, singers and players are not prepared in great numbers to accept the demands of weekly services and rehearsals. There are those, however, for whom the offering of musical skills in worship is part of their offering to God. For them it is a matter of Christian commitment and they serve the Church well and faithfully.

587.   There are other reasons for belonging to a choir. These range from the desire to make music, to meeting the wishes of parents. For some there is the enjoyment of the social life which may be offered by the Church and its musicians. Few join for the money, even where that is offered. It is necessary, therefore, to make as attractive as possible the opportunities and challenge of singing or playing in church. For youngsters in particular the personality of the director is as important as any musical qualifications.

Pastoral Care and Spiritual Development

588.   To have an *esprit de corps* is important for any choir. This is commonly fostered by the wearing of choir robes, competitions, chorister or musician training schemes, and a variety of out-of-church activities. There is an important pastoral role to be played by the director, and non-musical demands can be time-consuming. However, the Commission believes that time given in this way pays enormous dividends for a body of volunteer, amateur musicians and for those leading it. Experience suggests that it is not just valuable but essential for recruitment, as well as for effective working relationships and enhanced musical performance.

589.   There are those who have reservations about the value of choirs or other groups in worship, perhaps because of unhappy experience. All will recognise, however, the considerable potential for evangelism which is afforded by them. Evidence shows that people are often brought to Christ by membership of such a group.

590.   A band of singers or musicians also offers a context and an opportunity for training in Christian discipleship. It is not an opportunity which seems to be taken very often. All too frequently choirs and musicians, as well as servers, are taken for granted because of their being in church Sunday by Sunday. For many people, singing or playing at services is perhaps their only link with the Church, and it may well prove to be a temporary one. Young people particularly need special care. They find themselves involved in what is a mainly adult activity and they may be quickly bored by a church service. Their spiritual development must be the responsibility of the clergy, perhaps with the help of others. The clergy ought also to have a part with the director of music in the pastoral care of the choir or music group.

The Music Group

591.   Repeated reference is made in this Report to music groups. These consist of two or more instrumentalists, with or without singers, involving almost any combination of instruments. Suitable arrangements for the instruments available have to be made and this requires some skill. If this is not available from the director of music or some other person in the church, a local musician may be prepared to help. The huge value of a band of instrumentalists is as yet largely unexploited by the Church. Not the least of its benefits is that a music group provides a means of involving more people, especially youngsters, in its life. The growth of instrumental tuition in schools means that large numbers of children with some musical ability are available to be recruited.

592.   A music group adds to the variety of music used in worship and it may help a congregation to experiment and explore new possibilities. In view of the Commission's belief that churches generally should be more adventurous in their choice of music, the formation of a music group is strongly recommended. For several reasons this could be a positive step forward.

593.   Music groups and choirs are usually drawn to differing styles of music and varying degrees of formality. Experience has shown that this can lead to rivalry or even friction between the two. If there is no

overall director of music for the church, the leaders of the two groups will need to ensure a close relationship and positive co-operation with each other. Where necessary, the incumbent may need to be involved, for it is vital to the church's life and worship that there be mutual respect and the acceptance of the distinctive and complementary contributions of all its musicians.

Boys and Girls

594.   A complicating factor in recruitment for church choirs may be the boy/girl issue. Elsewhere in this Report there is some discussion of the question as it affects cathedrals. It relates more particularly to parish churches, which rarely have single-sex choirs in these days. Where there are boys alone in the front rows there may need to be parallel opportunities for girls, either by turn or by the formation of a second choir. When girls have been introduced into a formerly all-male top line, most of the boys have disappeared. Among the reasons for this is that girls seem to volunteer more readily for singing and the recruitment of boys is not given priority. A particular effort is in any case demanded, to ensure a supply of trebles both for their own sake and in order to provide the tenors and basses of the future.

595.   Boys, more than girls perhaps, face the problem of 'street credibility' with their contemporaries because of the public's perception of a church choir. This underscores the need for it to provide more than musical training for its members. If it can offer the fellowship of a club, young people may well risk the scorn of their peers to belong to it. Its reputation in encouraging a variety of worthwhile activities will then gain increasing acceptance in the community.

596.   Remuneration offered to children in parish church choirs is usually at the level of pocket money. It provides perhaps little incentive for most youngsters in today's affluent society. However, where funds can be found, the award of bursaries for education and music tuition has much to be said for it. The Commission commends the example of parishes such as St. Mary's, Portsea, which have a scheme of this kind. It has parallels with the cathedral and collegiate traditions.

The Children Act (1989)

597.   Those who have charge of young people in choirs ought to be aware of the provisions of The Children Act (1989). It is designed to

protect children and to ensure that care is taken in making appointments to any post which involves contact with children. These might include clergy, vergers and others, in addition to directors of music. The screening of applicants must be thorough and names may need to be checked against 'List 99'. This is a record of those convicted of crimes against juveniles. Names can also be submitted to the police computer.

Recruitment and Future Organists

598.   An imaginative and sustained programme of recruitment for choirs and music groups is required, not only to ensure their future but also to train tomorrow's directors of music. Many of today's leading musicians, both in the sacred and in the secular spheres, began their careers through belonging to a church choir. Learning to play the organ can also lay the foundation for wider musical skills, including the ability to direct a group of choral or instrumental musicians.

599.   A recent survey in the Archdeaconry of Wiltshire suggests that the need is urgent. Only one organist in five there is under the age of forty, and of all those serving, 40% are more than sixty years of age. There is every reason to think that these findings are typical of many rural areas in England.

600.   Assuming that the organ is likely to remain the most common instrument for worship, the Commission urges parishes and dioceses to set up schemes to encourage people to learn the organ. The warm response to the successful National Learn the Organ Year in 1990 suggests that there are many people who are interested in doing so. Consequently, its work is to be continued by a number of bodies, chiefly the newly-formed National Organ Teachers' Encouragement Scheme (NOTES). A few dioceses already have bursary schemes to encourage young organists, and extending this, both at diocesan and parish level, could prove immensely valuable. A modest financial investment now could ensure the continuing and improved provision of church music in the future.

601.   Every church ought to provide ready access to its organ for those who are learning or may wish to learn the instrument. The Commission has been saddened to hear of cases where clergy and organists make it difficult or impossible for serious pupils to practise. It is important for the organ to be properly covered by insurance, but making it available to students costs little and is again an investment for the future. Also to

be commended is the example of those churches which purchase orchestral instruments for members of their music groups.

602.   The recruitment of potential church musicians could be helped by the development of links with local high schools and colleges which offer music courses. It is often possible to gain the services of a competent student for a year or two, either as an organist or as an organ scholar. This is not only helpful to the church but provides valuable experience for the person concerned. We should not overlook the possibility of attracting professional musicians into church music, and the teaching profession in particular contains people who might need only a little persuasion to help, at least on an occasional basis.

603.   All church musicians should be afforded opportunities to sing or play alone, with others listening. The balance between congregational and other music is one which has to be worked out in each church, with the advice of the worship committee where there is one. The contribution that a good choir, singing or instrumental group can make to the worship of a parish cannot be underestimated. If it is to give of its best, however, it must be appreciated and affirmed by being allowed to perform on its own, in addition to leading the singing of the whole congregation.

604.   It is obvious that this requires a high degree of commitment to regular practice, with punctuality and concentration during rehearsals. Much unseen work, including individual practice where that is required, is put into even a short public performance. In a service, the musicians are often the focus of attention. Even when they are silent their example in attitude and behaviour has a direct bearing upon the way their role is perceived by the congregation. Poor discipline shows in whispering and giggling, and in fussy 'busyness' with music or musical instruments. It is a distraction to other worshippers and detracts from the importance of church musicians. As part of the whole, they are expected to enable all who are present to make their offering to God as fully and as well as they can, in addition to making their own contribution for him.

RECOMMENDATIONS

That organists or directors of music be fully supported by clergy and parishes in their efforts to recruit people for choirs and music groups (586–588).

That clergy, in particular, recognise the value of choirs and music groups for evangelism and nurturing in the Christian faith, and ensure that children participating in them receive spiritual and pastoral care (589–590).

That organists or directors of music give consideration to the formation of a music group, where there is none, and ensure its close working relationship with any existing choir (591–593).

That organists or directors of music work to recruit both boys and girls for their choir, and that both sexes be given equal opportunities and encouragement (594–597).

That dioceses and parishes give immediate attention to setting up schemes to encourage people to learn the organ, and make their instruments available for practice (598–601).

That parishes give consideration to forming links with musicians in local educational institutions (602).

That choirs and music groups be given opportunities in church services to sing and play on their own (603–604).

25

Educating for the Future

605.   Until the passing of the Forster Education Act in 1870, most training in music was obtained primarily, if not solely, through singing or playing in churches, chapels and cathedrals. With the foundation of music colleges, the Church's responsibility for producing future musicians diminished. But church choirs continued to have an active role in music education, together with the schools, many of which remained in close association with the Church. Continuing co-operation between Church and school will be needed if the music in our services is to improve and, indeed, if the presence of young people is to guarantee the future of our congregations.

CHILDREN IN CHURCH AND SCHOOL

606.   Children are part of today's Church. However, when they are separated from a Sunday morning congregation in a Sunday School they can easily be made to feel as if they are the Church of tomorrow. For this reason, young people with their varied musical and other gifts should be encouraged from an early age to make their contribution to the corporate worship of the church family. At first this might be a mixture of music, dance and drama, in a regular 'children's slot'. Later it could develop into music groups consisting of a variety of instruments and voices, bands, instrumental ensembles or dance groups. As soon as possible, young musicians should be encouraged to become part of regular adult groups, and an all-age orchestra could play for occasional services.

607.   Additional encouragement and training for children might be provided by congregational 'creative' days, when young and old alike meet together to make music, as well as to take part in other activities. This Report has already pointed out that something more than singing and playing may be needed if boys and girls are to remain part of a choir or music group. If the Church is to keep its teenagers, especially, it has to compete successfully with many other attractions and activities which appeal to the young.

608.   It is vital that young people feel not only welcome in the church, but also valued and needed there, whether in bands, music groups, orchestras or choirs. The power of music should be harnessed to encourage them to belong. If the congregation accepts them as they are, and if lively and attractive leaders give them time and energy, young people are likely to stay in the Church. If not, they will vote with their feet when they are old enough to do so.

609.   The question of children's spiritual development and formation has previously been discussed in this Report, and many former girl and boy choristers testify to the benefits, spiritual as well as musical, of belonging to a good choir. These can last for a lifetime.

The Educational Value of Choirs

610.   The fine choral tradition of this country owes much to the vocal foundation laid in so many of our churches and cathedrals down the ages. This suggests that the Church has a continuing responsibility to promote choral music and to provide challenging opportunities for young singers in its choirs. This is the more necessary, the Commission believes, at a time when the bias in schools has shifted towards instrumental music and composition, although a fair number of state secondary and senior independent schools continue to maintain a strong tradition of choral singing.

611.   A survey on singing in schools was conducted in 1988 on behalf of the British Federation of Young Choirs, and the results have recently been published ('Singing in Schools', British Federation of Young Choirs, 1991). These indicated that of those questioned, 73.8% of secondary schools and 43.1% of primary schools believed that there had been a decline in the quantity of choral singing provided in schools. Both reported a decline also in its quality (secondary 46.7%, primary 28.4%). The Commission expresses its anxiety that the pro-posed syllabus in the revised music curriculum allows less time than hitherto for choral music. It also notes that teachers' present contracts make it difficult for them to find time to run extra-curricular activities like choirs.

Singing in Schools

612.   An additional cause for disquiet is the present shortage of music teachers in primary and secondary schools. This has now been officially recognised and it is expected that extra student places will be provided

to make up the deficiency. This is encouraging, for, as HM Inspectors have said, 'the development of music in primary schools depends very largely on the level of expertise and quality of teaching available' (*The Teaching and Learning of Music*, Aspects of Primary Education series, HMSO, 1991). Where there are no music specialists in post in primary schools, general class teachers are often driven to almost exclusive use of schools' broadcasts, both for assembly and for class music. These are admirable programmes. But the Commission believes that no radio or television presenter can adequately take the place of a live teacher, and that no school should depend almost wholly on a centralised choice of music, particularly of hymns or songs. The recent government commitment to providing an element of specialist music teaching in primary schools is greatly to be welcomed.

613.   Concern has been voiced to the Commission over the lack of a repertoire of music common both to schools and to the Church. It should be possible for clergy and teachers to ensure both that churches include some of the school's repertoire in their own, and that schools make room in their assemblies for some traditional hymns.

614.   The Commission recognises that many schools are undergoing a period of rapid and difficult change, in the wake of the 1988 Education Reform Act. The demands of the National Curriculum have put great pressure upon the educational service in new forms of school management and there have been problems of staffing and funding. It is unlikely that music will receive the same emphasis or resources as the 'core' subjects of English, Mathematics and Science in most schools, in spite of its designation as a 'foundation' subject. Significant among the changes in the school music curriculum (distilled in the reports of the National Curriculum Music Working Group, 1991), is the emphasis on performing, composing and listening. The inevitable reduction in the amount of time likely to be given to singing challenges the Church to remedy this deficiency. Only so may choral opportunities be provided for future generations of children.

Young Instrumentalists

615.   The Commission welcomes the much improved standard of instrumental playing which is one of the schools' greatest recent success stories. It is already proving beneficial to many churches, and the Commission has urged earlier in this Report that those churches which have not taken advantage of it should do so. This is an area in which young people's enthusiasm has been well and truly

aroused at school. Given the opportunity, many more would doubtless welcome the chance to exercise their new-found skills in the context of church services. They may not come from a church-going background, but with encouragement they might well respond to an invitation to be part of the Church's music, at least occasionally.

Co-operation between School and Church

616.   The Commission urges teachers who are church members to involve children with musical talent in the worship of their church. Churches in rural areas in particular could benefit from co-operation of this kind.

617.   In their training of instrumentalists, schools offer the Church a golden opportunity to develop church bands, orchestras or music groups in which youngsters can participate, often on an equal basis, alongside adult musicians. Far from taking this supply of trained musicians for granted, the local church should be providing its own kind of expertise to complement and augment that which comes from the schools. It is unreasonable to look to the school to supply all the musical needs of the parish. In its training of young people to sing, however, the Church will be making a welcome and reciprocal contribution towards the musical life of schools.

618.   In line with an earlier discussion in this Report, the Commission recommends that local churches establish close working links with school music departments. These could be most advantageous to both parties and could facilitate the recruitment of church musicians at an early age. Without it, there may be few coming forward to serve the Church in the twenty-first century.

THE TRAINING AND RE-TRAINING
OF CHURCH MUSICIANS

619.   Many of the suggestions made in this Report presuppose a higher degree of expertise and commitment in church organists or directors of music in the future than is often the case at present. The Commission believes, therefore, that specific initial and in-service training needs to be provided urgently for church musicians if significant progress is to be made.

620.   There are many who require not only the further enhancement of their musical skills, but also some training in liturgy and theology.

Where a director of music has an inadequate knowledge of the liturgy, the musical contribution may be at best out of keeping with the rest of the celebration, and at worst destructive of it. Teaching, communication and pastoral skills are also needed by those with responsibility for the training and direction of others.

A National Scheme

621.   The first requirement is for a nationally co-ordinated scheme devised by all the churches, together with theological colleges and those educational and professional bodies which are concerned with church music. An encouraging start to this has been made in the recent establishment of the Churches' Initiative for Music Education (CHIME). This exists to enable co-ordination and co-operation in training, and the issuing of qualifications, by church music organisations of all denominations.

622.   Any scheme of training will need to have methods of study which are flexible and tailored, as far as possible, to individual needs. Inter-related courses might fit into a modular plan. It would thus be possible for studies to be pursued either full- or part-time, before or during employment as a church musician. Courses would have elements which applied to both professional and to amateur musicians. A modular structure would also have the advantage of helping to avoid too rarefied an approach. Some modules could be shared with other musical and theological courses.

623.   A comprehensive syllabus would include performing, accompanying, improvising, composing, arranging and orchestrating, voice training, rehearsing, recording and the use of electronics (including computers and word processors), liturgy and theology, and communication and management skills. Its aim would be to produce people with versatile musicianship and proven teaching ability, based upon religious conviction. The pastoral and spiritual care of students on the course would be no less important than their academic or technical instruction.

624.   Just as teaching practice is prescribed for student teachers, so the course would include a 'sandwich' element. This would involve several periods of working in the field alongside experienced practitioners. Placements could be arranged for both observation and practice in several contrasting situations, such as a cathedral, an inner city parish, or a village church. Tutors would supervise their students' work

in the manner of teacher trainers. In this way, church music students would have varied opportunities to put into practice the theory learnt in their studies. They would be rooted in reality. Those who are considering a professional career would also gain a valuable overview of the various fields open to them when deciding where their future might lie.

The Organisation of the Scheme

625.   It is tempting to the Commission to recommend the establishment of a church music staff college, perhaps building upon the foundation of the Royal School of Church Music. This would provide a base and headquarters for the proposed educational programme. However, realism leads to the suggestion rather of a joint enterprise between one or more designated colleges of music or polytechnics and some theological colleges, under the auspices of CHIME or some other body.

626.   Its brief would be to devise, offer and supervise a comprehensive course devoted to the training of church musicians in all aspects of their craft. The course would be a total entity in its own right, and not a subsidiary subject taken for one term by full-time students during the second year of a degree or graduate equivalent course in general musicianship. Whilst making some use of material offered in other courses, it would be free-standing and designed to produce well-qualified and committed 'ministers of music'. Colleges, cathedrals and other churches which offer organ and choral scholarships might well consider widening the scope of their awards, so as to be an integral part of such a programme.

In-service and Amateur Training

627.   The scheme outlined above would be designed chiefly with intending professional musicians in mind. With sufficient flexibility and with the expertise gained by staff in operating it, however, it should be possible for serving church musicians, both amateur and professional, also to take advantage of it. In addition to part-time study, there could be vacation or weekend courses at a regional level, and country-wide summer and winter schools, after the successful pattern pioneered by the Open University. These might be organised at those colleges which are part of the scheme and could also involve such organisations as CHIME, the RSCM, the Benslow Music Trust and the

British Federation of Young Choirs. In this way, new ideas would be widely disseminated.

Local Training for Musicians

628.   It is important that parish directors of music be encouraged to take opportunities for in-service training. The proposed scheme would offer facilities for this. More local training initiated by dioceses and parishes should also be encouraged. The RSCM has been offering a wide range of courses for many years, and there is a well-established pattern of deanery, archdeaconry or diocesan events and festivals in many places. A fresh look could be taken at some of these, in order to determine their effectiveness in helping parishes both to respond to the liturgical changes of recent years and to explore a wider repertoire of music.

Renewal Music

629.   For many people contemporary music meets a need which more traditional music does not. Help may well be needed, therefore, for those churches which are beginning to include more modern styles of composition, instrumental and vocal music in their services. Quite a number of the musicians who are at home in the 'renewal' idiom have grown up outside the Church. Whilst they bring a welcome freshness and enthusiasm to worship, they may also lack a sympathetic under-standing of the Church's liturgy and tradition. Moreover, for home-produced music and self-taught instrumental playing, the only role models for many young vocalists and groups are provided through television and pop concerts. It is not therefore surprising if there is sometimes an over-provision of microphones and electronic equip-ment and a prevalence of noise, not least the persistent beat of a drum kit.

630.   Sensitive guidance may be needed for young musicians. With-out in any way discouraging them, they may need advice on providing music for worship which is acceptable to the many different people in a congregation. There is an ever-growing amount of musical material in this genre and musicians and clergy need to be wise and selective in their choice of it. Skill is also required to arrange it for a particular choir, group or instruments.

631.   Training for the selection and use of music in a contemporary style is offered by an increasing number of workshops initiated by

people such as Chris Bowater, Dave Fellingham, Andrew Maries, Christopher Norton and David Peacock. The programme of the RSCM is also expanding, to cover a wider range of instruments and styles. The linking of a church having good resources and experience with another which is struggling could provide a useful and manageable means of learning, and both churches would derive benefit from it.

EDUCATING THE CONGREGATION

632.   It is essential that the training of children and church musicians is supported by our congregations. The emphasis in most of this Report is upon the importance of the whole people of God gathered for worship. Unless the proposals of the Commission have their understanding and support, little will change in church music, except for the worse. The people in the pew, not to mention the clergy and the musicians themselves, have to be convinced of the priority of worship, and the indispensability of first-rate music within it. Otherwise, schemes for producing well-trained professional and amateur musicians will meet with little success.

Variety and Preferences

633.   It came as little surprise to the Commission in its work to be reminded both of the rich diversity which exists in the field of church music and of the very different attitudes and preferences to be found within our congregations. Some place their emphasis upon the transcendent otherness of God and the traditional 'good' music which expresses it. Others seek to worship through readily understandable services and music which speaks of a personal relationship to God in Christ, and the dynamic working of the Holy Spirit. Whilst generalising for the sake of simplicity, the Commission does not believe that there is any essential conflict between these two categories. Each has much to offer to the other and there is no question of one tradition being right and the other wrong.

Conflict in a Congregation

634.   Because music is so universally popular in society, and because feelings on the subject run deep, attitudes can harden and objectives diverge. It can easily become a cause of friction, and is sometimes made the scapegoat for disagreement and discontent in other areas of a congregation's life. When this happens, it is vital that the conflict be resolved and that broken or strained relationships which may have given rise to the problem be repaired. This Report has already

discussed the matter of resolving disagreements. Those between clergy and musicians often spill over into the parish, and sides will be taken. Whatever the cause of division, there must be opportunities for the parties involved to air their grievances, to talk through the areas of conflict and to find a satisfactory resolution. In achieving reconciliation, Myers-Briggs, Enneagram and similar personality-typing methods can be helpful. In extreme situations, it may be necessary to resort to arbitration.

CONCLUSION

635. Some of the contents and recommendations of this Report may themselves be the cause of controversy in places. If so, the Commission will at least have provoked thought and debate. It hopes it may encourage congregations and others to consider important and urgent issues relating to music in worship. It urges clergy and others to disseminate widely those parts of this Report which are relevant to the life of their local church, and also to help their congregations to recognise their responsibility in making progress possible. If we are to enhance the quality of our worship and church music, there will have to be a new awareness and fresh resolution on the part of all God's people. The implications in relation to resources are obvious, but the chief requirement will be the conviction and the will to achieve the necessary reforms.

RECOMMENDATIONS

That parishes seek to co-operate closely with local schools, partly for the recruitment of children for music in church and partly for mutual support in the music education of children (605, 615–618).

That children and young people, particularly those who are instrumentalists, be welcomed and encouraged to contribute to music in worship (606–609).

That schools be encouraged both to maintain their choral tradition and to liaise with local church musicians, in order to agree on a common repertoire of hymns and songs (610–614).

That a scheme for training church musicians be devised, suitable for students before and during employment, and for both professionals and amateurs, and that the Churches' Initiative for Music Education give consideration to this (619–627).

That dioceses and parishes consider the provision of local in-service training courses for church musicians (628).

That parishes enable musicians who are unfamiliar with the selection and use of music in contemporary styles to take advantage of any appropriate workshops (629–631).

That congregations be encouraged to support all endeavours to improve the musical offering of their church, and to appreciate the need for the best which is attainable (632–634).

26

The Cathedral Contribution

636.   Through the centuries the most influential centres of education in church music have been cathedrals and similar foundations. The place of cathedral music should not, therefore, be overlooked in this Report although the Commission sees its task as primarily one of helping parishes. As the chief guardians and developers of the tradition of church music, the role of cathedrals remains vital for both present and future.

Yesterday and Today

637.   Some people still perceive a cathedral in terms of Trollope's Barchester novels, but the reality is very different. Enormous changes have taken place in recent decades, dictated both by finance and by the tasks laid upon their clergy. No longer quiet, rather isolated places, many cathedrals are involved in the life of the wider Church and community. Chapter members are often busy people with diocesan or other responsibilities and are likely to have some consciousness of the Church's life at parish level and an informed awareness of contemporary issues. This was by no means always true. Musically, too, the remoteness of the past is being dispelled. Some cathedrals are also thinking imaginatively about their relationship to music and musicians in the parishes.

638.   The Commission pays warm tribute to the clergy and musicians of our cathedrals who have preserved so much that is precious in Britain's heritage and unique in the Western world. The constraints of finance and increasing demands from visitors make their continuing commitment to their music even more admirable. There is no doubt that the standards of singing and playing are much higher than they were fifty years ago.

639.   This is not to deny that in a number of our cathedrals there is a sense of complacency. This is perhaps concealed, and at the same time fostered, by constant public assertions of 'the excellence of the

cathedral tradition'. There are cathedrals in this country with feeble standards, even among the more prominent establishments with well-known choirs. Poor choir discipline, lack of commitment, lack of devotion, lack of liturgical sense in the choice of music and lack of balance in a limited repertoire are not uncommon. Cathedrals cannot rest comfortable and content any more than the rest of us in times of change and challenge for the Church.

640.   We belong to a generation which has grown up knowing little of the language of religion, or of the basic doctrines and faith of Christianity. Our culture is fragmented and secular, and for most people Choral Evensong, for example, has little to offer except beautiful music. This is true even for many younger Christians. The cathedral tradition is an undoubted musical gem. But a more truly popular liturgy is also required which will combine the demand of St. Teresa of Avila for something 'plain and homely' with that which has majesty, poetry, otherness and the power to communicate. A cathedral is in a particularly good situation to give the Church a lead in this area, and to offer an inspiring vision for the future. It has fewer constraints and more resources than the average parish, and as the mother church of the diocese and focus of the Bishop's ministry, it should be expected to show the way.

Worship and Resources

641.   The cathedral's greatest advantage is in its recognition that worship is the well-spring of all else. This is expressed by the daily services said or sung, morning and evening, every day of the year. From so solid a base it should not be difficult or daunting to make experiments. Except in the case of cathedrals with parishes, Chapters do not have the same obligations to their congregations as the parish clergy. Apart from a regular core of worshippers, every service involves a different group of people.

642.   The sheer scale of most cathedral buildings, with their different parts and open spaces which allow considerable flexibility, is another great asset. It invites exploration both of movement and of sound, and a lone instrument or the calling of one voice to another, as if from nowhere, can create a most powerful effect, as can a procession up the full length of a large building. Anyone who has witnessed the beginning of the Sung Eucharist in Liverpool's Anglican Cathedral will testify to this.

643.   Many cathedrals have a staff of up to half a dozen clergy, with varying experience and theological expertise. They also have an army of both voluntary and employed people upon whom to call for a wide range of tasks, from shifting furniture to guiding visitors. Such personnel are an important resource, although they are often fully stretched. Nevertheless, with good management and imaginative leadership many would be willing to assist with events and acts of worship which are out of the ordinary.

644.   There are also the musical resources of a cathedral. The organ and its players, the choir and its director, and a long tradition, all have a unique contribution to make to the exploration of new possibilities for worship. It is, however, the tradition which is often the inhibiting factor. The choral repertoire of many of our cathedrals remains somewhat restricted by the requirements of Choral Evensong from the Book of Common Prayer, of the Sunday morning Eucharist and of Matins. Occasional large services or special events may extend their repertoire, but the music is nearly always in the idiom which is identified with cathedral music.

A Call for Experimentation

645.   It would constitute a return to the worst of the Dark Ages if the cathedral musical tradition were lost. However, the Commission believes that, with the expertise which is available in our cathedrals, there should be a willingness to use and experiment with different styles of music. This would contribute towards the search for a new liturgical expression of worship, and would also help parishes in their search for excellence in whatever musical idiom they use in their services. For example, it ought not to be beneath the dignity of cathedral musicians to use occasionally very simple music set to good quality liturgical texts, and to demonstrate it to parishes with few resources.

646.   The Commission also recommends that cathedral musicians, with their vocal and instrumental expertise, should explore some of the many worship songs in contemporary style. In this way they would identify with those congregations which use them and would also set standards of performance, and maybe of composition as well. There could also be room for experimentation with modern religious music with a jazz-rock feel to it. Coming from the Negro-spiritual tradition, it represents the spiritual music of anger and liberation.

647.   There should, perhaps, be a greater wooing of contemporary composers. After a period of somewhat cerebral activity, music has returned to being an expressive art with a deep spiritual impact. Among modern writers, Henryk Górecki, Jonathan Harvey, Olivier Messiaen, Arvo Pärt, John Tavener and Michael Tippett use modality, plainsong, Byzantine chants and ragas in their compositions. Our cathedrals could well provide them with attractive opportunities of writing for musicians with professional standards, in a building which is sympathetic to their work.

648.   There are many possibilities to be explored with instruments other than the organ. The alternative does not have to be a full orchestra, and the imaginative use in a cathedral's acoustic of quite modest instrumental resources can be most effective. In particular, electronic music in so much space is stunning.

649.   Electronic organs are usually accepted as a substitute whilst the main instrument is undergoing an overhaul. However, people are often surprised to discover something approaching authentic pipe tone in the very large instruments which are sometimes installed. A few cathedrals have an electronic organ in addition to their traditional instrument. It may be sited in the nave, or placed wherever it is most convenient, and can provide a useful complement to the main organ. Although constant improvements are being made in digital or computer technology, it is to be hoped that cathedrals and large churches will continue to use the pipe organ in spite of the cost of doing so.

Cathedrals and Parishes

650.   Cathedrals offer the opportunity to be musically bold. A catholic attitude towards their repertoire and a generosity of spirit by cathedral musicians would do much to overcome the antipathy which is sometimes felt by parishes towards the cathedral and its resources. Inviting parishes and their musicians to lead worship in a cathedral is certainly helpful in creating good relationships. However, the invitations are usually issued when the cathedral choir is on holiday, and so parish musicians do not benefit from hearing and seeing the cathedral choir at work.

651.   A diocesan service in the cathedral may afford opportunities to hear the cathedral choir, but these occasions necessarily include a large proportion of congregational singing, and a correspondingly small amount of solo work. It is particularly in such services that items not in

the usual cathedral style or repertoire could be included. Special training events could also make use of the strengths of the cathedral musicians in their building. These could be courses for parishes, or musical workshops for children on Saturday mornings, in the same style as some of the theatre workshops; or summer music schools along the lines of the excellent cathedral camps for young people. There could also be master classes by a local composer or performer of renown, and budding organists would never forget an opportunity to play the cathedral's organ.

652.   It could also be enormously valuable for the cathedral organist and choir to move out on occasions into deaneries and parishes. Although difficult to organise, it would greatly help and encourage parish musicians. Some cathedrals, such as Salisbury and Oxford, already do this. One correspondent remarked to the Commission that the list of foreign tours by cathedral choirs gives the impression 'that it is some sort of virility test' and that he 'would prefer a list of parish churches visited in the Diocese'. It is appropriate, too, for cathedral musicians to be involved in an ordination or other episcopal event outside the cathedral where the cathedral Chapter is involved with the Bishop.

653.   From the musical base of a cathedral there is much that could be offered to the parishes and some dioceses have local workshops, services and events which are led by a musician from the cathedral. The demands of the cathedral's own services make it very difficult for the organist to be away very often. But many cathedrals now have more than an organist and a deputy. The creation of scholarships for organists and lay clerks means that more than one person could be available for diocesan work.

The Director of Music
654.   The Commission believes that there is a case for a cathedral to have a director of music who is not the same person as the organist. The director would have overall responsibility for all the music and musicians in the cathedral. Directing the choir, co-operating with the clergy and others in liturgical planning, and co-ordinating all music-making, services and events would constitute a full brief. In many places this is the *de facto* situation. The organist actually spends most time in conducting the choir, and the assistant or organ scholar plays the organ. It may be right to recognise and regularise this arrangement by a change of nomenclature and its reflection in a job description.

219

655.   The somewhat curious situation which at present pertains to the roles of organist and assistant needs to be recognised. If the 'organist' conducts and the assistant plays, then being an assistant is not a training for being an 'organist' one day. Consequently, excellent performers may be appointed to senior cathedral posts without having the necessary experience for training a choir. This can also be true of the training received by organ scholars. In addition to their musical tuition, they ought to be trained in worship and liturgy.

Training of Cathedral Organists

656.   During the last century, and the first half of this one, cathedral organists were the musical leaders of their communities. Cathedrals often attracted people with a national reputation. This is not generally true today, although a number of our cathedral organists could have pursued a career either as a conductor or as a recitalist. It is unlikely that cathedrals could reverse this trend by making the job more attractive, in terms of remuneration and prestige. So consideration needs to be given to accepting the present position and to providing training and support for a distinctive role. For some, at least, it is primarily a matter of having a vocation to serve God in this way.

657.   There is no specific training for cathedral organists and they have little guidance from experts as they practise on other people. The old system of apprenticeship served earlier generations well. But the current high professionalism in the arts means that more is required and there is a need to be able to train choral directors in the same way that we train instrumentalists. There is sometimes, for example, a woeful lack of knowledge in cathedrals about vocal production, the workings of the human voice and how it should be protected as well as used. Many cathedral choirs get by through the sheer discipline of daily singing.

658.   Better provision is made for organ players, although a thorough training in organ repertoire and styles has appeared only in the last twenty years. Some of our best-known cathedral musicians still deem this irrelevant, however, and British organists have long been regarded by musicians overseas as self-taught amateurs. Nevertheless, it is encouraging to note that among the younger generation of organists the standard of performance has risen, and continues to rise, dramatically.

Lay Clerks and Choral Scholars

659.   The most visible expression of the cathedral's music is its choir. The lay clerks (or lay vicars or songmen or singing men) require perhaps more consideration than is given to them. Their financial reward is generally meagre and most need a supplementary income. It is extremely difficult to obtain the kind of employment which allows availability for singing or rehearsing during working hours, especially in the small cities where many of our cathedrals are set. Moreover, there has to be a high degree of commitment in order to offer so much time at unsocial hours. Appropriate recognition is therefore due to the lay clerk's contribution to what is one of a cathedral's evangelistic ministries. Singing in a cathedral choir is quite different from singing in a professional chorus, and lay clerkship is not just another job.

660.   Choral scholars or students who sing in the choirs of cathedrals situated in or near universities or colleges should not be taken for granted either. It is easy to regard them as temporary replacements for, or additions to, the lay clerks. But the opportunity of singing lessons and more general musical studies should be available to them, so that they can be trained for permanent posts when their student days are ended. A valuable pool of singers could then be established.

The Cathedral Team

661.   All the musicians of a cathedral must be encouraged to feel that they are fully part of its life rather than mere employees. No matter how gifted and eminent, they should be able to feel proud to share in the cathedral's offering and witness. The music policy needs to be integrated with the overall aim of the cathedral, and in this the attitude of the clergy and senior administrators is crucial. Their attendance at worship is important if musicians are not to feel undervalued and discouraged.

662.   The responsibility of the director of music for the management of musicians needs to be matched by the responsibility of the Chapter in its management of senior cathedral staff. There is often too much capricious behaviour, by clergy and musicians alike, and traditional understandings of role are no longer adequate. This demands that cathedral authorities consult widely on appointments, provide detailed job descriptions and perhaps offer fixed-term contracts. Cathedral jobs must not be allowed to regress to the status of providing comfortable employment with little or no accountability. Both clergy

and musicians need to be willing to accept a measure of insecurity, although some continuity is required for the stable life of the community. One correspondent to the Commission noted that Minor Canons today tend to arrive without too much experience of cathedral music and seldom stay long enough to derive much understanding of it.

Choir Schools

663.   Many of the medieval foundations have schools attached to them. As an integral part of the cathedral community, those who are responsible for their management need also to be closely involved in the ordering of the cathedral's life. Choir schools offer particular opportunities for education in music and liturgy, in addition to the academic syllabus common to all schools.

664.   All but two choir schools in England are independent schools. Consequently, their pupils tend to come from the more advantaged socio-economic groups. The Commission believes that more places ought to be available to children from less wealthy backgrounds. It recognises, however, the problem which could face a child at the age of thirteen, after five or six years of subsidised fees. Without a scholarship or bursary thereafter, parents might not be able to afford continuing education in an independent school. A move to the maintained sector at that stage could be difficult for the child concerned after experience in a cathedral choir. It is perhaps a pity that closer links have still not been forged between state education and the cathedral tradition.

665.   The Children Act (1989) has already been mentioned. It applies particularly to boarding schools and the Social Services Department has automatic right of entry into them. The relevant document (The Children Act (1989): Guidance and Regulations, Volume 5, Independent Schools) is being distributed to all boarding schools. Further advice can be obtained from the Social Services Department. Where children leave school premises for their singing duties, it should be clear as to who assumes responsibility for them. At Worcester, for example, it has been agreed that the Dean and Chapter take responsibility once the choristers enter the cloisters.

Boys and Girls

666.   If, as the Commission affirms, singing as a cathedral chorister is a valuable educational experience, it is unjust to deny that experience to girls, as has been the case hitherto. It hopes that the examples set by

St. Mary's Cathedral, Edinburgh and by Salisbury Cathedral will be followed by others. Girls should be offered the same opportunities of musical training as boys in choir schools, and they should take part in the choral music of our cathedrals.

667.   There seems to be no agreement on whether the voices of boys and girls of the same age actually sound different or whether it depends upon the way they are trained. Even if there is a distinction, many would maintain that it does not matter, and point to the different sounds made by different boys' choirs. It is true, nevertheless, that the vocal development of boys and girls does not proceed equally. A boy's voice reaches its peak at about the age of thirteen, and a girl's voice normally two or three years later.

668.   A common reason for preferring a boys' choir is that for many people the sound of an unbroken voice symbolises a particular kind of innocence. A boy's voice is sometimes seen as especially precious because it is fragile and cannot last, any more than the snowdrops and crocuses of early spring.

669.   These are some of the factors in a reluctance to combine boys and girls in the same choir. There is also the question of gender-awareness. Boys of a near pubertal age commonly feel threatened and are easily embarrassed if they make mistakes or experience voice-breaking problems in the presence of girls. They may therefore be inhibited in their performance and difficult in their behaviour.

670.   Any choir combining boys and girls has to face the question as to when a girl would leave it, given that boys do so when their voices change. The loss of boys as they reach adolescence means that directors do not have their work with the younger children complicated by the lethargy and difficulties of the adolescent. But given that a girl's voice does not change in the same way, some criteria must be established. Younger boys and girls must not be prevented from entering the choir because all places are filled indefinitely. A further consideration is that the length of time a boy spends in a cathedral choir is generally dictated by his attendance at a preparatory school. If the same rule were applied to girls, they might perhaps have a less satisfactory experience of cathedral music, given the later flowering of their voices.

671.   These and other questions will have to be faced as cathedrals open their choirs to girls. But the Commission urges that this should be

widely considered. Girls should not be thought of as a substitute for boy choristers. The number of trebles must be maintained for reasons of tradition, proven excellence and the need for a supply of skilled tenors and basses. A high proportion of adult male singers in cathedral choirs are themselves former choristers. Opportunities for girls must therefore be provided in addition to those which exist for boys. As was said in a submission from the UK Council for Music Education and Training, 'the "gender bias" in church choirs should be resolved in a way consonant with the preservation of the established choral tradition'.

672.   Too many girls and women, however, have been lost to church music in the past because of lack of opportunity. This should be reversed, not simply to redress an inequality, but also because the addition of girls could bring a new dimension to music-making in cathedrals.

Costs

673.   The funds which would be required to provide choral scholarships for girls present an understandable deterrent, as they could only add to the already heavy, and constantly increasing, financial burden which faces cathedral Chapters. The Commission hopes that benefactors or other means may be found, not only to allow the inclusion of girls but also to make increased provision for their music. It acknowledges with appreciation the improvements that have been made in recent years. But the salaries of organists and their assistants, as well as what is paid to lay clerks and in choral scholarships, will have to be set at a more realistic level than has been true of the past. The Commission also notes with gratitude, and warmly commends, the very considerable help given to cathedrals by the Friends of Cathedral Music and the Department of Education and Science's chorister scheme.

The Cathedral's Mission through Music

674.   Expenditure on music benefits the cathedral itself and, less directly, the diocese and its parishes. It also provides the cathedral with something worthwhile to offer to the wider community. Every cathedral has a 'story' to tell. It may be a sharp, modern one like Coventry, or an heroic ancient one like Winchester, or a more unexceptional one like the majority of our cathedrals. Visitors come, in some cases in their thousands, and cathedrals seek to help them to become pilgrims by a ministry developed to meet their needs.

675.   Music can have an important role in this ministry. Those who come into our cathedrals solely for the music, either in services or concerts, are not to be despised. For casual visitors a special five- or ten-minute recital can sometimes be arranged, providing an extra performing opportunity for the choir. It offers a reminder of the worship for which the cathedral exists and stills the atmosphere into one of prayer. A video or audio recording telling the cathedral's story with a backing by the choir might be a good resource for visitors. Recordings of cathedral music are also very popular.

676.   Among the musical events which draw people to cathedrals in large numbers are performances of the orchestral Masses of Mozart, Haydn, Schubert and others. Offered as an act of worship in accompanying the liturgy, they make a powerful impact. A number of cathedrals already arrange such services and the Commission recommends that they form a regular part of every cathedral's programme.

677.   Worship, and the music within it, is first and foremost an offering to God by our cathedrals. It is also a means of evangelism in a way which is not true or possible within the ordinary congregational context. A different kind of person is reached by it and there are many who drop in to cathedrals for a whole host of reasons, including the desire for anonymity by those who are not comfortable within the more intimate context of a parish.

A Platform for Exploration

678.   Given the security of a regular pattern of worship, and the theological and musical resources of the staff, most cathedrals can afford to take some risks in offering a platform for experiments in liturgy, drama, art and music. Cathedrals which are involved in explorations of this kind know of the great demand for them and of the widespread interest they create. They are finding, however, that they are increasingly compelled to be selective in their response because of limited personnel and the tremendous wear and tear on their buildings.

679.   An agreed policy may be necessary to ensure that each event in some way displays the kingdom of God hidden in the folds of ordinary life, or advances the coming of the kingdom. It is tempting to book a famous orchestra, a prominent painter or an eminent playwright to generate a large audience, whether or not their particular contribution is appropriate for the setting. Sadly, many buildings have poor

acoustics and inadequate lighting. These can be a distraction to people who are used to high quality sound and vision in other places, and the beauty of the building does not always provide adequate compensation.

680.   Broadcasts on radio and television provide a wider platform. These are regularly offered to cathedrals, not least because of their professional approach and expertise in broadcasting. Most cathedrals welcome the large audiences which the media bring and they make the best of such opportunities in presenting services which are generally well-produced, if predictable. Again, the Commission would encourage some occasional experiments, with the co-operation of the producer. From time to time cathedrals should ask themselves whether they are using their platform in the most creative and imaginative way.

Laboratories for the Community

681.   Cathedrals have been described as laboratories. They enjoy a measure of independence from ecclesiastical structures. This allows them some freedom to experiment and to use their resources to build bridgeheads with society. For example, a cathedral might engage in a small prophetic employment project to point the way in an area of high unemployment. There is no reason why something comparable might not be set up for the artistic and musical life of a local community.

Conclusion

682.   Cathedrals have been called 'magical market-places'. They are part of our cultural heritage. Increasingly in recent years people have been coming to them, perhaps in search of that stillness and mystery which is at the heart of all things. It is, therefore, important to maintain all that is best in a cathedral's worship and to preserve its distinctive heritage of music. Its musical base might be broadened in order to meet more people on their journey, but there must be no diminution in the quality of its offering.

683.   The Commission considers that the careful preparation and meticulous 'production' of worship, far from working against the Holy Spirit, should take precedence over all else saving the worship itself. With their experience, cathedrals should set for all an example of the imaginative use of their resources and maintain the highest possible standards. They should not be slavishly imitated. But they may help

and encourage others to worship. The full meaning of a service or a piece of music does not always need to be totally clear to make an impact. Lives can be changed by something that is not fully understood. Worship is a sharp evangelistic instrument, as well as the offering of our best to God, and cathedrals excel in it.

RECOMMENDATIONS

That cathedrals, with their resources and a long tradition of church music, be expected to set an example of the highest possible standards of worship and music (636–639).

That cathedrals, in addition to maintaining the excellence of the cathedral tradition, be encouraged to explore and experiment in both liturgy and music, in commissioning music from contemporary composers, and in the use of instruments other than the organ (640–649).

That cathedral musicians take the initiative in forging links with deaneries and parishes for the purposes of mutual support and the musical enrichment of their worship (650–653).

That cathedral Chapters give careful thought to what they require of their organist, and consider whether, in any new appointment, a change of nomenclature is desirable, in order to indicate the importance of that person's role in the cathedral's life, as well as expertise in choir training, vocal technique and organ-playing (654–658).

That cathedrals give proper recognition to the contribution made by all their musicians, both in regarding them as an integral part of the cathedral staff and in finding the means for their remuneration at a realistic level (659–662, 673).

That those responsible for choir schools seek ways both of recruiting children from less wealthy backgrounds and of providing the same musical and liturgical education for girls as that enjoyed by boys (663–672).

That in addition to maintaining their rhythm of daily worship, cathedrals make the most of their opportunities for evangelism and mission within the wider community (674–681).

27

Resources and Instruments

684.   Although the primary musical resources of the Church are provided by people and their voices, some physical resources are essential. First, an organ or other instrument and printed music are required, and these are expensive items. According to replies to the Parish Survey questionnaire, the average urban church spends about £470 annually on its music, including its organist's salary, and those in rural areas spend on average £180. These sums represent respectively 2.3% and 1.7% of a parish's total expenditure. In many cases payment is made on an *ad hoc* basis, rather than forming part of an annual budget.

685.   In the Commission's view this level of expenditure by the Church on music in its worship is lamentably inadequate. It serves to confirm the impression that the Church of England gives church music a low priority. The Commission fully acknowledges the great financial difficulties which currently face parishes, but believes that the present situation relating to expenditure on music is the result of years of neglect. For too long we have traded on the goodwill of our church musicians. We have given them honoraria which began by being modest but which have not generally been increased even to match inflation. Choir members are sometimes prepared to pay for their own robes and music, and orchestral players provide their own instruments. But such generosity should never be taken for granted.

Budgeting
686.   An overnight cure for this problem may not be possible, given today's financial stringency, but parishes and dioceses should at least begin to work towards a solution. The first step is to ensure that in every parish the salaries of musicians and the costs of their music and instruments, together with insurance, has a place in the annual budget. It may not be possible to allocate very much money at the beginning, but at least the requirements of the church's music will be

drawn to the attention of the parish. It ought to be possible to allocate a larger amount for them as the parish's financial situation improves. Moreover, it makes it easier for those responsible for the music to plan expenditure when they are given a budget, and they can make the best use of the funds available.

The Organ, Pipe and Electronic

687.   A considerable outlay is required either for a modest pipe organ, with its long life-span but need for regular tuning and maintenance, or for a modern electronic instrument which demands little or no maintenance, but which may have a shorter life-span. Hard work and some imagination usually make it possible to raise the necessary funds. Various bodies may help, and the Council for the Care of Churches can offer advice on applying for grants. People are often more willing to contribute to the upkeep of their church's organ than to the maintenance of its fabric, although there will always be arguments about the rightness of spending money on a musical instrument to be used for a few hours a week, instead of meeting other needs.

688.   It is the view of the Commission that as part of our musical heritage, the organ has a claim on the Church with which it is particularly associated. It is also in tradition and in practice, peculiarly suited for music written for worship and there is no satisfactory substitute for it. It is most desirable, therefore, that our churches retain or replace their organs.

689.   The debate concerning the suitability of electronic instruments generates strong feelings. However, the Commission hopes that those facing the choice between pipe and electronic will not be persuaded by the common belief that bigger is better. A small, well-positioned pipe organ of good quality with perhaps no more than six ranks of pipes, can provide better musical results than a large electronic instrument with a dazzling variety of stops. The diocesan organ adviser should always be consulted at an early stage in the discussions held in the parish.

Other Instruments

690.   The provision of an organ does not preclude the use of other instruments, as they and their players become available. They offer a pleasing contrast to the organ and, where their pitch is compatible, splendid reinforcement and enhancement of it. Certain styles of music are better suited for a variety of instruments than for the organ and, for

reasons already given, a music group is an invaluable asset to the church.

691.   Portable instruments allow a good measure of flexibility in the placing of a band or music group, but they usually require a fair amount of space and their chairs, music stands, microphones, amplification equipment and electric cables can present a somewhat disordered appearance. Considerations of storage space for valuable and sensitive equipment should not be overlooked, especially if moveable platforms are also required. Adding to the already cluttered glory-holes in the tower, behind the organ or at the back of an aisle can create fire and safety hazards, and introduces the risk of damaging equipment.

Buildings

692.   Problems of storage and restricted space for musicians, and the siting of the organ, occur particularly in older churches. The vestry may be little larger than a walk-in cupboard; or nineteenth-century church restorers under the influence of the Oxford Movement may have cluttered the chancel; or buildings designed primarily for the preaching of the Word may still have galleries and pews to capacity. Sometimes a sensitive re-ordering can create some flexible space, although the Diocesan Advisory Committee must be consulted from the beginning about any plans for change. In its submission to the Commission, the Council for the Care of Churches suggests that churches contemplating the rearrangement of furnishings should consider the benefits of creating suitable space for eucharistic worship 'which would also be ideal for musical activities . . . plays, dance and so on'. Free-standing seating and free-standing mechanical action pipe organs are good in making for flexibility. The Council suggests that parish churches might advantageously develop 'their own style of music' and move away from 'traditional seating patterns'. Nevertheless, singers and musical instruments 'need to be closely related to the congregation, the organ and the liturgical action for acoustical and practical reasons'. There is also the need for all the musicians involved to be able to see each other.

693.   The Commission hopes that architects and others concerned with re-ordering, or with the design of new buildings, will take sympathetic account of the needs of musicians and their instruments, including sufficient space for the storage of equipment. This has not always been so in the past and many organs have been placed in positions which bottle up their sound and seem little more than an

obtrusive afterthought. Consideration should also be given to acoustics and sound enhancement systems, and here again advice may be sought from the Council for the Care of Churches.

Sound Reinforcement

694.   Careful thought needs to be taken when providing amplification in a church. The Commission warmly commends the installation of loop systems for the use of the deaf and hard-of-hearing, but there is often an unnecessary expenditure on sound reinforcement in quite small buildings. Most of us have become lazy listeners, due to the pervasiveness of electronic media, and many singers, speakers and players have become dependent upon the microphone. Some argue that sound enhancement obviates the necessity for people to raise their voices. They are able instead to address the congregation in a more intimate way, as if speaking to individuals. There may be a place for this, but it should not be forgotten that public worship is a corporate activity as well as an individual one.

695.   Certain instruments require amplification, but the sensitivity of modern equipment needs to be matched by the sensitivity of those who operate it. Clicks and crackles through loudspeakers set worshippers' nerves on edge and over-loud music can be enervating and distressing for congregations. It may be desirable for sound system operators to take part in rehearsals before some services.

Music on Tape

696.   A good sound system is certainly required, even in small churches, where pre-recorded music is used with any regularity. Both as a substitute for, and as a supplement to instruments and players, this can be effective when the sound is properly reproduced. It can provide a background to speech or set a mood, and can play pieces before, during or after services, or accompany congregational singing. If it is used to accompany hymns or other singing, it is important that the recording is appropriate for the local setting. Ideally, recordings of the instrument installed in the building itself might be made, and it is probably better to use recordings which do not include singers if the congregation is to feel fully involved. The use of pre-recorded music should always help and reinforce the singing of the congregation rather than replace it.

Visibility of Musicians

697.   Wherever possible, musicians should be seen as well as heard both by each other and by the congregation. This is so that the musicians can feel, and be perceived to be, fully part of those gathered for worship. In addition, the lead they give in the service should be visual as well as aural. This is helpful to congregational singing where there is a conductor, and to facilitate such minutiae as when to stand or sit. The eye may take in what the ear misses. Acoustics may dictate the decision, but worshippers generally prefer to see the musicians as well as hear them. Moreover, being in the public eye usually helps musicians to give of their best.

Robes or Uniform

698.   Where a choir has a prominent place, and especially if there is a formal procession for its entry and exit, there is a good case for some kind of uniform. The Parish Survey showed that 79% of choirs and music groups wear robes of some kind. Where they do not, the church may be unable to afford their cost, or may have decided that choir robes denote a wrong kind of separation from the rest of the congregation. The Commission makes no judgment, but notes that robes have the advantage of all uniforms. They create a sense of belonging; they help people wearing them to recognise that they are 'on duty'; they suppress individualism, rivalry and eccentricity in dress; and they present a neat, dignified and unified appearance to the congregation.

699.   Robes should not be too elaborate. They should be comfortable to wear and easy to keep clean. Although many churches have designed their own garments, perhaps to be consistent with the style of those worn by their servers and clergy, there is much to be said for the traditional cassock and surplice. Matching tops and skirts or trousers can be an economical and appropriate uniform. Certainly the cost of providing robes should be seen in relation to the financial priorities of the music budget and of the church. For example, it probably ought not to exceed the money allocated to the purchase of music.

The Music Library

700.   All published music, whether in sheet or book form, is very costly. For that reason alone it needs to be carefully handled and properly stored. The use of binders and folders helps to prolong its life, and any markings should only be made in pencil, so that they can be erased. A proper library and catalogue, as well as convenient cup-

boards for storage, helps to preserve an expensive asset and to build up a comprehensive library. It is tempting to throw away music of a past era, usually in order to create more space. But it should not be done too hastily. That music of yesterday which is spurned today may be tomorrow's exciting rediscovery. Many choirs have a librarian who is responsible for the custody and repair of the music. This should also apply to the organist's music – the litter around many a console speaks eloquently of the lack of facilities for proper storage in that church.

Copying and Copyright

701.   One of the problems posed by the amount of music being published today is that both musicians and congregation are often required to have more than one book. Sometimes a whole clutch of papers and books is needed. Alternatives are either to keep to one published book, or for the church to compile and print its own book, or for a special service sheet to be produced as necessary.

702.   The copying of published works, whether in a church's own collection or for an *ad hoc* occasion, raises questions of copyright. The law as it stands at present has already been described in this Report and the Commission believes that its provisions must be observed. The Church should be scrupulous in the matter, in order to give proper acknowledgment of its debt to composers and publishers.

703.   However, there are likely to be continuing difficulties. If these are to be avoided, the present laws on copyright need to be simplified or relaxed, and the licence at present sponsored by Christian Copyright Licensing Ltd. (formerly the Christian Music Association) needs to be broadened into a fully comprehensive licensing scheme for the texts and tunes of hymns as well as songs. The Commission urges support for the Pratt Green Trust and other organisations which are working to ensure that composers, writers and publishers are properly remunerated and that their texts and music are readily available for use in worship. It also commends the possibility of establishing one or more centres providing a sheet music loan service.

Overhead Projection

704.   Copyright is often breached out of ignorance. Nowhere does this happen more than in the increasingly common practice of projecting words, with or without music, on to a screen. This has obvious benefits, including that of raising people's eyes and mouths from their

books, so that the quality of their singing is improved. It can also contribute to a sense of unity in the congregation through offering a common visual focus. But not many churches are designed in such a way as to make a projected display possible without its being visually or liturgically intrusive. Convenient or not, it remains illegal without the necessary licence or written permission from the publisher.

Orchestral Arrangements of Music

705.   A piece of equipment perhaps more essential to the church musician than an overhead projector is a photocopier. Even though copyright material may not be reproduced without permission, anyone writing new music or arranging music for instrumental or vocal parts needs to have access to a good machine if the work is to be done efficiently.

706.   Few orchestrations of hymns and worship songs are as yet available, but Boosey and Hawkes, the Oxford University Press and the Royal School of Church Music publish some of the more traditional hymnody and pieces. More contemporary music is obtainable from the Music in Worship Foundation, the Jubilate Group, and Langham Arts (All Souls), who also offer some orchestrations of traditional hymnody. All publishers are urged to take note of the growing need for orchestrations for use in church.

Conclusion

707.   In financial terms, church musicians are generally under-funded, particularly by comparison with much else that appears on the parish budget. Given that they contribute so significantly to the worship which is the mainspring of the Church's life, their requirements are modest indeed. It is not a case of asking for luxuries nor of the bad workman who is said to blame his tools. Even a good musician cannot obtain the best results without the right kind of auxiliary resources, and a church which values its music will not begrudge their provision.

RECOMMENDATIONS

That parishes make provision in their budget for the costs of their music (684–686).

That parishes continue to maintain an organ, and that they seek advice, when that is necessary, from the diocesan organ adviser, who needs to have a thorough grasp of the technical and artistic aspects of both pipe and electronic organ design and construction (687–689).

That parishes use instruments in addition to the organ and, if helpful, pre-recorded music in church services (690, 696).

That those responsible for the construction or re-ordering of church buildings take full account of the needs of musicians and their instruments, and liaise closely from the beginning with the Diocesan Advisory Committee (691–693, 697).

That parishes avoid unnecessary extravagance on such items as sound enhancement systems and choir robes, and recognise the importance of the proper care and storage of their music and equipment (694–695, 698–700).

That the Church at all levels should be scrupulous in its observance of the laws of copyright, whilst fully supporting those who work for their simplification, as well as those who seek to make copyright material more easily accessible for reproduction (701–704).

That publishers of church music recognise the growing demand for instrumental arrangements of hymns and other music (705–706).

28

Support and Structures

708.   The work of the Commission has been wide-ranging and, in some respects, disparate. Those who seek to develop a vision and implement changes in their use of music in worship, in addition to creating and maintaining high standards may welcome help and advice to achieve these ends. The Commission therefore ends this part of its Report with some practical proposals addressed to the Church of England at national, diocesan and local levels.

Worship, Liturgy, Music and Buildings

709.   The Commission's proposals stem from its conviction that worship is the Church's priority. It believes that if it is to be offered worthily, there needs to be a greater commitment to it and an improvement in its quality. This in turn requires a new coherence whereby liturgists, musicians and architects bring their insights together. The Commission recognises the freedom, variety and individuality of churches in the ordering of their services, but is of the opinion that all public worship everywhere requires a proper relationship between the liturgy, the music and the building.

710.   The importance of this relationship has long been recognised by the Roman Catholic Church in England and Wales, and there is a department of the Bishops' Conference which is concerned with the ordering of worship. It embraces three committees, each with its own particular expertise. There is one which is responsible for pastoral rites, which includes the texts and the carrying out of liturgical celebrations; there is one for music; and there is one for art and architecture with an interest in liturgical buildings, their furnishings and artistic embellishments. A good deal of the work of these three groups is quite distinct and separate, but the structure allows for a proper relationship between them and for some overlap of both work and membership.

711.   The situation in the Church of England is rather different. Some provision is made for support in the three areas of liturgy, music and buildings, but the bodies responsible have no official relationship to each other. Moreover, in the case of music, there is no organisation officially recognised by the Church of England.

712.   The Liturgical Commission is appointed by the Archbishops and the Standing Committee of the General Synod and is mainly concerned with liturgical texts. In recent years its work has expanded to exercise considerable influence in the whole area of liturgical education and formation. This is chiefly through the individual work of its members around the country. The Commission has no full-time paid adviser or director. Its secretary is shared with other boards and committees of the Synod, with an office in Church House, Westminster. There is no Centre for Pastoral Liturgy in the Church of England, comparable to the Irish Institute of Pastoral Liturgy at Carlow.

713.   The world of church music is represented in the Liturgical Commission only when a consultant is appointed on an *ad hoc* basis, as in the past. The constitution makes no provision for a church musician to be included in the membership, and such consultation as is undertaken is somewhat arbitrary and is based upon personal relationships. Recently, however, church musicians and composers have been invited to take part at an early stage in the process of producing liturgical texts.

714.   The Council for the Care of Churches (CCC) is the body which most naturally deals with architectural questions as they affect the liturgy. There is already some co-operation between those involved in this work and those in the liturgical world. Although it too is a subordinate body of the General Synod, the CCC has a very different kind of constitution and role from that of the Liturgical Commission, and works from a different building. The relationship between the two is, therefore, fairly tenuous.

715.   A combination of the work of these two statutory bodies would be enormously valuable for the whole area of liturgical education and formation. But there would still be a gap, because of a lack of formal involvement by church musicians. In addition, there is at present neither a full-time person working in the field of worship nor a centre to which people could come in order to learn. It might be the musicians who could help in meeting these two needs.

716.   There is no statutory body for church music, equivalent to those for liturgy and buildings. Everything in this area relies at present upon the unofficial provision of a number of organisations devoted to various aspects of music in worship. Without in any way denigrating the value and work of any of them, it is usual to regard the Royal Society of Church Music as being pre-eminent. The combination of its constitution, history, work, resources and publications and the high reputation it has achieved in many circles gives it a semi-official status in the Church. Being one of several organisations concerned with church music, its effectiveness has been limited, and its focus confined mainly to traditional church music. However, the broadening of its formerly conservative approach to church music will have done much to dispel suspicion of it in those circles where traditional music has given way to new forms.

A Recognised Body for Church Music

717.   There seems good reason to suggest that the RSCM should be recognised as the Church's body for church music. There would need to be the assurance that in addition to promoting traditional church music, it would continue to widen its range of activities. It would be required to embrace the emphasis in many churches on instrumental music of various kinds, with loosely-defined music groups as well as robed choirs, and a variety of contemporary styles of church music. Only so would it be right to give this organisation a special place in the structures of the Church and to single it out for a relationship not accorded to other musical bodies.

718.   A change in the constitution of the RSCM, and in the method of making new appointments within its organisation, would also be required. Without creating any threat to the essential independence of the RSCM, some relationship to the General Synod would be necessary. Thus, that body might have the right to nominate some members of the Council, which is the RSCM's governing body, and Synod would thereby have at least some part in the appointment of RSCM staff.

719.   Given that these conditions could be met, the Commission would like to propose that the RSCM be given formal recognition by the Church of England. It would be the third party, with the Liturgical Commission and the CCC, for the establishment of working relationships between those with a special concern for public worship. The Commission does not recommend particular amalgamations, or the winding up, of any of the other church music organisations. It foresees

that, with a broader RSCM as part of the Church's official structure, some rationalisation and a reduction in the number of organisations whose common purpose is the promotion of good church music could follow in due course.

Working Together for Worship

720.   A case could be made for a structure based on the Roman Catholic model, where liturgical rites, musical needs and issues of architecture and art are brought together within one organisation. This might, however, weaken the increasingly effective work of the Liturgical Commission, the CCC, and the RSCM. It would also require major new resources which are not likely to be available to the Church in a time of financial stringency. Instead, the Commission proposes a small liaison group, to be called the Consultative Council for Worship (CCW).

721.   This Council would have a concern for the whole area of worship in the Church of England and would consist of three members each from the Liturgical Commission, the RSCM and the CCC, with a diocesan bishop, appointed by the House of Bishops, as chairman. It might also have a secretary from Church House. The expenses of its members would be paid by the constituent bodies and there would be no need for additional funding for the Consultative Council for Worship by the General Synod.

722.   The CCW would ensure a close relationship between three areas of concern which at present relate through the unofficial liaison of a few overworked people who happen to have a foot in more than one camp. In particular, the CCW would have responsibility for the work of teaching and presentation, which is where the three areas most need to be brought together.

723.   In the longer term, the Consultative Council for Worship could take the foremost role in the Church's strategy for worship, with initiative passing to it from its three constituent bodies. However, this is not the Commission's present proposal and any greater responsibility should evolve rather than be imposed. For the present, the education of the Church is a priority if its worship and music are to attain a consistently high standard. In order to ensure speedy progress in this crucial area, the CCW should be brought into being as soon as possible.

A Liturgy Centre

724.   One of the resources missing in recent years has been a centre of pastoral liturgy in the Church of England. Without it, liturgists and liturgical reform have lacked the means to help the Church make the best use of new rites. It could be that the implementation of the Commission's recommendations relating to the CCW might create the right conditions for such a centre. Of the three bodies proposed, only the RSCM has at present adequate teaching and training facilities, but it has lacked organised input from those concerned with liturgy and architecture. If a trained liturgist were to be appointed to the head-quarters staff of the RSCM, there could be the gradual development, from small beginnings and under the same roof, of a pastoral centre. This would also prove a great enrichment of the wider Church, for the RSCM is an ecumenical body and therefore this facility would also be available to other churches. It might be welcomed particularly by the Roman Catholic Church, which has experienced problems similar to those of the Church of England in providing resources for this kind of work.

725.   The Commission is aware that the funding of such a project might not be possible for the RSCM or for the General Synod. However, it hopes that the need for a full-time liturgy adviser will be seen to be sufficiently great for finance to be found from some source, to make such an appointment possible.

The Ecumenical Factor

726.   The RSCM is an ecumenical organisation, and for more than twenty years it has taken steps to encourage the participation and membership of other churches. In making its proposal that the RSCM should have a particular place in the life of the Church of England, the Commission does not believe that this is likely to create any significant tension. Indeed, it could prove to be a fruitful area of co-operation between denominations. Further advantages would accrue from and for the different churches which constitute the overseas membership of the RSCM.

727.   The Commission welcomes the recent ecumenical develop-ment in the formation of the Churches' Initiative for Music Education (CHIME), already mentioned in this Report. This in no way detracts from the need for an Anglican organisation. CHIME would have the

same kind of relationship to the RSCM as the ecumenical Joint Liturgical Group has to the Liturgical Commission.

Dioceses and their Committees

728.   At diocesan level the Commission suggests a structure similar to the one proposed for the Church of England as a whole. In the diocese, the one statutory body is the Diocesan Advisory Committee, with a concern for church buildings and their furnishings and decoration.

729.   Each diocese is obliged to have a committee for its buildings, but this is not true in the areas of liturgy and music. Until recently the existence of a Diocesan Liturgical Committee depended on the whim of the bishop. Now almost every diocese has some group with a clear teaching and training role, following a major initiative by the Liturgical Commission in the late 1980s. The constitution of these committees differs from diocese to diocese, but there is usually some recognition of the need for close liaison with the Diocesan Advisory Committee. This is often provided by some overlap of membership.

Diocesan Music Committees

730.   There is much greater variation in the provision made by dioceses for the encouragement of church music. Like liturgical committees, Diocesan Music Committees are not legally required, but all dioceses have one in some form. Most of them are served by an area RSCM Committee. This, in spite of its description for ecumenical purposes, generally coincides with the area of a diocese. Its officers are appointed directly by the Director of the RSCM, after local consultation which is not necessarily with the bishop or other church leaders.

731.   Six dioceses have their own Diocesan Music Committee, one of the most interesting of which is that in the Diocese of Rochester, where a Diocesan Committee and the RSCM area committee have been brought together with a careful constitution and clear guidelines, resulting in a broad and creative brief. In contrast, most Diocesan Music Committees have no terms of reference and their activities do not extend much beyond holding choral festivals. A specimen constitution, based on the Rochester scheme, is set out in Appendix 3.5.

732.   In considering how best to provide for a body officially responsible for music in a diocese, it may be better to modify what already exists rather than create a new body. In some cases few changes would

be necessary. In others, some careful restructuring may be required in order to bring the constitution of the music committee more into line with those of the Diocesan Advisory Committee and the Diocesan Liturgical Committee. Where an RSCM committee is involved, the question of how its members are appointed would need to be resolved if it is to be given new work and a status relating to diocesan structures.

733.   Part of the purpose of any restructuring would be to ensure a close relationship with the other bodies, with a possible overlap of membership. For example, the diocesan organ adviser belongs to the Diocesan Advisory Committee, but any relationship to the other two bodies would need to be carefully considered. In some dioceses the cathedral and its musicians are not represented on the music committee, whilst in others the committee is dominated by the cathedral and its approach to music. It is clear that cathedral musicians have a vital role to play in the life of a diocese, and membership of a music committee is one excellent way in which they could fulfil it. It is to be hoped that they would take an active part in a body with a broad base and wide sympathies. The relationship between cathedral and diocese is at its most vital in the area of liturgy, and of its music in particular.

Diocesan Consultative Council for Worship

734.   The existence of three diocesan bodies responsible for liturgy, music and buildings will require a small liaison group. This would be along the lines of the Consultative Council for Worship already described. The Commission therefore suggests the creation of a Diocesan Consultative Council for Worship (DCCW). It would coordinate the work of the three committees and ensure the provision at local level of good teaching and adequate training in liturgical skills, including music.

A Diocesan Music Adviser

735.   Were more resources available, the Commission would be proposing a diocesan liturgical adviser as the local equivalent of the proposed appointment to the RSCM headquarters staff. However, more urgently recommended is the appointment of diocesan music advisers. Their task would be to help local churches to review and improve their music and to broaden their repertoire. They might assist with the recruitment and training of musicians and give advice on resources and music available. They would also provide a consultation service, aimed as much at clergy as at musicians. They would visit

parishes and deaneries as invited, and would be essentially peripatetic in much the same way as the RSCM's Regional Commissioners.

736.   Diocesan music advisers might also be given a particular brief for small congregations. To this end they could arrange deanery or archdeaconry days for parish representatives to meet and be given help and encouragement with ideas and resources. Among the topics for these might be the use of pre-recorded accompaniments and sound systems, how to lead unaccompanied singing, the choice of service settings, ways of singing or saying the Psalms and advice on cheaper instruments. Help could also be given to 'reluctant organists'.

737.   People undertaking work such as this would need to have wide musical experience and to be gifted teachers. But there is no reason to doubt the availability of suitable candidates if the funding can be provided. The Commission has no illusions about the difficulty of finding the finance for such appointments and it is probably unrealistic to think that any diocese is in a position to do so *in toto*. However, there are various possibilities which ought to be considered.

738.   The first is that a number of dioceses might combine to fund such a person, or that different denominations might contribute to the cost of an ecumenical appointment. Alternatively, the RSCM might increase the number of its Regional Commissioners, aided by financial help from dioceses and churches. A network of perhaps ten Commissioners, instead of the present three, could be created across the country, each with responsibility for four or five RSCM areas (or dioceses). A modest amount in the budget of the dioceses involved would make this feasible.

739.   Another possibility would be to make use of newly-retired people with musical experience and skills, working on perhaps a five-year contract. Rather than pay a salary, the diocese would offer a generous honorarium, as well as full expenses, to someone who might be glad to serve the Church in this way on a part-time basis. Many dioceses could probably find a music adviser of this kind, but it might be difficult to ensure a good appointment in every place.

740.   A possible diocesan role for cathedral musicians has already been mentioned in this Report. A few dioceses have a music adviser who is employed by the cathedral, with or without some financial help from the diocesan budget. This is another model which might be

explored and has the benefit of relating parishes to the cathedral. Work in the diocese is likely to be more possible for the assistant organist, or even a lay clerk, than for the director of music.

741. Many schools employ music teachers on a part-time basis and it might be possible to create a post which is part school-based and part church-based. Given the Commission's conviction of the vital importance of music education in schools for providing a solid basis for church musicians, such an appointment could be of enormous benefit. An additional advantage could be the part-finance which might be obtained, if not from the Local Education Authority then from the many educational trusts which exist.

Diocesan Action

742. The Commission hopes that dioceses will look at these options as practical possibilities for the future. It urges them to take steps as soon as possible to set up or to regularise their music committee, in order to consider ways and means of appointing a diocesan music adviser as its first task. At the same time, the existence of the diocesan liturgical committee may need to be formalised. Thereafter, the DCCW would be established.

743. An important educational opportunity for liturgical formation is, indirectly, provided by special diocesan services. These provide an ideal context for local congregations to experience liturgy of the first order and the DCCW should have a part in their planning. In this way diocesan, archdeaconry, deanery and perhaps ecumenical services may succeed in illustrating good practice, in addition to fulfilling the purposes for which they are arranged.

At Parish Level

744. New and creative structures for liturgy and music at national and diocesan level will be of limited value unless parishes are motivated and equipped to benefit from fresh initiatives. The Commission has already recommended the creation of a worship committee or group in those parishes where there is none. This would be the appropriate body to assist the incumbent and Parochial Church Council (PCC) in all matters concerning the liturgy, the music and the building as they relate to the worship of the parish. It would also have links with the DCCW. Where there is no worship committee, the PCC would take a more direct interest in matters concerning worship,

subject again to the incumbent's rights and responsibilities in this area. However, the tradition that an organist who is an employee should not be a member of the PCC is an unhelpful one. It is essential for the church's musical director either to be co-opted or to be present during any meetings in which the services and their music are discussed.

745.   Throughout this Report, the Commission has been well aware of the limitations of finance. It has therefore avoided making recommendations which require a huge injection of money by the General Synod or other central body. There are some proposals which need a process of consultation, however, leading to their implementation. The Commission asks therefore that the Archbishops set up a small working party as soon as possible in order to implement the structural proposals which are outlined in this chapter.

746.   This request is made in the belief that at both national and diocesan level a new approach is needed to establish a truly creative and fruitful relationship between the different areas of liturgical interest, including music. There are people with the time and skills available. They are needed to teach and to train the Church to use its worship more effectively for the glory of God, the good of his people and the extension of his kingdom here on earth.

RECOMMENDATIONS

That, in recognition of the primary place of worship in the life of the Church, the Archbishops be asked to appoint as soon as possible a small working party to implement the recommendations which follow (708–709, 745–746).

That a Consultative Council for Worship be established for the Church of England (710–715, 720–723).

That the Royal School of Church Music be recognised as the Church of England's official body for church music, on the understanding that it continue to broaden its approach to church music and that it be related in some way to the General Synod (716–719).

That means be found for the appointment of a full-time national liturgy adviser and the establishment of an ecumenical liturgy centre (724–727).

That dioceses modify or set up, as appropriate, a Diocesan Liturgical Committee and a Diocesan Music Committee and establish a Diocesan Consultative Council for Worship (728–734, 742–743).

That dioceses appoint a diocesan music adviser to parishes (735–741).

That parishes ensure the involvement of their organist or director of music in all discussions by the Parochial Church Council relating to their church's worship (744).

PART 6

CONCLUSION AND
RECOMMENDATIONS

29

Conclusion

747. Although this Report has pointed to the generally unsatisfactory state of music in our churches, the Commission would not wish to end on a note of pessimism. The fact that the subject of music in worship arouses widespread interest and evokes a strong response in many people is enough to suggest that it is still very much an important issue.

748. In those places where music is taken seriously the standards of performance are much improved, and a musically literate public demands, and often receives, the very best. There is also an impressive development of instrumental groups and a growth of new writing in less traditional musical idioms. Even where this is not of the highest quality, it indicates considerable activity, and points to possibilities for the recovery of the proper place of music in the Church's services.

749. The significant commitment to music by many cathedrals and other foundations and by countless church organists and choirs all over the land is a source of much encouragement. They faithfully and unostentatiously make their musical offering week by week, and many of them carry on against heavy odds without complaint. Their dedication also offers hope for the future.

750. Some church musicians, and the clergy and congregations to which they belong, may feel that many of the suggestions made in this Report are not for them. The Commission's description of a director of music may seem laughably idealistic to a parish which can barely find a 'reluctant organist'; some of the resources here described as necessary are likely to be dismissed as wholly unrealistic by a church with a handful of worshippers struggling to meet its diocesan quota, as well as to repair its roof.

751. The Commission has been conscious throughout its work of the reality of the problems facing many parishes, especially those in Urban Priority Areas and in rural situations. However, it has seemed right to

aim high and describe the ideal rather than settle for something less than the best, even if it is more immediately attainable. To have done so might have suggested acquiescence in the present situation, instead of a desire to help the Church into new directions and towards a better future for its music. The Commission's recommendations for new structures and specialist personnel are made in the belief that these will enable parishes and dioceses to implement, in due course, other recommendations in this Report, without necessarily incurring huge expenditure.

752.   Clearly, the director of music is a key person, not least for the recruitment and employment of people in choirs and music groups. It is encouraging to see an increasing recognition in many places of the director as part of a church's ministerial team. Musicians and clergy are professional people and so expect recognition for their skills, as well as personal respect. The Commission has therefore placed some emphasis upon the need for proper training and has stressed the importance of a healthy personal relationship between the incumbent and the organist in strengthening their working partnership.

753.   Their relationship to the congregation is also significant. This Report has underlined the importance of congregational singing and has noted that the variety of people in most churches demands a variety of music to meet their needs in worship. There should be a willingness to explore and to experiment, with the full co-operation of the congregation.

754.   When the value of music for the fostering and deepening of Christian unity is recognised, the widening of the repertoire assumes a greater importance. The Commission has appreciated the insights brought by two of its members from other traditions and gladly acknowledges the need for all denominations to share their riches with each other.

755.   Music also has an evangelistic dimension. Its drawing power should not be underrated and a parish with a lively musical tradition is more likely to grow in membership than one where the musical contribution to worship is insignificant. A strong musical element can greatly enhance services and add to their effect in motivating people for mission.

756.   We return, however, to the points made early in this Report

Conclusion

which run as a thread right through it: that music in worship is employed for God, and that worship is the most vital of all the activities of the Church and of the individual. Without worship our music in church is largely irrelevant. But with it, our singing and playing can become something beautiful for God and a blessing for all who are present.

30

Recommendations

The bracketed reference after each recommendation is to the paragraph or paragraphs in the Report.

TO THE CHURCH AT ALL LEVELS

1. That clergy, musicians and congregations alike give fresh consideration to the place and value of music in the services of the Church (494–499, 501–502, 511).

2. That clergy and musicians recognise the value of music as an ingredient in evangelism, both in worship and outside it, and take opportunities afforded by the media (505–510).

3. That the potential of music for fostering ecumenical relationships be utilised to the full by the Church at all levels (503–504).

4. That the Church at all levels should be scrupulous in its observance of the laws of copyright, whilst fully supporting those who work for their simplification, as well as those who seek to make copyright material more easily accessible for reproduction (701–704).

IN PARISHES

To Clergy, Musicians and others Responsible for Planning and Leading Worship

5. That clergy and musicians do all in their power to ensure close and amicable working relationships (557–559, 562).

6. That those responsible for the choice of music in our churches take account of the varying tastes and preferences of their congregations, and set up a system for congregational feedback (526–527).

Recommendations

7. That congregations be given ample opportunity to sing in services, even where they have to be unaccompanied (528–529, 540).

8. That congregations be encouraged to support all endeavours to improve the musical offering of their church, and to appreciate the need for the best which is attainable (632–634).

9. That congregations be helped to explore and experiment with new music (550–554).

10. That choirs and music groups be given opportunities in church services to sing and play on their own (603–604).

11. That congregations be taught to regard solo anthems, songs, and organ and other instrumental pieces, as integral parts of a service (542–545).

12. That congregations be taught to use opportunities of silence and the value of listening, and that those responsible for planning services ensure a proper balance between the spoken and the sung (517–521).

13. That those responsible for the choice of hymns and worship songs be guided by the quality of their doctrinal content, language and musical idiom, and that both the new and the old be included in the repertoire (530–533, 538–539, 541).

14. That clergy and musicians be prepared to plan and lead worship imaginatively, to blend different styles, and to allow themselves to be guided both by the needs of the congregation and by sound liturgical principles in devising church services (514–516, 522–523).

15. That clergy and musicians ensure the continuing place of psalmody in Anglican worship, whether it be sung or said (535–537).

16. That those responsible for planning and leading worship make as thorough a preparation for each service as is possible, including the preparation of prayer (500).

To Clergy

17.   That, where it is appropriate, clergy seek out and train others for the leading of worship (560–561, 573–575).

18.   That organists or directors of music be fully supported by clergy and parishes in their efforts to recruit people for choirs and music groups (586–588).

19.   That clergy, in particular, recognise the value of choirs and music groups for evangelism and nurturing in the Christian faith, and ensure that children participating in them receive spiritual and pastoral care (589–590).

To Organists or Directors of Music

20.   That children and young people, particularly those who are instrumentalists, be welcomed and encouraged to contribute to music in worship (606–609).

21.   That organists or directors of music work to recruit both boys and girls for their choir, and that both sexes be given equal opportunities and encouragement (594–597).

22.   That parishes seek to co-operate closely with local schools, partly for the recruitment of children for music in church and partly for mutual support in the music education of children (605, 615–618).

23.   That organists or directors of music give consideration to the formation of a music group, where there is none, and ensure its close working relationship with any existing choir (591–593).

24.   That parishes use instruments in addition to the organ and, if helpful, pre-recorded music in church services (690, 696).

25.   That parishes give consideration to forming links with musicians in local educational institutions (602).

26.   That parishes find ways of encouraging composers to write music for their particular needs and resources (546–548).

Recommendations

To Parochial Church Councils

27. That parishes aim to have an organist or director of music with Christian commitment, together with personal and leadership skills, as well as musical ability (570–572, 576–578).

28. That parishes ensure the involvement of their organist or director of music in all discussions by the Parochial Church Council relating to their church's worship (744).

29. That parishes set up a worship committee, where there is none, in order to advise the incumbent and Parochial Church Council, and to support their organist or director of music (555–556, 579–580).

30. That parishes work towards a realistic level of remuneration for their organist or director of music and make provision for their continuing training (581–584).

31. That parishes enable musicians who are unfamiliar with the selection and use of music in contemporary styles to take advantage of any appropriate workshops (629–631).

32. That parishes provide melody line editions of hymn and song books for their congregation (534).

33. That parishes continue to maintain an organ, and that they seek advice, when that is necessary, from the diocesan organ adviser, who needs to have a thorough grasp of the technical and artistic aspects of both pipe and electronic organ design and construction (687–689).

34. That parishes avoid unnecessary extravagance on such items as sound enhancement systems and choir robes, and recognise the importance of the proper care and storage of their music and equipment (694–695, 698–700).

35. That parishes make provision in their budget for the costs of their music (684–686).

IN CATHEDRALS

To Chapters and Foundations

36. That cathedrals, with their resources and a long tradition of church music, be expected to set an example of the highest possible standards of worship and music (636–639).

37. That in addition to maintaining their rhythm of daily worship, cathedrals make the most of their opportunities for evangelism and mission within the wider community (674–681).

38. That cathedrals give proper recognition to the contribution made by all their musicians, both in regarding them as an integral part of the cathedral staff and in finding the means for their remuneration at a realistic level (659–662, 673).

39. That cathedral Chapters give careful thought to what they require of their organist, and consider whether, in any new appointment, a change of nomenclature is desirable, in order to indicate the importance of that person's role in the cathedral's life, as well as expertise in choir training, vocal technique and organ-playing (654–658).

40. That those responsible for choir schools seek ways both of recruiting children from less wealthy backgrounds and of providing the same musical and liturgical education for girls as that enjoyed by boys (663–672).

To Organists and Directors of Music

41. That cathedrals, in addition to maintaining the excellence of the cathedral tradition, be encouraged to explore and experiment in both liturgy and music, in commissioning music from contemporary composers, and in the use of instruments other than the organ (640–649).

42. That cathedral musicians take the initiative in forging links with deaneries and parishes for the purposes of mutual support and the musical enrichment of their worship (650–653).

Recommendations

IN DIOCESES AND PARISHES

43. That dioceses modify or set up, as appropriate, a Diocesan Liturgical Committee and a Diocesan Music Committee and establish a Diocesan Consultative Council for Worship (728–734, 742–743).

44. That dioceses appoint a diocesan music adviser to parishes (735–741).

45. That dioceses and parishes give immediate attention to setting up schemes to encourage people to learn the organ, and make their instruments available for practice (598–601).

46. That dioceses and parishes consider the provision of local in-service training courses for church musicians (628).

MISCELLANEOUS

To the Archbishops of Canterbury and York

47. That, in recognition of the primary place of worship in the life of the Church, the Archbishops be asked to appoint as soon as possible a small working party to implement the recommendations which follow (708–709, 745–746).

48. That the Royal School of Church Music be recognised as the Church of England's official body for church music, on the understanding that it continue to broaden its approach to church music and that it be related in some way to the General Synod (716–719).

49. That a Consultative Council for Worship be established for the Church of England (710–715, 720–723).

50. That means be found for the appointment of a full-time national liturgy adviser and the establishment of an ecumenical liturgy centre (724–727).

To Those Providing Theological Training

51. That theological colleges and courses, as well as those responsible for post-ordination training and continuing ministerial training, review their provision for the training of ordinands and clergy in

257

the art of preparing for and conducting public worship, and the use of music within it (563–569).

To Church Architects and Diocesan Advisory Committees

52. That those responsible for the construction or re-ordering of church buildings take full account of the needs of musicians and their instruments, and liaise closely from the beginning with the Diocesan Advisory Committee (691–693, 697).

To the Churches' Council for Health and Healing

53. That the therapeutic use of music in the Church's ministry of healing be further investigated, perhaps under the auspices of the Churches' Council for Health and Healing (512–513).

To the Churches' Initiative for Music Education

54. That a scheme for training church musicians be devised, suitable for students before and during employment, and for both professionals and amateurs, and that the Churches' Initiative for Music Education give consideration to this (619–627).

To Schools

55. That schools be encouraged both to maintain their choral tradition and to liaise with local church musicians, in order to agree on a common repertoire of hymns and songs (610–614).

To Church Music Publishers

56. That publishers of church music recognise the growing demand for instrumental arrangements of hymns and other music (705–706).

APPENDICES

1

The Commission

1.1   Terms of Reference

To consider the place of music in the Church's worship and life; to survey the present situation with regard to music and musicians in the Churches both in Britain and world-wide; and to make recommendations.

An appended note reads:
[Some of the areas] in which it may give guidance include: the use of music in the worship of parish churches and cathedrals, music for modern liturgies (the Eucharist, family services, charismatic renewal), music for choir and congregations, the use of organs and other instruments, the recruitment and training of musicians, the training of clergy and education of the Church, new church music and its composers and the use of the media.

1.2   Membership

The Rt. Revd. Timothy Bavin, OGS (Chairman)   Bishop of Portsmouth

Mr. Harry Bramma   Director of the Royal School of Church Music; Honorary Treasurer of the Royal College of Organists; Organist of All Saints' Church, Margaret Street, London

Dr. Lionel Dakers, CBE — Formerly Director of the Royal School of Church Music

The Revd. Canon John Davies — Director of Theological and Religious Studies, University of Southampton; Honorary curate of St. Alban's, Swaythling, Southampton

Mr. Philip Duffy — Master of the Music, Liverpool Metropolitan Cathedral; nominee of the Roman Catholic Church

Mrs. Susan Page — Teacher of Drama and Communication Skills; Reader in country parishes; member of General Synod

The Revd. Michael Perham — Rector of the Oakdale Team Ministry, Poole; member of the Liturgical Commission; member of the Council for the Care of Churches

Mr. Patrick Salisbury (Secretary) — Organist of All Saints' Church, Sutton Courtenay; formerly HM Staff Inspector for Music, DES

The Very Revd. Canon Colin Semper — Canon of Westminster; former Provost of Coventry; formerly Head of Religious Programmes, BBC radio

Mr. Richard Shephard — Headmaster of the Minster School, York

The Revd. Jane Sinclair — Lecturer in Worship and Pastoral Studies, St. John's College, Nottingham; member of the Liturgical Commission

Mr. Noël H. Tredinnick	Organist and Director of Music, All Souls Church, Langham Place, London; Professor of the Guildhall School of Music and Drama; freelance conductor and musical arranger
Professor Richard Watson	Professor of English, University of Durham; nominee of the Free Church Federal Council
Mrs. Jacquie Webb	Director of Music, St. Andrew's Church, Chorleywood
Dr. Allan Wicks, CBE	Formerly Organist of Canterbury Cathedral
Virginia Vincent Jennifer Robinson Jean Maslin }	Secretariat

1.3 Dates and Places of Meetings

1. 12–13 July 1988   St. Columba's House, Woking

2. 5 September 1988   The Church Commissioners, London

3. 9–10 January 1989   The Royal School of Church Music, Addington Palace, Croydon

4. 7 April 1989   The Church Commissioners, London

5. 5–6 July 1989   Church House, Ogleforth, York

6. 2 November 1989   Jerusalem Chamber, Westminster Abbey, London

7. 4–5 January 1990   The Royal School of Church Music, Addington Palace, Croydon

8. 3 May 1990   Jerusalem Chamber, Westminster Abbey, London

9.   11–13 July 1990   The Minster School, York

10. 31 October 1990   The Faculty Office of the Archbishop of
                            Canterbury, London

11. 23–24 January 1991   The Anglican Cathedral, Liverpool

12. 24 April 1991   Jerusalem Chamber, Westminster
                            Abbey, London

13. 17–19 July 1991   The Minster School, York

14. 16–17 October 1991   The Royal School of Church Music,
                            Addington Palace, Croydon

1.4   Finance

The work of the Commission took nearly four years. Most of
its expenditure was incurred in respect of travel and accommodation
for its members and those who made presentations in person to
the Commission. Expenses were also paid for clerical assistance,
stationery, photocopying, postage and the purchase of some publications.

The expenses of the Chairman and of much secretarial work, stationery
and postage were paid by the Church Commissioners. In addition to
these costs, it is estimated that the total expenditure of the Commission amounted to £16,500.

Two most generous grants towards this were made by the Proprietors
of *Hymns Ancient and Modern*. Grants were also received from the
Fox Memorial Trust; Westminster Abbey; the Goldsmiths' Company;
the Ouseley Trust; and Miss Ingrid Slaughter. The cost of the parish
survey was borne by Mr. Nicholas Wills. The balance of expenditure
was contributed by the Central Church Fund.

To all these the Commission expresses its thanks and appreciation for
the generosity which enabled it to do its work.

The cost of printing and producing the Report has been carried by the
joint publishers, Church House Publishing and Hodder and Stoughton
Ltd.

The Commission

1.5 Working Papers written by Members of the Commission and the Chapters to which these papers related

Chapter 1   The case for an Archbishops' Commission on Church Music

Chapter 2   An Historical Survey of Church Music

Chapter 3   God, Music and Creation

Chapter 4   Worship, Prayer and the Liturgy of the Church

Chapter 5   Roles of Music in Worship
Singing in Tongues

Chapter 6   Hymns
The Language of Worship

Chapter 7   The Physical Setting of Worship
The Worshipping Community

Chapter 8   An Account of a Myers-Briggs Weekend attended by three members of the Commission
Music and Spirituality
Quality, Styles, Standards and Choice
Worshippers are People

Chapter 9   Music in Parish Churches
Where the Organ is rarely heard

Chapter 10   Cathedral Music – a few thoughts
Music in Cathedrals

Chapter 11   Changes in Patterns of Free Church Worship
Music in the Roman Catholic Church in England

2

The Evidence

2.1 Publications

A letter was written by the Chairman of the Commission in September 1988 to various publications, as follows:

> The appointment by the Archbishops of a Commission to review music in church has aroused considerable interest, and care has been taken to ensure that membership of the Commission is well-balanced and representative of many musical traditions.
>
> However, it also needs to obtain the widest possible range of views from people of all denominations. So we would be pleased to hear from anyone with interest, skill or experience in any aspect of church music and will be glad for your readers to write to: The Secretary, Archbishops' Commission on Church Music, 7 Chapel Lane, Sutton Courtenay, Abingdon, Oxon. OX14 4AN.

This was sent to the following journals and newspapers:

British Journal of Music
   Education

Church Music Quarterly
Church of England Newspaper

Church Times
Classical Music
Daily Telegraph
English Churchman
Music Teacher
Musical Times
Organists' Review

The Guardian
The Independent
The Listener
The Times
The Times Educational
 Supplement

It is not known how many people wrote to the Commission in direct response to this letter, although many of the letters listed in Appendices 2.2 and 2.3 may have been prompted by it. In addition, the correspondence columns of some publications carried letters from their readers, and the Royal School of Church Music's *Church Music Quarterly* included an article in its October 1988 issue, with letters from readers in subsequent issues.

A letter seeking evidence was also written directly to twenty-eight organisations having an interest in church music.

2.2 Correspondence from Individuals

Graham Alsop, St. Albans, Hertfordshire

Geoffrey M. Atkinson, Brighton

Jonathan Backhouse, Crediton, Devon

Leon Bailey, Worcester

Mr. and Mrs. J. W. C. Baker, Cowes, Isle of Wight

Derek Baldwin, Tunbridge Wells, Kent

Frank Ball, London NW9

Evelyn M. Barnett, Southall, Middlesex

Charles Barnham, Sutton Courtenay, Oxon.

G. R. M. Beadle, Canterbury

Margaret Bearfoot, Bexley, Kent

The Revd. Dr. Jeremy Begbie, Cambridge

Adrian Bell, Linthorpe, Middlesbrough

The Revd. John Bell, Glasgow

The Revd. David R. Bird, Kinson, Bournemouth

Anne Bond, South Godstone, Surrey

The Revd. Canon Andrew Bowden, Coates, Cirencester

Christopher Brain, Crookes, Sheffield

Dr. Ursula Brett, Chiswick, London

The Revd. Dr. David L. E. Bronnert, Southall, Middlesex

The Revd. Prebendary A. T. Budgett, Bruton, Somerset

Margaret and Arthur Carr, Lenton Abbey, Nottingham

Liz Carrington, West Bridgeford, Nottingham

Helen Chambers, Alveston, Bristol

John Chapman, Stroud, Gloucestershire

Petronella Clarke, London N22

Peter Cook, Surbiton, Surrey

The Revd. Peter Cornish, South Croydon, Surrey

The Revd. Canon Martin Coombs, Pershore, Worcestershire

Trevor Cowlett, Kennington, Oxford

M. C. Cox, Wheathampstead, Hertfordshire

Bob Craven, Heathfield, East Sussex

Vincent Cross, Weston Favell, Northamptonshire

The Revd. Alastair Cutting, Adwick-le-Street, Doncaster

Adrian Daffern, Durham

The Revd. Canon Hugo de Waal, Cambridge

Anne Dunn, Basingstoke, Hampshire

G. A. Earl, St. Leonards-on-Sea, Sussex

Dr. Graham Elliott, Chelmsford, Essex

John Ewington, Bletchingley, Surrey

Janny Faulkner, Fareham, Hampshire

Jan A. Fischer, Caterham, Surrey

Roger Fisher, Chester

Dr. Kieran Flanagan, Bristol

The Revd. Ian Forrester, Chelmsford

Dr. John Forster, Knaresborough, Yorkshire.

The Revd. M. Garland, Kingshurst, Birmingham

David Gedge, Powys

The Revd. Peter Godden, Maidstone, Kent

The Revd. Canon Bruce Grainger, Keighley, West Yorkshire

Michael F. Griffiths, Bridgend, Mid-Glamorgan

The Revd. R. Grigson, West Bromwich

John S. Hack, Woking, Surrey

Marilyn Harper, Forest Hill, London

The Revd. Canon Michael Harper, Haywards Heath, Sussex

John Harris, Marsh, Huddersfield

The Revd. T. R. Hatwell, Tonbridge, Kent

Stanley Haydock, Nottingham

Paul Herrington, Oxford

W. B. Hesmondhalgh, London SW1

Dr. Berkeley Hill, Ashford, Kent

Arthur E. Hooper, Liskeard, Cornwall

The Revd. Bob Hopper, Gateshead

The Revd. David Holloway, Jesmond, Newcastle

Alison Howell, Earls Court, London

John Humphrey, Sevenoaks, Kent

Paulette Huntington, Emley, Huddersfield

The Revd. Alun J. Hurd, Chertsey, Surrey

The Revd. Courtney Johns, Axminster, Devon

Dr. J. D. Jones, Newport, Isle of Wight

Judyth Knight, London NW10

The Revd. Graeme Knowles, Leigh
Park, Portsmouth

The Revd. Roderick Leece,
Portsmouth

D. J. Littlewood, Enfield,
Middlesex

The Revd. Christopher Lowson,
Eltham, London

Adrian Lucas, Portsmouth

The Revd. Alan Luff, Westminster,
London

Sir David Lumsden, London NW1

Sir John Manduell, Manchester

Andrew R. Maries, York

Dr. Alwyn Marriage, Guildford,
Surrey

The Revd. Dr. John Marsh, Ossett,
Yorkshire

Geoffrey Marshall-Taylor, BBC,
London

Christopher S. Martin, Bristol

The Revd. Canon Michael McLean,
Norwich

The Revd. Hugh Mead, Chiswick,
London

John Measures, Basingstoke,
Hampshire

The Revd. Brian Meney, London
E13

The Revd. Brian Morris, Rochester

The Revd. L. Mortimer, Coventry

The Revd. Peter Moss, Hempnall,
Norfolk

The Revd. J. C. Naumann, South
Ruislip, Middlesex

Michael Nicholas, Norwich

Peter Nickol, Kettering,
Northamptonshire

Peter Oakes, Walsall, West
Midlands

The Revd. Stephen Oliver, BBC,
London

Rowland Owen, Haslemere, Surrey

Michael Paget, Bridgwater,
Somerset

Eric Pask, Harpenden,
Hertfordshire

The Revd. Michael Perry,
Tonbridge, Kent

Marlene Phillips, Milnthorpe,
Cumbria

John and Jane Pickering, Rowlands
Castle, Hampshire

Dr. Lionel Pike, Egham, Surrey

Thomas Pitfield, Bowdon, Cheshire

Sidney Place, Johannesburg, South
Africa

The Revd. Prebendary Michael
Pollit, Shrewsbury

Michael Procter, Hitchin,
Hertfordshire

Iain Quinn, Llandaff, Cardiff

John Radford, Portsmouth

Dr. Robin Rees, Abingdon,
Oxfordshire

Br. Reginald SSF, Chichester

Stephen Rhys, East Sheen, Surrey

The Revd. Harvey Richardson,
Haywards Heath, West Sussex

Frank S. Rider, Bradfield,
Berkshire

E. D. Rowley, Shanklin, Isle of
Wight

Mark Rowlinson, Manchester

The Revd. Canon Michael Saward,
St. Paul's Cathedral, London

Ian Sharp, Liverpool

Philip and Iris Sizer, Bucklebury,
Berkshire

The Revd. David Smith, Malvern,
Worcestershire
Geoffrey Smith, Boston,
Lincolnshire
Dr. Michael Smith, Llandaff,
Cardiff
The Revd. M. K. Snellgrove,
Sutton Coldfield
F. Gordon Spriggs, Earley, Reading
Jennifer Standage, Blackheath,
London

Professor John Tarn, Liverpool
The Revd. Canon Cyril Taylor,
Petersfield, Hampshire
Dr. Berj Topalian, Clifton, Bristol
Dr. June B. Tillman, London SW16
J. Turner, Plaistow, London
Dr. Peter Underwood,
Loughborough, Leicestershire

Arthur Wallis, Highgate, London
Stuart Ward, Hampton Hill,
Middlesex

Dr. Derek Watson, Charlton Kings,
Cheltenham
The Revd. Dr. Fraser Watts,
Cambridge
John A. W. Webber, Beckenham,
Kent
Mrs. M. Wharton, Alderbury,
Wiltshire
Dr. Graham Whettam, Ingatestone,
Essex
Malcolm Wilson, Dunblane,
Perthshire
A. J. Winfield, Heelands, Milton
Keynes
Ian Wishart, Dundee
Dr. Kenneth M. Wolfe, Dulwich,
London
A. A. R. Wood, Lymington,
Hampshire
Frederick P. A. Wood, Siddington,
Macclesfield, Cheshire
The Revd. Christopher Wren,
Bensham, Gateshead

2.3   Submissions received from Organisations

Baptist Union of Scotland
Bexley District Organists' and
Choirmasters' Association
British Federation of Young Choirs

Cathedral Organists' Association
Central Readers' Conference
Chelmsford Cathedral and the
Anglia Higher Education College
Choir Schools' Association
Christian Music Association
Churches' Initiative for Music
Education (CHIME)
Council for the Care of Churches

Friends of Cathedral Music

Guild of Church Musicians

Hymn Society of Great Britain and
Ireland

Incorporated Society of Musicians
Independent Local Radio
International Ministerial Council of
Great Britain

Joint Committee for Church Music
in Ireland
Jubilate Group

Liturgical Commission (General
Synod of the Church of England)

Methodist Association of Youth
 Clubs
Methodist Church Music Society
Music in Worship Trust
Music Masters' and Mistresses'
 Association

National Early Music Association
North Wales Organ Music
 Foundation

Panel of Monastic Musicians
Presbyterian Church in Ireland

Religious Broadcasting, Network
 and Local Producers, BBC
Royal Academy of Music
Royal Air Force
Royal College of Organists
Royal School of Church Music

St. Michael-le-Belfry Church, York
Salvation Army
Scottish Episcopal Church
Scottish Catholic Liturgy
 Commission
Society of St. Gregory
'Songs of Praise', BBC TV

Theological College Principals'
 Conference

Unitarian Church Music Society
United Kingdom Council for Music
 Education
United Reformed Church
 Musicians' Guild

Wren Music

2.4   Presentations made in person to the Commission

Mr. Robin Sheldon, Music in Worship Foundation	7 April 1989
Mr. Andrew Maries, Director of Music of St. Michael-le-Belfry, York	5 July 1989
The Revd. Dr. John Marsh, Christ Church, South Ossett, West Yorkshire	6 July 1989
The Revd. Peter Moss, Team Rector of Hempnall, Norwich	2 November 1989
Mr. Paul Leddington Wright, Organist of Coventry Cathedral and formerly Music Adviser to the Methodist Association of Youth Clubs	4 January 1990
Professor John Tarn, Nelson Professor of Architecture, Liverpool University	4 January 1990
Dr. Alwyn Marriage, exponent of Liturgical Dance	5 January 1990
Lt. Col. Norman Bearcroft of the Salvation Army	3 May 1990
The Revd. Roger Hutchings of BBC TV's 'Songs of Praise'	3 May 1990

The Revd. Christopher Wren, St. Chad's, Bensham, Gateshead	11 July 1990
The Revd. John Bell, Iona Community, Convener of the Panel of Worship of the Church of Scotland	12 July 1990
Mr. Graham Kendrick, song writer	31 October 1990
The Revd. David Lewis, St. Cyprian's, Liverpool	23 January 1991
The Revd. John Catlin, St. Chad's, Kirkby	23 January 1991
The Revd. Michael Perry of Jubilate Hymns	24 April 1991

2.5 Parish Survey Summary and the Questionnaire

Introductory: the Survey 'Music in Parish Worship'

A postal survey was carried out in October 1988 on behalf of the Commission by the Statistics and Computer Department of the Central Board of Finance of the Church of England. The Questionnaire had been drawn up by members of the Commission and was distributed to the incumbents of parishes included in the sample, accompanied by an explanatory letter from the Chairman. A full analysis of the results of the survey was carried out by Jacqui Cooper BA, MSc and copies of her 81-page report are obtainable by remitting £5.00 to The Secretary, ACCMUS, 7 Chapel Lane, Sutton Courtenay, Abingdon, Oxon. OX14 4AN.

Composition of the Sample and Distribution of the Questionnaire

In order to keep costs to a minimum, the Commission decided to make use of an earlier sample which had been constructed in 1986. 680 parishes had then been identified by the Statistics Department, using a selection method which combined stratified and random sampling to provide a balanced sample of all parishes in England. Distribution of the questionnaire to these 680 parishes produced 545 returns, of which 524 could be included in the analysis, thus representing nearly 80% of the parishes approached. 63% of these returns came from rural and 37% from urban parishes. 23% of the churches in the sample described themselves as having an evangelical form of worship, 41% as having a central form of worship and 36% as having a catholic form of worship. It emerged that a higher percentage of urban churches are evangelical or catholic, whereas a higher percentage of rural churches are central. Rural churches seem to have been less affected by the Renewal/ Charismatic Movement than urban ones; evangelical churches are much more likely to have been affected than those practising other forms of worship.

The Role of Music in Worship

The most important purpose of church music according to all groups in the sample is to worship and praise God. Urban churches thought that its second most important role was to promote corporate awareness and fellowship, whereas rural churches gave a higher priority to its function of uplifting the soul. Evangelical and central churches thought its role in promoting corporate awareness and fellowship was more important than did catholic churches. The latter gave high priorities to its roles in illuminating and intensifying the words of the service, and in helping people to pray. 97% of the groups in the sample thought that the order of priority that they gave was being partially or completely achieved in their church.

Personnel

29% of the groups in the sample had a worship committee and 65% had a director of music. Both worship committees and directors of music are more commonly found in urban churches, whilst the minister is more likely to take sole responsibility for the church's policy in worship in rural areas. Over two-thirds of the churches had one or more organists; this proportion was higher in central churches (75%) and lower in catholic churches. 63% of churches had a choir and 21% had a separate singing group. Urban churches are more likely to have a choir or singing group or both; singing groups are more common in evangelical churches. The average choir has fifteen members of which six are male and nine female, four are aged thirteen or under, two are aged between fourteen and eighteen, and nine are nineteen or over. 20% of the sample had a separate music group. Again these were more common in urban (35%) and evangelical (44%) churches. The average group consists of nine members of which five are female, although in catholic churches the average number in the group is thirteen.

Services

The average number of services of all forms in a month is six, of which three are Eucharists and two are services of Evening Prayer. Urban churches tend to have more services with a choir than do rural ones. Catholic churches have more Eucharists with a choir than do evangelical churches which are more likely to have family services or services of Morning or Evening Prayer with a choir. In those churches with a music group, the average number of services in which the group takes part in a month is three.

The Evidence

Hymn Books
Mission Praise (Marshall Pickering, 1985) or *Junior Praise* (Marshall Pickering, 1986) were the most popular of all the hymn books listed in the questionnaire. They were used by 36% of churches in the sample, although this proportion was nearly twice as high in evangelical churches, and much lower (17%) in catholic churches. The next most popular book was *Hymns Ancient and Modern New Standard* which was used by 28% of churches, particularly central churches. The average number of publications used by churches in the sample was two.

Repertoire
85% of churches in the sample included organ music in their repertoire and over 50% included congregational settings of the Eucharist (particularly in catholic churches), choruses or songs (particularly in evangelical churches), choir/singing group anthems and psalms/canticles to Anglican chants (particularly central churches). Urban churches were significantly more likely to use the first three of these than were rural ones.

Minister, Musical Director and Congregation
Two-thirds of the sample had a director of music currently in post; in urban churches this figure was 77%. He/she was more likely to have a musical qualification or to earn his/her living as a musician if working for an urban church. Nearly two-thirds of respondents said that their congregations were supportive of innovations; in urban churches this figure was 77%. Music is also more likely to be given as a reason for individuals leaving an urban church.

Resources
Over 60% of those who had a director of music provided finance to cover his/her remuneration, and this figure rose to 72% in urban areas. 50% of the groups in the sample said they provided finance for the organist's remuneration and 34% provided the finance for payments to choir members. Urban churches were more likely than rural ones to finance choir and congregational music, training for church musicians and the purchase of musical instruments (e.g. electric keyboards, guitars, etc.). The average amount spent by urban churches on church music is nearly £470 a year (2.3% of expenditure) compared with £180 (1.7% of expenditure) by rural churches. Urban churches are more likely to provide this finance through their annual budget, as opposed to on an *ad hoc* basis, than rural ones. Evangelical or catholic churches also spend more in cash terms than central churches, but the amount

represents a higher percentage of total parish expenditure in central and catholic churches. A director of music is more likely to receive £600 or more a year if he/she works in an urban church or a catholic church.

The Questionnaire

The Questionnaire was accompanied by a letter from the Chairman of the Commission, as follows:

My dear Incumbent,

As you will know, I think, the Archbishops have appointed a Commission on Church Music and as its Chairman I write to seek your help.

One of our tasks is to 'survey' the present situation of music in church and one of the ways we hope to do this is by means of a questionnaire, which is being sent to a balanced selection of parishes from the whole country.

May I, then, ask you to complete the enclosed questionnaire, in the knowledge that we shall have no means of identifying the parish from which it is returned so that your replies will be 'anonymous'.

The questions have been asked in such a way as to make them simple to answer and require only a 'yes/no' or numerical response, so that I hope not to take more than a few minutes of your time. Even so, you may wish to consult with others, in particular with your 'director of music' (which is used in the questionnaire as a portmanteau term to describe the person with executive responsibility for the music in your church).

Should there be more than one church in the parish, may I suggest that you either complete the questionnaire for one of them or make and complete further copies of the document in respect of your other church/es – or additional copies can be had from the Secretary of the Commission, using the stamped addressed envelope which is enclosed for your convenience. Please reply as soon as possible, and in any case not later than 1st January, 1989.

In anticipation, I thank you for your assistance in doing a piece of work which is of very considerable importance for the life and work of the church.

With all good wishes,

Yours sincerely,

The Evidence

The full text of the Questionnaire appears below.

1.   PRELIMINARY

(a)   Tick the box opposite the category which most closely describes
        the character of your parish:

Scattered rural		Large town		Suburban	
Village		New town		Urban or inner city	
Market town		Large housing estate			

(b)   Give the approximate number on your electoral roll by ticking
        the appropriate box:

0–100	
100–300	
300–500	
More than 500	

(c)   Tick the box opposite the description which most nearly fits the
        form of worship currently practised in your church:

(i) Evangelical	
(ii) Moderate Evangelical	
(iii) Central	
(iv) Moderate catholic	
(v) Catholic	

(d)   Has the worship of your church been affected by the Renewal/
        Charismatic Movement?

Greatly	
Somewhat	
Not at all	

2.   THE ROLE OF MUSIC IN WORSHIP

(a)   Here is a list of 7 possible roles/purposes for church music to
        fulfil; please rate them in order of priority (1 to 7) by placing
        the appropriate figure opposite each statement.

(i) To provide a medium for evangelism	
(ii) To provide contrast or establish mood	
(iii) To uplift the soul	
(iv) To worship and praise God	
(v) To help people to pray	
(vi) To promote corporate awareness and fellowship in worship	
(vii) To illuminate and intensify the words of the service	

(b)   Do you feel that, in your church, this order of priority is being
        achieved?

Yes	Partially	No

3.   PERSONNEL

(a)   Who in practice takes responsibility for your Church's policy in worship?

(i) The minister and director of music together	
(ii) The minister alone	
(iii) The director of music alone	
(iv) A worship committee (or its equivalent)	

(b)   Do you have a worship committee or equivalent?

Yes	No

(c)

		Yes	No
(i)	Do you have a choir?		
(ii)	Do you have a separate singing group?		
(iii)	If the answer to (i) or (ii) is 'yes', does either wear robes?		
(iv)	Do you have a separate music group?		

(d)   Indicate the number of persons actively engaged in leading the music of your church:

		Male	Female	Total
(i)	The director of music			
(ii)	The assistant director of music			
(iii)	The organist (if other than (i) or (ii))			
(iv)	Reluctant organist(s) (e.g. 're-cycled' pianists or others who help out)			
(v)	Choristers under the age of 13			
(vi)	Choristers aged between 14 and 18			
(vii)	Choristers aged 19 and above			
(viii)	Members of music/instrumental group (even if only occasional)			
	GRAND TOTAL			

4.   SERVICES

In the course of an average 4-week month, how many times will the following Sunday services (in which music is a constituent part) take place in your church?

	With Choir	Without Choir	With Music Group	Without Music Group
(a) Eucharist				
(b) Family service (non-Eucharist)				
(c) Morning Prayer				
(d) Evening Prayer				
(e) Other				

5. HYMN BOOKS

Are any of the following recent publications currently in use in your church?

	Yes	No
(a) Ancient and Modern New Standard		
(b) New English Hymnal		
(c) Hymns for Today's Church		
(d) With One Voice		
(e) Mission Praise/Junior Praise		
(f) Sounds of Living Water/Fresh Sounds		
(g) Celebration Hymnal		
(h) Songs of Fellowship		
(i) Hymns of Faith		
(j) Other (but do not specify)		

6. REPERTOIRE

Does your church's musical repertoire include:

	Yes	No
(a) Congregational setting(s) of the Eucharist		
(b) Choir settings of the Eucharist		
(c) Choir/singing group anthems		
(d) Choruses or songs		
(e) Psalms and/or canticles to Anglican chants		
(f) Responsorial psalms		
(g) Psalms sung in other styles		
(h) Plainsong		
(i) Taizé music		
(j) Organ music		
(k) Instrumental music		
(l) Recorded music		

7.   MINISTER, MUSICAL DIRECTOR AND
     CONGREGATION

		Yes	No
(a)	Do you currently have a director of music in post?		
(b)	Is he/she appropriately trained?		
(c)	Does he/she have a musical qualification?		
(d)	Does he/she earn his/her living as a musician?		
(e)	Is your congregation supportive of innovations in the music of your church?		
(f)	Do you consider that your knowledge of church music is adequate to provide the necessary support for your church musicians?		
(g)	Is your working relationship with your director of music a comfortable one?		
(h)	Is the music of your church one of the things that attracts people into it?		
(i)	If the answer to (h) was YES, is it partly because they wish to participate in the choir, music group etc.?		
(j)	Has the music of your church ever been given as a reason for individuals leaving your congregation?		

8. RESOURCES

(a)   Does your church provide finance to cover the following?

		Yes	No
(i)	The director of music's remuneration		
(ii)	The assistant director of music's remuneration		
(iii)	The organist's remuneration (assuming a different person)		
(iv)	Payments to choir members		
(v)	Training for church musicians		
(vi)	Choir music		
(vii)	Congregational music		
(viii)	Choir robes		
(ix)	Maintenance of the organ (and pianos if any)		
(x)	The purchase of other musical instruments (e.g. electric keyboards, guitars, percussion, music stands etc.)		

(b)   By what means does your church finance these items?

ANNUAL BUDGET	AD HOC BASIS

(c)   What is the average amount spent on church music each year?

£

(d)   What percentage of the parish budget does this represent?

%

(e)   Indicate the approximate amount of the director of music's remuneration (excluding fees for weddings, funerals etc.)

£100–£300	
£300–£600	
£600–£1,000	
More than £1,000	

(f)   How much of it does he/she accept?

ALL	SOME	NONE

9.   ADDITIONAL COMMENTS (please be very brief):

Please return your completed questionnaire as soon as possible (and not later than 1 January 1989) to Patrick Salisbury, Secretary to the Archbishops' Commission on Church Music, 7 Chapel Lane, Sutton Courtenay, Abingdon, Oxon. OX14 4AN.

2.6 Cathedrals

The Chairman wrote to the Chairmen both of the Deans' and Provosts'
Meeting and of the Precentors' Conference, inviting them to make a
submission to the Commission. Letters were also sent to all Deans and
Provosts individually and an enquiry was received from the informal
Deans' and Organists' group.

Some replies took the form of an acknowledgment or a brief
comment. Those which offered something more substantial came
from:

Canterbury (Precentor and Organist)
Carlisle (Dean)
Chester (Dean and Organist)
Chichester (Dean)
Derby (Chapter Clerk)
Norwich (Organist)
Portsmouth (Provost)
Ripon (Dean)
Rochester (Dean)
St. Paul's Cathedral (Canon Residentiary)
Sheffield (retired Provost)
Southwell (Provost)
Wakefield (Provost and Precentor)

2.7 Dioceses

Two separate questions were addressed at different times to Diocesan
Secretaries, for answer either by themselves or by some other person.
One enquiry related to the salary scales of parish organists, the other
sought information about diocesan music organisations. Replies were
received from:

Bath and Wells	Assistant Diocesan Secretary, Ms. Jean Routley
Birmingham	The Revd. Michael Garland
Blackburn	Diocesan Secretary
Bradford	Diocesan Secetary
Bristol	Diocesan Secretary, the Revd. Canon John Simpson
Canterbury	Diocesan Secretary
Carlisle	Diocesan Secretary
Chelmsford	Dr. Graham Elliott

Chichester	Diocesan Secretary, Mr. R. Bayfield and Mr. John Springford
Coventry	The Revd. Robert Mighall
Derby	Mr. David Bott, Mr. Peter Gould
Durham	Diocesan Secretary, Assistant Diocesan Secretary
Ely	Diocesan Secretary, Mr. Christopher Moore
Exeter	Mr. F. H. Pearce Richards
Gloucester	Assistant Diocesan Secretary, Mr. J. Postbury
Guildford	Mr. Leslie Mason, Mr. Andrew Millington
Hereford	Diocesan Secretary, Dr. Roy Massey
Leicester	Assistant Diocesan Secretary
Lichfield	Mr. Jonathan Rees-Williams
Lincoln	Diocesan Secretary, Ms. Joan Buckley, Ms. Grace Hesp, Mrs. M. Packman
Liverpool	Diocesan Secretary
London	Diocesan Office Manager, Mr. Nigel Osborn
Manchester	Assistant Diocesan Secretary
Newcastle	Diocesan Secretary
Norwich	Diocesan Secretary, Mr. Michael Nicholas
Oxford	Secretary of the Board of Finance Secretary of the Advisory Committee
Portsmouth	Bishop of Portsmouth
Ripon	Mr. David Salter
Rochester	Diocesan Secretary, Assistant Diocesan Secretary, Mr. Andrew Norcott
St Albans	Diocesan Secretary
St Edmundsbury and Ipswich	The Revd. Michael Booker, Mrs. Jill Staplehurst
Salisbury	Diocesan Secretary
Sheffield	Diocesan Secretary, Mr. Paul Ward

Southwark	P.A. to the Diocesan Secretary, Deputy Diocesan Secretary
Southwell	Diocesan Secretary, Miss Constance Drake
Truro	Diocesan Secretary, Mrs. Ann Robinson
Wakefield	Diocesan Secretary, the Revd. Canon David Baxter
Winchester	Diocesan Secretary, the Revd. Neil Crawford-Jones, the Revd. Canon Roger Job, the Revd. Canon Basil Trevor-Morgan
Worcester	Diocesan Secretary
York	Diocesan Secretary, Mr. Richard Shephard

2.8 Other Christian Traditions and Ecumenical Congregations in England

Among those consulted by the Commission for Chapters 11 and 12 of the Report, gratitude is due especially to the following people, although not all of them belong to the church or congregation on which they helped with information.

Fr. Athanasius and Fr. Gregorios (Orthodox)

Mrs. Jennifer Demolder and Canon Charles Walker (Roman Catholic)

The Revd. Ronald England, Miss Marjorie Gottschalk Trone and Mr. Peter Lea-Cox (Lutheran)

Mr. Ralph Bailey and Mr. Charles Cleall (Methodist)

The Revd. George Bexon (Baptist)

Lt. Col. Norman Bearcroft (Salvation Army)

Mr. Phil Rogers, the Revd. J. Stevens (House churches)

The Revd. David Bronnert, the Revd. Christopher Cartwright, the Rt. Revd. Bishop Howell Davies, Mrs. Bryony Davis, the Revd. Michael Eastman, Mr. Bob Gardner-Hopkins, Dr. Nimmi Hutnik, the Revd. Ernest Kamran, Mr. Graham Kendrick, the Revd. and Mrs. David Kitley, Miss Tjutju Koswara, Mr. and Mrs. Sewa Mehat, Mr. Keith Sedgebear, the Revd. Dr. John Sentamu, Mrs. Helen Steven, Mr. D. Dummers (Ethnic congregations)

The Rt. Revd. Bishop Lloyd Rees (HM Prisons)

The Staff Chaplain to the Chaplain of the Fleet, the staff of the Royal Army Chaplains' Department at Bagshot Park and the

Revd. John Morley on behalf of the Chaplain-in-Chief, RAF
(H.M. Forces)

2.9 Overseas

In order to fulfil its brief to include church music outside England in its
survey, the Commission sought evidence from correspondents in
various parts of the world. In his letter the Chairman wrote:

> Obviously our survey of music in the churches outside this
> country will be somewhat haphazard and incomplete, given the
> time and resources available to us, but it would be enormously
> helpful to us if you were able to write up to 1,500 words saying how
> you see the state of music in the churches in your part of the world.
>   We are not looking for precise statistics (unless you have some)
> but more for impressions by people on the spot, and we would like
> to know, in particular, about areas such as:
>
> (a) whether the use of music in church has declined or increased
> over the past twenty-five years (and if there is any correlation
> of this with new services);
>
> (b) the recruitment and use of choirs, music directors/organists
> and music groups;
>
> (c) whether church musicians are encouraged, recruited and
> trained to a high standard and, if professional, paid at a
> realistic level;
>
> (d) relationships between church musicians and the clergy;
>
> (e) what instruments are used in worship;
>
> (f) the use of new music and hymns (especially that which is
> 'indigenous' and/or connected with 'renewal'), and the en-
> couragement of composers;
>
> (g) what hymn book/s is/are most popular;
>
> (h) what is exciting and hopeful – and why;
>
> (i) what is disturbing or depressing – and why;

(j)   your view of the future of Church music in your country.

There is, of course, no need to cover all these points, but they are set out to help you. You may wish to ignore them, but anything that you like to send us will be very much appreciated.

Written replies were received as follows:

Australia
> Mr. Charles Clark
> Mr. Ray Holland
> Miss Kay McLennan
> Mr. Bruce Naylor
> The Rt. Revd. Bishop Newell
> Mr. Stewart Perkins
> Archbishop Keith Rayner
> G. Westacott
> RSCM ACT and Southern Region Branch

Canada
> Mr. Giles Bryant
> The Revd. Stephen Crisp
> Mr. Peter Shepherd
> Mr. John Tuttle

Europe
> The Ven. John Lewis

Hong Kong
> The Revd. Canon David Leigh

New Zealand
> Mr. G. J. Bowler
> Professor Peter Godfrey
> Dr. Douglas Mews
> Mr. N. W. Werry
> Mr. Roger Williams

South Africa
> The Rt. Revd. Bishop Frederick Amoore
> Mr. Richard Cock
> The Revd. Owen Franklin
> The Revd. Chich Hewitt
> The Revd. Canon Winston Ndungane
> Ms. Karen Pratt
> Dean John Salt
> The Rt. Revd. Thomas Stanage

Uganda	The Very Revd. Misuseva Bugimbi
United States of America	Mr. John Fenstermaker
	Mr. James Litton
	Mrs. Dorothy Lyall
	Mrs. Betty Carr Pulkingham
	Dr. Frederick Swann
Zimbabwe	Ms. Beth Atkins
	Mr. James Peto
	Mrs. M. E. Shelton
	The Revd. Andrew Thomson

No reply was received from correspondents in East Africa or the Middle East.

2.10 Anglican Religious Communities in Britain

All the communities listed in the *Church of England Year Book 1990* received a copy of the Commission's working paper on Music in Religious Communities, for their comments and suggestions.

Replies were received from:

Priory of Our Lady, Burford
Community of the Glorious
  Ascension
Community of the Resurrection
Community of the Servants of the
  Will of God
Ewell Monastery
Society of St. Francis
Society of St. John the Evangelist
Society of the Sacred Mission
St. Mary's Abbey, West Malling
Community of Reparation to the
  Blessed Sacrament
Community of St. Francis
Community of St. John Baptist
Community of St. Mary the Virgin
Community of St. Peter
Community of St. Peter, Horbury
Community of St. Wilfrid

Community of the Companions of
  Jesus the Good Shepherd
Community of the Epiphany
Community of the Holy Cross
Community of the Holy Family
Community of the Holy Name
Community of the Holy Rood
Community of the Presentation
Community of the Servants of the
  Cross
Community of St. Andrew
Order of St. Elizabeth of Hungary
Order of the Holy Paraclete
St. Saviour's Priory
Sisters of Charity
Sisters of the Church
Society of All Saints
Society of the Precious Blood

The Evidence

Particular thanks go to Fr. Mark Hartley, OCSO, Honorary Secretary of the Panel of Monastic Musicians; the Revd. Canon Jeremy Davies, Precentor of Salisbury Cathedral; Sr. Theresa Margaret, CHN; Fr. Peter Allen, CR; Mother Allyne, CSMV; Fr. Gregory, CSWG; Sr. Hilary, CSF; Sr. Susan, OHP; Sr. Mary John, Abbess, OSB; and Br. Reginald, SSF.

2.11 Questionnaire to Theological Colleges and Courses

The following questionnaire, addressed to the Principals of the thirty-three Anglican or ecumenical theological colleges and ministerial training courses in England, Scotland and Wales was completed either by them or by one of their staff or by a student. Twenty-nine replies (an 88% response) were received, of which sixteen were from colleges and fourteen from courses.

Name of Theological College/Course ....

(Please tick as appropriate)

Are your students given instruction or training in:

1. The place of music in life and its use in worship (a 'theology' of music)?

    Much .... Some .... Little .... None ....

    Comments

2. Preparing and conducting services which include music?

    Much .... Some .... Little .... None ....

    Comments

3. The role in worship of organists, choirs and other musicians and the relationship of the clergy with them?

    Much .... Some .... Little .... None ....

    Comments

4.   The choice of hymns (both words and music)?

   Much ....   Some ....   Little ....   None ....

   Comments

5.   The use of settings, anthems and other music?

   Much ....   Some ....   Little ....   None ....

   Comments

6.   Voice production and singing in church?

   Much ....   Some ....   Little ....   None ....

   Comments

Any other comments

Please return to The Chairman, ACCMUS, Bishopswood, Fareham, Hants. PO14 1NT

3

Miscellaneous

3.1 Canon B.20 'Of the Musicians and Music of the Church'
3.2 Specimen Job Specification for a Parish Organist or Director of Music
3.3 Specimen Agreement for the Appointment of an Organist (and Choir Director)
3.4 Royal School of Church Music Salary Scales for Parish Organists and Choir Directors 1992
3.5 Specimen Constitution for a Diocesan Music Committee
3.6 Addresses of Some Organisations mentioned in the Report

3.1 Canon B.20 'Of the Musicians and Music of the Church'

1. In all churches and chapels, other than in cathedral or collegiate churches or chapels where the matter is governed by or dependent upon the statutes or customs of the same, the functions of appointing any organist or choirmaster (by whatever name called), and of terminating the appointment of any organist or choirmaster, shall be exercisable by the minister with the agreement of the parochial church council, except that if the archdeacon of the archdeaconry in which the parish is situated, in the case of termination of an appointment, considers that the circumstances are such that the requirement as to the agreement of the parochial church council should be dispensed with, the archdeacon may direct accordingly. Where the minister is also the archdeacon of the archdeaconry concerned, the function of the archdeacon under this paragraph shall be exercisable by the bishop of the diocese.

2. Where there is an organist or choirmaster the minister shall pay due heed to his advice and assistance in the choosing of chants, hymns, anthems, and other settings and in the ordering of the music of the church; but at all times the final responsibility and decision in these matters rests with the minister.

3. It is the duty of the minister to ensure that only such chants,

hymns, anthems, and other settings are chosen as are appropriate, both the words and the music, to the solemn act of worship and prayer in the House of God as well as to the congregation assembled for that purpose; and to banish all irreverence in the practice and in the performance of the same.

3.2 Specimen Job Specification for a Parish Organist or Director of Music

1.   All Saints,   , wish to appoint an Organist/Director of Music/Choirmaster from . . .

2.   The parish seeks a committed Christian/practising communicant member of the Church of England who will identify fully with the work and life of the Church.

3.   The appointment will be made by the incumbent and Parochial Church Council, in accordance with Canon B.20.

4.   The successful applicant will be required to sign a contract with the incumbent and PCC.

5.   The Organist/Director of Music will be expected to work closely with the incumbent and will be a member of the Worship Committee, who will wish to designate specific areas of responsibility (such as who chooses the hymns) and make recommendations about the musical aspects of worship. He/she will be a member/attend meetings of the PCC.

6.   He/she will be responsible for supervising the upkeep of the organ (and other instruments in the church).

7.   He/she will be allowed to use the organ for teaching and will be encouraged to foster the interest in music of young people. He/she should be aware of the relevant provisions of the Children Act 1989.

8.   He/she will be responsible for the recruitment and training of the choir and will be expected to co-ordinate the Christian education of choristers.

9.   He/she will be expected to discharge a pastoral role in dealings with other musicians.

10.   He/she will be expected to see that different groups (choirs, music groups, congregations) work together as one family as they make their contribution to the Sunday Liturgy.

11.   He/she will be entrusted with the administration of a budget for the purchase of music, robes, etc.

12.   The normal weekly practices are:

13.   Sunday Services at present are:

14.   There are also weekday services on important Holy Days such as Epiphany, Ash Wednesday and Ascension Day.

15.   The Organist/Director of Music will be required to be present at Christmas, Holy Week and Easter, unless there are good reasons against this.

16.   He/she will be required to work in close co-operation with the assistant organist or other recognised deputies, and to make sure that all musical services are covered.

17.   The annual salary will be £ ..... Essential expenses, if approved in advance, will be paid.

18.   The Organist/Director of Music will be entitled to .... weeks' holiday per annum. Some flexibility in this area may be necessary and communication with the incumbent will be required in respect of necessary absences at other times.

19.   He/she is entitled to play at all occasional services (weddings, funerals, memorial services, etc.).

20.   The closing date for applications is .... A letter of application, including curriculum vitae, with the names of two referees, should be forwarded to .... as soon as possible.

3.3   Specimen Agreement for the Appointment of an Organist (and Choir Director)

This document has been issued on the authority of The Incorporated Association of Organists, The Incorporated Society of Musicians, The

Royal College of Organists, The Royal School of Church Music and the Legal Adviser to the General Synod of the Church of England.

NOTES:

1.   Where an asterisk * appears in the text, delete as necessary.

2.   Paragraph 5 should be omitted if the Organist is not also to be Director of the Choir.

3.   Where a priest-in-charge has been appointed, this draft should be adapted.

4.   Attention is drawn to the *Organists' Guide to Employment* issued by The Incorporated Society of Musicians.

AN AGREEMENT made the .... day of 19

between the Reverend ....

Incumbent/Priest-in-Charge of the Benefice of ....

in the Diocese of .... (hereinafter called

'the Incumbent') of the first part, the Parochial Church Council

of the Parish of ....

(hereinafter called 'the Council') of the second part

and ....

of ....

(hereinafter called 'the Organist') of the third part.

WHEREBY IT IS AGREED as follows:

1. THE INCUMBENT (with the agreement of the Council) hereby appoints the Organist to act as Organist (* and Choir Director) of the Church of

    .... in the Parish of

    .... aforesaid.

2. (a) THE COUNCIL shall pay to the Organist the salary of £ .... per annum to be payable on the usual quarter days the first payment (which may be a proportionate payment) to be made on the .... day of .... One thousand nine hundred and ....

    (b) THE COUNCIL shall review the salary annually.

3. SUBJECT to the general direction of the Incumbent the Organist shall have the care and control of the music in the above-mentioned Church.

4. (a) THE ORGANIST shall play the organ at all the ordinary Sunday Services and at Services on the Holy Days of the Church listed in the Schedule to this Agreement.

    (b) When the organ is required for Services in addition to those referred to in sub-paragraph (a) hereof the matter shall be agreed between the Incumbent and the Organist for which an agreed additional fee shall be payable.

5. (a) THE ORGANIST shall also act as the Choir Director which shall entail the training of the Choir and shall arrange regular weekly practices for this purpose.

    (b) Only choristers who have been approved both by the Incumbent and the Organist shall be admitted to the Choir.

    (c) The power to dismiss choristers shall be that of the Organist subject to the concurrence of the Incumbent.

6. THE ORGAN shall be reserved for the personal use of, and

the giving of lessons by the Organist, also for the practice of his/her * pupils and for that of a recognised assistant at such times as will not interfere with the Services of the Church. The use of the organ shall not be granted to others without the consent of the Organist.

7. THE ORGANIST shall have the sole right to play at Wedding Services, Funeral Services and other special services, and to be paid the fee for so doing by those who engage him/her * according to the scale in force at the time at the said Church. The Organist may allow some other competent person to play at any such Service but in that event the Organist shall be entitled to receive the fee.

8. Where pursuant to the Performers' Protection Acts 1958–72, the Organist agrees to a sound recording or a video recording being made of a service, he/she * shall be entitled to the payment of an additional fee or fees.

9. THE ORGANIST shall be entitled to .... weeks holiday in each year to be taken at such times as shall be agreed between the Organist and the Incumbent. The Council shall defray the cost of supplying a deputy for .... weeks each year.

10. THE ORGANIST when absent other than for reasons of illness or holiday shall provide and pay a competent deputy to carry out his/her * duties. If the Organist shall be incapacitated by illness from performing his/her * duties the cost of supplying a competent deputy shall be borne by the Council for a period not exceeding .... consecutive weeks. Should such incapacity exceed that period the Council may decide that the Organist shall be on unpaid leave of absence.

11. (a) Subject to the provisions of Canon B.20 of the Canons of the Church of England this AGREEMENT may be terminated either by the Incumbent with the agreement of the Council giving notice to the Organist or by the Organist giving notice to the Incumbent and to the Secretary of the Council.

    (b) In this paragraph 'notice' means not less than one

quarter's notice in writing to be given to the other party to expire on one of the usual quarter days.

12.   THIS AGREEMENT shall automatically terminate when the Organist attains the age of .... years unless the Incumbent with the agreement of the Council decide that he/she * should continue in office after that date for a further period not exceeding twelve months and thereafter subject to annual review by the Incumbent and the Council.

13.   Any questions or differences whatsoever which may at any time hereafter arise between the parties hereto touching this agreement or the subject matter thereof arising out of or in relation thereto shall be referred to the archdeacon in whose archdeaconry the parish is situated or a person nominated by the archdeacon.

AS WITNESS the hand of the Incumbent and the Organist and, on

behalf of the Council, the hands of the Chairman presiding and two

other members present at a meeting of the Council held on the

.... day of .... 19..... at which a resolution was passed

authorising the signature of this agreement.

SIGNED by the Incumbent   ....

SIGNED on behalf of the
Parochial Church Council
of the Parish of   ....

....
                                              Chairman

....

....
                                 Two members of the Council

SIGNED by the Organist
(and Choir Director)   ....

THE SCHEDULE

Holy Days on which the Organist shall play the organ pursuant to paragraph 4 (a) of this Agreement:

3.4 Royal School of Church Music Salary Scales for Parish Organists and Choir Directors 1992

The following are the *minimum* recommended rates for amateur organists and choirmasters in 1992. The term 'amateur' refers to those church musicians who earn their living principally outside the world of music. It is not a reflection of their importance or ability.

1. *Smaller village or suburban church; no choir, simple services*
    Salary   £1,040 per annum
    *Fee for weddings and funerals   £15.75 per service

2. *Larger village or suburban church; choir with one rehearsal per week*
    Salary   £1,300 per annum
    *Fee for weddings and funerals   £21.00 per service

3. *Town church; choir with at least two rehearsals per week*
    Salary   £1,820 per annum
    *Fee for weddings and funerals   £26.25 per service

N.B.   * The fees for weddings should be increased by 50% if a tape recording is made, and by 100% if a video recording is made. Written permission of the organist should be sought in each case.

Notes
(1)   The above figures assume duty at two services on each Sunday. They do not include any allowance for travel costs, or postage, telephone and other expenses.

(2)   Incumbents and Parochial Church Councils are strongly recommended to enter into a written agreement with the organist and choirmaster. Copies of an *Agreement for the Appointment of an Organist* may be obtained from the RSCM, price £1.25 including postage.

(3)   In cases of divided posts, churches should use these minimum rates as a basis.

3.5   Specimen Constitution for a Diocesan Music Committee

CONSTITUTION OF THE .... *DIOCESAN CHURCH MUSIC COMMITTEE*

(in association with the ROYAL SCHOOL OF CHURCH MUSIC)

President: The Diocesan Bishop

Title
1.   The committee shall be called 'The Diocesan Church Music Committee, (in association with The Royal School of Church Music)' (hereinafter referred to as 'The Diocesan Committee' or 'The Committee').

Objects
2.   The objects of the Committee are as follows:
The promotion of high standards of church music in the Diocese, and in particular:
- (i)   to arrange diocesan choir and music festivals, whether in the cathedral or elsewhere;
- (ii)   to arrange courses of instruction for church musicians (instrumentalists, singers and directors of music);
- (iii)   to arrange training and other events relevant to church music;
- (iv)   to offer practical advice and help to individual churches, choirs, music groups, organists and worship committees;
- (v)   to liaise with the Diocesan Liturgical Committee and the Diocesan Advisory Committee through its representatives on the Diocesan Consultative Council for Worship.

The Committee is concerned with all styles of church music and churchmanship. It encourages selection of the most appropriate music and the most effective presentation for any particular occasion and location.

Method of Working
3.   The Diocesan Committee shall meet at least twice a year.

4.   Events arranged by the Committee shall be regarded (either)

as 'diocesan events' (e.g. diocesan renewal celebrations, diocesan choir festivals, chorister award examinations), in which case the responsibility shall rest with the Diocesan Committee; (or they shall be regarded as 'local RSCM events', in which case they shall be directed by RSCM–approved personnel and organised in liaison with RSCM Headquarters).

5. The Committee shall establish .... sub-committees, to be called .... and .... District Committees; they shall cover the geographical areas of the Archdeaconries of the Diocese. The duties of these District Committees shall be:

   (i) to draw up each year and submit to the Diocesan Committee a programme of 'local area events' (or 'local RSCM events'); then, after approval or amendment by the Diocesan Committee, to carry out this programme;

   (ii) to make contact with churches, choirs, music groups (and RSCM affiliates) in their District; to help, encourage and support them, particularly in the use of new or unfamiliar music and services;

   (iii) to identify churches which are severely lacking in musical resources (musicians, instruments, sheet music, etc.), and to work with the Diocesan Music Adviser with the aim of encouraging the use of appropriate music in worship;

   (iv) to establish and maintain links with local deaneries, clergy chapters and ecumenical fraternals, organists' associations and other groups concerned with church music in their district;

   (v) to help organise any diocesan events that the Diocesan Committee may hold in their District.

6. The Diocesan Committee shall also establish a Standing Committee, which shall meet as necessary to take administrative decisions not requiring the presence of the full Committee. The Standing Committee shall have no authority to make decisions regarding the policy of the Committee.

7. An Open Meeting shall be arranged once a year at which the Diocesan Music Adviser shall present a report on the work of the Committee during the preceding year. The meeting should also include a discussion on a topic of particular interest or concern for those involved with church music.

Membership
8. It is desirable that non-Anglican churches be represented.

9. The Diocesan Committee shall consist of:

Officers: Chairman – appointed by the Bishop (after consultation with the RSCM)
Diocesan Music Adviser

Treasurer ⎫ appointed by the Committee, either from serving members or from outside the Committee
General Secretary ⎬
Music Secretary ⎭

Members: the Chairmen of the District Committees
the Secretaries of the District Committees
up to three members appointed directly by the Bishop
(up to three members appointed directly by the RSCM)
up to three members co-opted by the Committee
(the RSCM Commission for the region, ex officio)

10. The District Committee shall consist of:

Chairman – appointed by the Bishop (after consultation with the RSCM)

Secretary ⎫ appointed by the Diocesan Committee (in consultation with the RSCM)
Up to four other members ⎬

11. The Standing Committee shall consist of:
– the officers of the Diocesan Committee

– up to two other members of the Diocesan Committee. Others may be invited as appropriate.

12. Small working groups may be established to undertake specific tasks. Members of these groups shall be chosen from the Diocesan Committee and may invite others to work with them.

13. The Chairman of the Diocesan Committee shall be appointed for a term specified by the Bishop, and shall be eligible for re-appointment. The other Officers and Members of the various committees will retire, and be eligible for re-appointment, on every third anniversary of this Constitution becoming effective.

Responsibilities
14. The responsibilities of the Diocesan Committee officers shall be as follows:

(a) the Chairman shall be responsible for calling meetings of the Diocesan Committee and of the Standing Committee. Seven clear days' notice shall be given of Diocesan Committee meetings, together with an agenda of business;

(b) the Diocesan Music Adviser shall act as consultant to the Committee in all matters concerning choice of music and the structure and content of courses;

(c) the Treasurer shall keep proper accounts of the funds of the Committee. The accounts must be audited at the end of the financial year (..........) by a qualified auditor appointed by the Committee. Cheques and other orders for payment shall be signed by any one of three members of the Committee, one of whom shall be the Treasurer;

(d) the General Secretary shall be responsible for:
– sending out notices and agendas for meetings of the Diocesan and Standing Committees;
– maintaining an up-to-date register of organists and choir directors in the Diocese;
– administrative work involved in the organisation of 'diocesan events' arranged by the Committee.
Secretarial assistance may be funded from the Com-

mittee's income, at the discretion of the Committee. Committee members shall be included on the mailing list for all general circulars sent to musical representatives.

(e) The Minutes Secretary shall keep Minutes of all meetings of the Diocesan and Standing Committees, and shall circulate copies of all such Minutes to Diocesan Committee members as soon as possible.

15. The responsibilities of the District Committee officers shall be as follows:

(a) the Chairmen shall be responsible for calling meetings of their committee as necessary;

(b) the Secretaries shall be responsible for ensuring that the necessary administrative work is carried out in organising 'local events' (or 'local RSCM events').

Amendment to the Constitution

16. Amendments or additions to this Constitution may only be made with the approval of the Bishop, (after consultation with the RSCM, and) after discussion by the Committee at a meeting at which two-thirds of all the members are present (in person or by proxy). Any proposed amendment or addition shall first be circulated to every member with the agenda.

Date of Effect

17. This Constitution becomes effective on ....

3.6 Addresses of Some Organisations mentioned in the Report

Anglia Polytechnic, East Road, Cambridge CB1 1TT (0223 63271)

Anglican Communities Consultative Council, (Secretary), 9 Stafford Road, Eccleshall, Stafford ST21 6JP (0785 850588)

Association of Independent Radio Companies, 46 Westbourne Grove, London W2 5SH (071 727 2646)

Benslow Music Trust, Little Benslow Hills, Ibberson Way, Benslow Lane, Hitchin, Hertfordshire SG4 9RB (0462 59446)

British Broadcasting Corporation, Broadcasting House, London W1A 1AA (071 580 4468)

British Broadcasting Corporation, TV Centre, Wood Lane, London W12 7RJ (071 743 8000)

British Federation of Young Choirs, 2 Heathcote Street, Loughborough, Leicestershire LE11 3BW (0509 211664)

Cathedral Organists' Association, Royal School of Church Music, Addington Palace, Croydon, Surrey CR9 5AD (081 654 7676)

Choir Schools' Association, Minster School, Deansgate, York YO1 2JA (0904 625217)

Christian Copyright Licensing Ltd, 26–28 Gildridge Road, Eastbourne, East Sussex BN21 4SA (0323 417711)

Christian Music Publishers' Association, c/o P.O. Box 75, Eastbourne, East Sussex BN23 6NW

Church House Publishing (formerly **Church Information Office**), Church House, Great Smith Street, London SW1P 3NZ (071 222 9011)

Churches' Initiative for Music Education, (Secretary), 1 Lyoncroft Cottages, Upwood Road, Bury, Huntingdon, Cambridgeshire PE17 1PA (0487 813549)

Colchester Institute, Sheepen Road, Colchester, Essex CO3 3LL (0206 570271)

Council for the Care of Churches, 83 London Wall, London EC2M 5NA (071 638 0971)

Ecclesiastical Insurance Group, Beaufort House, Brunswick Road, Gloucester GL1 1JZ (0452 28533)

Friends of Cathedral Music, 19 Sellerdale Rise, Wyke, Bradford BD12 9LL

Guild of Church Musicians, Hillbrow, Godstone Road, Bletchingley, Surrey (0883 843168)

Hymn Society of Great Britain and Ireland, 7 Little Cloister, Westminster Abbey, London SW1P 3PL

Incorporated Society of Musicians, 10 Stratford Place, London W1N 9AE (071 629 4413)

Independent Radio Authority, 70 Brompton Road, London SW3 1EY (071 581 2888)

Independent Television Commission, 70 Brompton Road, London SW3 1EY (071 584 7011)

Jubilate Hymns, 2 All Souls' Place, London W1N 3DB

Langham Arts, 2 All Souls' Place, London W1N 3DB
Liturgical Commission (General Synod of the Church of England), Church House, Great Smith Street, London SW1P 3NZ (071 222 9011)

Mechanical Copyright Protection Society Ltd., 41 Streatham High Road, London SW16 1ER (081 769 4400)
Music in Worship Foundation, 151 Bath Road, Hounslow, Middlesex, TW3 3BU (081 570 1465)
Music Publishers' Association, 103 Kingsway, London WC2B 6QX (071 831 75910)

National Federation of Old Choristers' Associations, 73 Lansdown Road, Gloucester GL1 3JD
National Organ Teachers' Encouragement Scheme (NOTES), Hon. Secretary, 44 Church Lane, Rickmansworth, Hertfordshire WD3 2HD

Panel of Monastic Musicians, Mount St. Bernard Abbey, Coalville, Leicester LE6 3UL
Pratt Green Trust, 191 Creighton Avenue, East Finchley, London N2 9BN

Royal Academy of Music, Marylebone Road, London NW1 5HT
Royal College of Organists, 7 St. Andrew's Street, Holborn, London EC4A 3LQ (071 936 3606)
Royal School of Church Music, Addington Palace, Croydon, Surrey CR9 5AD (081 654 7676)
Rural Music Schools' Association, Little Benslow Hills, Ibberson Way, Benslow Lane, Hitchin, Hertfordshire SG4 9RB

Salvation Army, 101 Queen Victoria Street, London EC4P 4EP (071 236 5222)
Society of St. Gregory, St. Gregory's Priory, Welcombe Road, Stratford-upon-Avon, Warwickshire CV37 6UJ

UK Council for Music Education and Training, 13 Beck Lane, South Luffenham, Oakham, Rutland, Leicestershire ME15 8NQ (0780 721115)

Index

317

United States of America 113, 115,
116, 117, 158
Universa Laus 97
University 128–129
Urban Priority Area (UPA) 84, 249

Vatican II 93, 94, 95, 120, 122
Vaughan Williams, Ralph 30, 94, 160
Venantius Fortunatus 55
Veni Creator Spiritus 55
Versicles 65
Vigils 119
Vincent, Virginia 12, 263
Viola 152
Violin 152
Violoncello 152
Vivaldi, A. 128
Voluntary, instrumental 47, 57, 100,
184, 185

Wagner 35
Walker, Christopher 97
Walmisley, Thomas 29
Wantage, Community of St. Mary the
Virgin 120
Washington, Henry 94
Watson, Richard 263
Watts, Isaac 27, 56, 100
Webb, Jacquie 263
Webb, Dr. John 145
Wedding March 82
Welsh male-voice choirs 135
Wesley, John and Charles 28, 56, 100

Wesley, S. S. 29
West Malling, St. Mary's Abbey 12
123
Westminster
Abbey 264
Cathedral 94
Dean and Chapter of 12
Diocesan Liturgy Centre 96
Hymnal, New 95
Western Wynde Mass 26
Wicks, Allan 263
Wills, Nicholas 11, 264
Wiltshire, Archdeaconry of 202
Winchester Cathedral 224
World War II 29, 30
World-wide Church 111–118
Wood, Charles 20, 29, 162
Woodward, G. R. 30
Worship 77, 172–173, 174, 175
differing styles in 176
Worship Committee 67, 79,
189–190, 244
Worship Song 82, 100, 104, 106, 115
183; *see also* Song
Wren, Brian 163
Wycliffe, John 25

York 12, 89
Young people 200, 201, 205
Youth group(s) 189
Youth orchestras, bands, etc. 133

Zimbabwe 111, 115, 117